LONDON

THE MINI ROUGH GUIDE

D0638237

Rough Guides online
www.roughguides.com

Rough Guide credits

Text editor: Caroline Osborne
Series editor: Mark Ellingham
Production: Dan May
Cartography: Stratigraphics and Katie Lloyd-Jones

Publishing Information

This 3rd edition published May 2003
by Rough Guides Ltd,
80 Strand, London WC2R 0RL

Distributed by the Penguin Group:

Penguin Books Ltd, 80 Strand, London WC2R 0RL
Penguin Putnam, Inc. 375 Hudson Street, New York 10014, USA
Penguin Books Australia Ltd, 487 Maroondah Highway,
PO Box 257, Ringwood, Victoria 3134, Australia
Penguin Books Canada Ltd, 10 Alcorn Avenue,
Toronto, Ontario, Canada M4V 1E4
Penguin Books (NZ) Ltd,
182–190 Wairau Road, Auckland 10, New Zealand

Typeset in Bembo and Helvetica to an original design by Henry Iles.
Printed in Spain by Graphy Cems.

© Rob Humphreys
400pp, includes index
A catalogue record for this book is available from the British Library.

ISBN 1-8453-112-7

We set out to do something different when the first Rough Guide was published in 1982. Mark Ellingham, just out of university, was travelling in Greece. He brought along the popular guides of the day, but found they were all lacking in some way. They were either strong on ruins and museums but went on for pages without mentioning a beach or taverna. Or they were so conscious of the need to save money that they lost sight of Greece's cultural and historical significance. Also, none of the books told him anything about Greece's contemporary life – its politics, its culture, its people, and how they lived.

So with no job in prospect, Mark decided to write his own guidebook, one which aimed to provide practical information that was second to none, detailing the best beaches and the hottest clubs and restaurants, while also giving hard-hitting accounts of every sight, both famous and obscure, and providing up-to-the-minute information on contemporary culture. It was a guide that encouraged independent travellers to find the best of Greece, and was a great success, getting shortlisted for the Thomas Cook travel guide award, and encouraging Mark, along with three friends, to expand the series.

The Rough Guide list grew rapidly and the letters flooded in, indicating a much broader readership than had been anticipated, but one which uniformly appreciated the Rough Guide mix of practical detail and humour, irreverence and enthusiasm. Things haven't changed. The same four friends who began the series are still the caretakers of the Rough Guide mission today: to provide the most reliable, up-to-date and entertaining information to independent-minded travellers of all ages, on all budgets.

We now publish more than 200 titles and have offices in London and New York. The travel guides are written and researched by a dedicated team of more than 100 authors, based in Britain, Europe, the USA and Australia. We have also created a unique series of phrasebooks to accompany the travel series, along with an acclaimed series of music guides, and a best-selling pocket guide to the Internet and World Wide Web. We also publish comprehensive travel information on our Web site: www.roughguides.com

Help us update

We've gone to a lot of trouble to ensure that this Rough Guide is as up to date and accurate as possible. However, things do change. All suggestions, comments and corrections are much appreciated, and we'll send a copy of the next edition (or any other Rough Guide if you prefer) for the best letters.

Please mark letters "Rough Guide Mini London Update" and send to:

Rough Guides, 80 Strand, London WC2R 0RL or
Rough Guides, 4th Floor, 345 Hudson St, New York NY 10014.

Or send an email to mail@roughguides.com
Have your questions answered and tell others about your trip at
www.roughguides.atinfopop.com

Acknowledgements

The author would like to thank Polly Thomas for wanting to edit the book, Helena for nearly editing it, and Caroline for actually editing it. Thanks, too, to Val for her contributions, to Dan May for typesetting, Nicky Twyman for proofreading and Maxine Repath for cartography.

CONTENTS

CONTENTS

MAP LIST

Introduction

With a population of just under eight million, **London** is Europe's largest city, spreading across an area of more than 620 square miles from its core on the River Thames. Ethnically it's also Europe's most diverse metropolis: around two hundred languages are spoken within its confines, and more than thirty percent of the population is made up of first-, second- and third-generation **immigrants**. Despite Scottish, Welsh and Northern Irish devolution, London still dominates the national horizon, too: this is where the country's news and money are made, it's where the central government resides and, as far as its inhabitants are concerned, provincial life begins beyond the circuit of the city's orbital motorway. Londoners' sense of superiority causes enormous resentment in the regions, yet it's undeniable that the capital has a unique aura of excitement and success – in most walks of British life, if you want to get on you've got to do it in London.

For the visitor, too, London is a thrilling place – and in the last few years, the city has been in a relatively buoyant mood. Thanks to the national lottery and the millennium-oriented funding frenzy, virtually every one of London's world-class museums, galleries and institutions has been reinvented, from the Royal Opera House to the British Museum. In the Tate Modern and the London Eye, the city can now boast the world's largest modern art gallery and Ferris wheel, and the first new bridge to cross the Thames for over a hundred years. Furthermore, following sixteen years of being the only major city in the world not to have its own governing body, London finally acquired its own elected assembly in 2000, along with a mayor who's determined to try and solve one of London's biggest problems: transport.

In the meantime, London's traditional sights – Big Ben, Westminster Abbey, Buckingham Palace, St Paul's Cathedral and the Tower of London – continue to draw in millions of tourists every year. **Monuments** from the capital's more glorious past are everywhere to be seen, from medieval banqueting halls and the great churches of Christopher Wren to the eclectic Victorian architecture of the triumphalist British Empire. There is also much enjoyment to be had from the city's quiet Georgian squares, the narrow alleyways of the City of London, the riverside walks, and the quirks of what is still identifiably a collection of villages. And even London's traffic problems are offset by surprisingly large expanses of greenery: Hyde Park, Green Park and St James's Park are all within a few minutes' walk of the West End, while, further afield, you can enjoy the more expansive countryside of Hampstead Heath and Richmond Park.

You could spend days just **shopping** in London, too, mixing with the upper classes in the tiara triangle around Harrods, or sampling the offbeat weekend markets of Portobello Road, Camden and Greenwich. The **music**, clubbing and gay/lesbian scenes are second to none, and mainstream **arts** are no less exciting, with regular opportunities to catch brilliant theatre companies, dance troupes, exhibitions and opera. **Restaurants**, these days, are an attraction, too. London is now on a par with its European rivals, and offers a range from three-star Michelin establishments to low-cost, high-quality Chinese restaurants and Indian curry houses. Meanwhile, the city's

pubs have heaps of atmosphere, especially away from the centre – and an exploration of the farther-flung communities is essential to get the complete picture of this dynamic metropolis.

What to see

Stretching for more than thirty miles at its broadest point, London is a big place. The majority of its sights are situated to the north of the River Thames, which loops through the city from west to east. However, there is no single predominant focus of interest, for London has grown not through centralized planning but by a process of agglomeration – villages and urban developments that once surrounded the core are now lost within the amorphous mass of Greater London.

One of the few areas that you can easily explore on foot is **Westminster** and **Whitehall**, the city's royal, political and ecclesiastical power base, where you'll find the **National Gallery** and a host of other London landmarks, from **Buckingham Palace** to **Westminster Abbey** and Big Ben. The grand streets and squares of **St James's**, **Mayfair** and **Marylebone**, to the north of Westminster, have been the playground of the rich since the Restoration, and now contain the city's busiest shopping zones.

East of Piccadilly Circus, **Soho**, **Chinatown** and **Covent Garden** are also easy to walk around and form the heart of the West End entertainment district, containing the largest concentration of theatres, cinemas, clubs, flashy shops, cafés and restaurants. To the north lies the university quarter of **Bloomsbury**, home to the ever-popular **British Museum**, and, to the east, the secluded quadrangles of Holborn's **Inns of Court**, London's legal heartland.

The City – the City of London, to give it its full title – is at one and the same time the most ancient and the most

INTRODUCTION

modern part of London. Settled since Roman times, it is now one of the world's great financial centres, yet retains its share of historic sights, notably the **Tower of London** and a fine cache of Wren churches that includes **St Paul's Cathedral**. Despite creeping trendification, the **East End**, to the east of the City, is not conventional tourist territory, but to ignore it entirely is to miss out a crucial element of contemporary London. Docklands is the converse of the down-at-heel East End, with Canary Wharf's skyscrapers, including the country's tallest building, epitomizing the pretensions of the smash-and-grab culture that has gripped the nation since the 1980s.

A small slice of central London south of the Thames is definitely worth exploring. First off, there's the **South Bank Centre**, London's little-loved concrete culture bunker, which is enjoying a new lease of life thanks to inspired artistic direction and its proximity to the giant observation wheel known as the **London Eye**. Further east along the river in Bankside is the **Tate Modern**, one of the world's greatest modern art museums, now linked to the City by the funky pedestrian-only Millennium Bridge.

The largest segment of greenery in central London is **Hyde Park**, which separates wealthy **Kensington** and **Chelsea** from the city centre. The **museums** of South Kensington – the Victoria and Albert Museum, the Science Museum and the Natural History Museum – are a must; and if you have shopping on your agenda, you'll want to check out the hive of plush stores in the vicinity of Harrods.

The capital's most hectic weekend market takes place around Camden Lock in **north London**. Further out, in the literary suburbs of Hampstead and Highgate, there are unbeatable views across the city from half-wild **Hampstead Heath**, the favourite parkland of thousands of Londoners. The glory of south London is **Greenwich**, with its nautical associations, royal park and observatory (not to mention its Dome). Finally, there are plenty of rewarding day-trips along the Thames from **Chiswick to Windsor**, most notably **Hampton Court Palace** and **Windsor Castle**.

When to go

Considering the temperateness of the English climate, it's amazing how much mileage the locals get out of the subject – a two-day cold snap is discussed as if it were the onset of a new Ice Age, and a week in the upper seventies starts rumours of drought. The fact is that English summers rarely get hot and the winters don't get very cold, though they're often wet. The bottom line is that it's impossible to say with any degree of certainty that the weather will be pleasant in any given month. May might be wet and grey one year and gloriously sunny the next, and the same goes for the autumnal months – November stands an equal chance of being crisp and clear or foggy and grim.

As far as crowds go, tourists stream into London pretty much all year round, with **peak season** from Easter to October, and the biggest crush in July and August, when you'll need to book your accommodation well in advance. Costs, however, are pretty uniform year-round.

	AVERAGE C°		RAINFALL (MM)
	AVERAGE DAILY MAX	AVERAGE DAILY MIN	AVERAGE MONTHLY
Jan	43	36	54
Feb	44	36	40
March	50	38	37
April	56	42	37
May	62	47	46
June	69	53	45
July	71	56	59
Aug	71	56	59
Sept	65	52	49
Oct	58	46	57
Nov	50	42	64
Dec	45	38	48

BASICS

BASICS

Arrival

Londonʼs international **airports** are all less than an
hour from the city centre, and the cityʼs **train** and
bus terminals are all pretty central, with tube stations
close at hand.

BY AIR

Heathrow (☎0870/000 0123, ⓦwww.baa.co.uk), fifteen
miles west of the city centre, has four terminals, and two
train/tube stations: one for terminals 1, 2 and 3, and a
separate one for terminal 4. The high-speed **Heathrow
Express** trains travel non-stop to Paddington Station
(every 15min; 15–20min) for £13 each way or £23
return (ten percent less if you book online at
ⓦwww.heathrowexpress.co.uk, more if you buy your
ticket on board). A much cheaper but slower alternative is
to take the Piccadilly **Underground** line into central
London (every 5–9min; 50min) for £3.70. If you plan to
make several sightseeing journeys on your arrival day, buy
a Day Travelcard (zones 1–6) for £5.10. There is also
Airbus #2, which runs from outside all four Heathrow
terminals to several destinations in the city (every 30min;
1hr) and costs £8 single, £12 return. From midnight,
youʼll have to take **night bus** #N9 to Trafalgar Square

(every 30min; 1hr) for a bargain fare of £1. **Taxis** are plentiful, but cost at least £40 to central London, and take around an hour (longer in the rush hour).

Gatwick (℡0870/000 2468, ⓦwww.baa.co.uk), thirty miles to the south, has two terminals, North and South, connected by a monorail. The non-stop **Gatwick Express** train runs between the South Terminal and Victoria Station (every 15–30min; 30min) for £11. Other options include the **South Central** services to Victoria (every 15–20min; 40min) for £8.20, or **Thameslink** to King's Cross (every 15–30min; 50min) for around £10. A taxi ride into central London will set you back £50 or more, and take at least an hour.

Stansted (℡0870/000 0303, ⓦwww.baa.co.uk), London's swankiest international airport, lies roughly 35 miles northeast of the capital, and is served by the **Stansted Express** to Liverpool Street (every 15min; 45min), which costs £13 single, £23 return. **Airbus** #6 also runs every 24 hours a day to Victoria Coach Station (every 30min; 1hr 30min), and costs £8 single, £12 return. A taxi into central London will cost £75 or more, and take at least an hour.

Luton airport (℡01582/405100, ⓦwww.london -luton.com) is roughly thirty miles north of the city centre, and mostly handles charter flights. A free shuttle bus takes five minutes to transport passengers to Luton Airport Parkway station, connected by **rail** to King's Cross and other stations in central London, with **Thameslink** running trains every fifteen minutes, plus one or two throughout the night; the journey takes thirty to forty minutes and is £10 for a single fare. Alternatively, **Green Line** buses run from Luton to Victoria Station (every 30min; 1hr 30min), costing £7.50 single, £12 return. A **taxi** will cost in the region of £70 and take at least an hour to reach central London.

ARRIVAL

London's smallest airport, **City Airport** (☏020/7646 0000, ⓦwww.londoncityairport.com), is situated in Docklands, nine miles east of central London. It handles European flights only, and is connected by shuttle bus with Canning Town tube (every 5min; 5min; £2.50), Canary Wharf (every 10min; 10min; £3), and Liverpool Street (every 10min; 30min; £6). A taxi into the city's financial sector will cost around £20 and take half an hour or so.

BY TRAIN OR BUS

Eurostar trains arrive at **Waterloo International**, just south of the river. Trains from the Channel ports arrive at **Charing Cross** or **Victoria** train stations; boat trains from Harwich arrive at **Liverpool Street**. Arriving by train from elsewhere in Britain, you'll come into one of London's numerous main-line stations, all of which have adjacent Underground stations linking into the city centre's tube network. Coaches terminate at **Victoria Coach Station**, a couple of hundred yards south down Buckingham Palace Road from Victoria train station and Underground.

Information

The chief British Tourist Authority (BTA) office in London is the **Britain Visitor Centre**, near Piccadilly Circus at 1 Regent Street (Oct–July Mon–Fri 9am–6.30pm, Sat & Sun 10am–4pm; Aug & Sept same times except Sat 9am–5pm; ⓦwww.visitbritain.com). London also has its very own **London Tourist Board**, or LTB (ⓦwww.londontouristboard.com), with a desk in Arrivals at Waterloo International (daily 8.30am–10.30pm).

Individual boroughs also run tourist offices, the most central one being on the south side of St Paul's Cathedral (April–Sept daily 9.30am–5pm; Oct–March Mon–Fri 9.30am–5pm, Sat 9.30am–12.30pm; ⓣ020/7332 1456, ⓦwww.cityoflondon.gov.uk). Although this office deals primarily with the financial district, they will accept phone enquiries, whereas LTB only offers a premium-rate pre-recorded information line (ⓣ09068/663344).

Most offices hand out a useful reference **map** of central London, plus plans of the public transport systems, but to find your way around every nook and cranny of the city you need to invest in either an *A–Z Atlas* or a *Nicholson Streetfinder*, both of which have a street index covering every street in the capital. You can get them at most bookshops and newsagents for under £5. The two best, simple, fold-out maps are *London: The Rough Guide Map* and *Benson's London Mini Map*.

The only comprehensive and critical weekly **listings** magazine is *Time Out*, which costs £2.20 and comes out every Tuesday afternoon. In it you'll find details of all the latest exhibitions, shows, films, music, sport, guided walks and events in and around the capital.

WEBSITES

London Tourist Board

Ⓦ **www.londontouristboard .com** The official LTB website is full of useful information, including an online accommodation service and news about what's new in the city's museums and galleries.

Ⓦ **www.londontown.com** Another LTB website, this time aimed more at first-time visitors from abroad, with a basic rundown of the top sights, hotels and restaurants.

Smooth Hound Systems

Ⓦ **www.s-h-systems.co.uk /tourism/london** A very simply designed and basic tourist info site, which covers London in exhaustive A–Z categories.

Streetmap

Ⓦ **www.streetmap.co.uk** Type in the London address or postcode you want, and this site will located it for you in seconds.

City transport

London's transport network is among the most complex and expensive in the world. The London Transport (LT) **travel information office**, at Piccadilly Circus tube station (daily 8.45am–6pm), will provide free transport maps; there are other desks at Oxford Circus and St James's Park (Mon–Fri only) tubes, Victoria Coach Station plus Euston, King's Cross, Liverpool Street, Paddington and Victoria train stations. There's also a 24-hour phone line and a website for transport information (☏020/7222 1234, ⓦ www.londontransport.co.uk). If you can, avoid travelling during the **rush hour** (Mon–Fri 8–9.30am & 5–7pm), when tubes become unbearably crowded, and some buses get so full they won't let you on.

THE TUBE

Except for very small journeys, the Underground – or **tube** – is by far the quickest way to get about. Each line has its own colour and name, and all you need to know is which direction you're travelling in: northbound, eastbound, southbound or westbound. Services operate from around 5.30am Monday to Saturday, and from 7.30am on Sundays, and end around midnight every day; you rarely have to wait more than five minutes for a train between central stations.

TRAVELCARDS

To get the best value out of the transport system, buy a Travelcard. Available from machines and booths at all tube and train stations, and at some newsagents (look for the sticker), these are valid for the bus, tube, Docklands Light Railway, Tramlink and suburban rail networks.

Day Travelcards come in two varieties: Off-Peak – which are valid after 9.30am on weekdays and all day during the weekend – and Peak. A Day Travelcard (Off-Peak), costs £4.10 for the central zones 1 and 2, rising to £5.10 for zones 1–6 (including Heathrow); the Day Travelcard (Peak) starts at £5.10 for zones 1 and 2. Weekend Travelcards, for unlimited travel on Saturdays and Sundays, start at £6.10 for zones 1 and 2. Weekly Travelcards are even more economical, beginning at £19.60 for zones 1 and 2; these cards can only be bought by holders of a Photocard, which you can get, free of charge, from tube and train station ticket booths on presentation of a passport photo. Those travelling to London from Australia, Ireland, New Zealand, South Africa or the US can also purchase a Visitor Travelcard, available for 2 to 7 days (zones 1–6), starting at £13.20, or for 3, 4 or 7 days (zones 1 & 2), starting at £12.80. However, these Travelcards must be purchased before entering the UK, or from Ⓦ www.ticket-on-line.com.

Tickets must be bought in advance from the machines or booths in station entrance halls; if you cannot produce a valid ticket, you will be charged an on-the-spot Penalty Fare of £10. A single journey in the central zone costs an unbelievable £1.60; a **Carnet** of ten tickets costs £11.50. If you're intending to travel about a lot, however, a Travelcard is by far your best bet (see above).

THE TUBE

BUSES

Tickets for all bus journeys within, to or from the central zone cost a flat fare of £1; journeys outside the central zone cost 70p. Normally you pay the driver on entering, but some routes are covered by older Routemaster buses, staffed by a conductor and with an open rear platform. Note that at request stops (easily recognizable by their red sign) you must stick your arm out to hail the bus you want (or ring the bell if you want to get off). In addition to the Travelcards mentioned overleaf, a **One-Day Bus Pass** (zones 1–4) is also available for £2 and can be used before 9.30am.

Regular buses run between about 6am and midnight; **night buses** (prefixed with the letter "N") operate outside this period. Night bus routes radiate out from Trafalgar Square at approximately twenty to thirty-minute intervals; more frequently on some routes and on Friday and Saturday nights. Fares are the same as for daytime buses, and Travelcards are valid.

SUBURBAN TRAINS

Large areas of London's suburbs are best reached by the **suburban train** network (Travelcards valid). Wherever a sight can only be reached by overground train, we've indicated the nearest train station and the central terminus from which you must depart. If you're planning to use the railway network a lot, you might want to purchase a **Network Railcard**, which is valid for a year, costs £20, and gives you up to 34 percent discount on fares to destinations in and around the southeast. To find out about a particular service, phone **National Rail Enquiries** on ☎08457/484950 or check timetables on their website (ⓦ www.railtrack.co.uk.)

TAXIS

Compared to taxi fares in most capital cities, London's metered **black cabs** are an expensive option unless there's three or more of you – a ride from Euston to Victoria, for example, will cost around £10 (more after 8pm and on the weekend). A yellow light over the windscreen tells you if the cab is available – just stick your arm out to hail it. (If you want to book one in advance, call ☎020/7272 0272.)

Minicabs look just like regular cars and are considerably cheaper than black cabs, but are a bit of a law unto themselves. There are hundreds of minicab firms in the phone book, but the best way to pick one is to take the advice of

THE LONDON PASS

If you're thinking of visiting a lot of fee-paying attractions in a short space of time, it's probably worth buying a London Pass (ⓦ www.londonpass.com), which gives you entry to a mixed bag of attractions including Buckingham Palace, Hampton Court Palace, Kensington Palace, London Aquarium, St Paul's Cathedral, the Tower of London, Westminster Abbey and Windsor Castle, plus a whole host of lesser attractions, and various discounts at selected outlets. You can choose to buy the card with or without an All-Zone Travelcard thrown in; the saving is relatively small, but it does include free travel out to Windsor. The pass costs around £25 for one day (£16.50 for kids), rising to £70 for six days (£36.50 for kids), or £30 with a Travelcard (£19 for kids), rising to £107 (£56 for kids). The pass can be bought online or over the phone (☎ 0870/242 9988), or in person from Exchange International bureaus at Heathrow and Gatwick airports and London's main-line train or major Underground stations.

the place you're at, unless you want to be certain of a woman driver, in which case call Ladycabs (☎020/7254 3501), or a gay/lesbian-friendly driver, in which case call Freedom Cars (☎020/7734 1313). Avoid illegal taxi touts, and establish the fare beforehand, as minicabs are not metered.

BOATS

Boat services on the Thames do not form part of an integrated public transport system. Fares are expensive, and Travelcards currently only give the holders a 33 percent discount on tickets.

All services are keenly affected by demand, tides and the weather, and tend to be drastically scaled down in the winter months. **Timetables and services** are complex, and there are numerous companies and small charter operators – for a full list, pick up the Thames River Services booklet from an LT travel information office, phone ☎020/7222 1234 or visit ⓦ www.londontransport.co.uk.

The busiest part of the river is the central section between **Westminster and the Tower of London**, with several points at which to get on and off, and fares averaging around £3 single. There are also frequent services from central London **to Greenwich** (every 30–40min; 1hr): typical fares are around £6.50 single, £8 return. If you're taking the Docklands Light Railway (DLR), it's worth finding out about Rail River Rover tickets (see p.106). From April to October, you can also take a boat from Westminster via Kew and Richmond **to Hampton Court** (journey time is 3hr 30min one way; £12 single, £18 return; see p.168).

SIGHTSEEING TOURS

Sightseeing **bus tours** are run by several rival companies, their open-top double-deckers setting off every fifteen minutes from Victoria Station, Trafalgar Square, Piccadilly, and other tourist spots. Tours take roughly two hours (though you can hop on and off as often as you like) and cost around £15. Alternatively, you can hop aboard one of the bright-yellow World War II amphibious vehicles used by Frog Tours (☎020/7928 3132, ⓦwww.frogtours.com) for a combined **bus and boat tour**. On departure from behind County Hall, near the London Eye, you spend fifty minutes driving round the usual sights, before plunging into the river for a half-hour cruise. Tours need to be pre-booked either online or over the phone, with tickets again costing £15. A money-saving option is to skip the commentary and hop on a real London bus – the Routemaster **#11 from Victoria Station** will take you past Westminster Abbey, the Houses of Parliament, up Whitehall, round Trafalgar Square, along the Strand and on to St Paul's Cathedral.

CONGESTION CHARGE

Driving in central London is to be avoided if at all possible – a slow, frustrating process now made even more unappealing by the controversial congestion charge, pioneered by Ken Livingstone in his first term as Mayor of London. Since early 2003, all vehicles entering central London between 7am and 6.30pm are liable to a congestion charge of £5 per vehicle. Drivers can pay for the charge online, over the phone and at garages and shops, and must do so before 10pm the same day or they incur a £5 surcharge. The congestion charging zone is bounded by Marylebone and Euston Road in the north, Commercial Street and Tower Bridge in the east, Kennington Lane and Elephant & Castle in the south, and Edgware Road and Park Lane in the west

SIGHTSEEING TOURS

THE GUIDE

Westminster and Whitehall

Political, religious and regal power has emanated from **Westminster** and **Whitehall** for almost a millennium. It was Edward the Confessor who first established Westminster as London's royal and ecclesiastical power base, some three miles west of the City of London. The embryonic English parliament met in the abbey in the fourteenth century and eventually took over the old royal palace of Westminster. In the nineteenth century, Whitehall became the "heart of the Empire", its ministries ruling over a quarter of the world's population. Even now, though the UK's world status has diminished, the institutions that run the country inhabit roughly the same geographical area: Westminster for the politicians, Whitehall for the civil servants.

The monuments and buildings covered in this chapter also span the millennium, and include some of London's most famous landmarks – **Nelson's Column**, **Big Ben** and the **Houses of Parliament**, **Westminster Abbey** and **Buckingham Palace**, plus two of the city's finest permanent art collections, the **National Gallery** and **Tate Britain**. Since it's also one of the easiest parts of London to walk round, this is a well-trodden tourist circuit, with all the major sights within a mere half-mile of each other and linked by two of London's most triumphant avenues, **Whitehall** and **The Mall**.

TRAFALGAR SQUARE

Map 4, G9. ⊖ Leicester Square or Charing Cross.

Despite the pigeons and the traffic noise, **Trafalgar Square** is still one of London's grandest architectural set pieces. John Nash designed the basic layout in the 1820s, but died long before the square took its present form. The Neoclassical National Gallery filled up the northern side of the square in 1838, followed five years later by the square's central focal point, **Nelson's Column**; the famous bronze lions didn't arrive until 1868, and the fountains – a real rarity in a London square – didn't take their present shape until the eve of World War II.

As one of the few large public squares in London, Trafalgar Square has been both a tourist attraction and a focus for political demonstrations since the Chartists assembled here in 1848 before marching to Kennington Common. On a more festive note, the square is graced each December with a giant Christmas tree, donated by Norway in thanks for liberation from the Nazis, and on **New Year's Eve** thousands of inebriates sing in the New Year.

Stranded on a traffic island to the south of the column, and predating the entire square, is the **equestrian statue of Charles I**, erected shortly after the Restoration on the very spot where eight of those who had signed the king's death warrant were disembowelled. Charles's statue also marks the original site of the thirteenth-century **Charing Cross**, from where all distances from the capital are measured – a Victorian imitation now stands nearby, outside Charing Cross train station (Map 4, H8).

The northeastern corner of the square is occupied by James Gibbs' church of **St Martin-in-the-Fields** (ⓦ www .stmartin-in-the-fields.org), fronted by a magnificent Corinthian portico and topped by an elaborate, and distinctly unclassical, tower and steeple. Completed in 1726, the interior is purposefully simple, though the Italian plasterwork on the barrel vaulting is exceptionally rich; it's best appreciated while listening to one of the church's free lunchtime concerts. There's a licensed café in the roomy crypt, not to mention a shop, gallery and brass-rubbing centre (Mon–Sat 10am–6pm, Sun noon–6pm).

The National Gallery

Map 4, G8. Daily 10am–6pm, Wed till 9pm; free; ⓦ www .nationalgallery.org.uk ⊖ Leicester Square or Charing Cross.

Unlike the Louvre or the Hermitage, the **National Gallery**, on the north side of Trafalgar Square, is not based on a royal collection, but was begun in 1824 when the government reluctantly agreed to purchase 38 paintings belonging to a Russian émigré banker, John Julius Angerstein. The gallery's canny acquisition policy has resulted in a collection of more than 2300 paintings, but the collection's virtue is not so much its size, but the range, depth and sheer quality of its contents.

To view the collection chronologically, begin with the **Sainsbury Wing**, the softly-softly, postmodern 1980s adjunct which playfully imitates elements of the original gallery's Neoclassicism. However, with more than a thousand paintings on permanent display in the main galleries, you'll need real stamina to see everything in one day, so if time is tight your best bet is to home in on your areas of special interest, having picked up a gallery plan at one of the information desks. A welcome innovation is the **Gallery Guide Soundtrack**, with a brief audio

TRAFALGAR SQUARE

commentary on a large selection of the paintings on display. The soundtrack is available free of charge, though you're asked for a "voluntary contribution". Another possibility is to join up with one of the gallery's **free guided tours** (daily 11.30am & 2.30pm, plus Wed 6.30pm), which set off from the Sainsbury Wing foyer.

Among the National's **Italian** masterpieces are Leonardo's melancholic *Virgin of the Rocks*, Uccello's *Battle of San Romano*, Botticelli's *Venus and Mars* (inspired by a Dante sonnet) and Piero della Francesca's beautifully composed *Baptism of Christ*, one of his earliest works. The fine collection of Venetian works includes Titian's colourful early masterpiece *Bacchus and Ariadne*, his very late, much gloomier *Death of Acteon*, and Veronese's lustrous *Family of Darius before Alexander*. Elsewhere, Bronzino's erotic *Venus, Cupid, Folly and Time* and Raphael's trenchant *Pope Julius II* keep company with Michelangelo's unfinished *Entombment*. Later Italian works to look out for include a couple by Caravaggio, a few splendid examples of Tiepolo's airy draughtsmanship, and glittering vistas of Venice by Canaletto and Guardi.

From **Spain** there are dazzling pieces by El Greco, Goya, Murillo and Velázquez, among them the provocative *Rokeby Venus*. From the **Low Countries**, standouts include van Eyck's *Arnolfini Marriage*, Memlinc's perfectly poised *Donne Triptych*, and a couple of typically serene Vermeers. There are numerous genre paintings, such as Frans Hals' *Family Group in a Landscape*, and some superlative landscapes, most notably Hobbema's *Avenue, Middleharnis*. An array of Rembrandt paintings that features some of his most searching portraits – two of them self-portraits – is followed by abundant examples of Rubens' expansive, fleshy canvases.

Holbein's masterful *Ambassadors* and several of Van Dyck's portraits were painted for the English court, and there's home-grown **British** art, too, represented by important works such as Hogarth's satirical *Marriage à la Mode*, Gainsborough's translucent *Morning Walk*, Constable's ever-popular *Hay Wain*, and Turner's *Fighting Téméraire*. Highlights of the **French** contingent include superb works by Poussin, Claude, Fragonard, Boucher and Watteau, and the only two paintings in the country by David.

Finally, there's a particularly strong showing of **Impressionists and Post-Impressionists** in rooms 43–46 of the East Wing. Among the most famous works are Manet's unfinished *Execution of Maximilian*, Renoir's *Umbrellas*, Monet's *Thames below Westminster*, Van Gogh's *Sunflowers*, Seurat's pointillist *Bathers at Asnières*, a Rousseau junglescape, Cézanne's proto-Cubist *Bathers* and Picasso's Blue Period *Child with a Dove*.

The National Portrait Gallery

Map 4, G8. Daily 10am–6pm, Thurs & Fri till 9pm; free; Ⓦ www.npg.org.uk ⊖ Leicester Square or Charing Cross.

Around the east side of the National Gallery lurks the **National Portrait Gallery** (NPG), founded in 1856 to house uplifting depictions of the good and the great. Though it has some fine works in its collection, many of the studies are of less interest than their subjects, and the overall impression is of an overstuffed shrine to famous Brits rather than a museum offering any insight into the history of portraiture. However, it is fascinating to trace who has been deemed worthy of admiration at any moment: aristocrats and artists in previous centuries, warmongers and imperialists in the early decades of the twentieth century, writers and poets in the 1930s and 1940s, and, latterly, retired footballers, and film and pop stars.

The NPG's **new extension**, opened in 2000, has proved a great success, providing a bigger Tudor gallery, and a new

TRAFALGAR SQUARE

contemporary gallery to expand the section that's by far the most popular. There's also a computer gallery, lecture theatre and rooftop café/restaurant with a view over the cityscape. The NPG's **Sound Guide**, which gives useful biographical background information to some of the pictures, is provided free of charge, though you're strongly invited to give a "voluntary contribution" of £3.

THE MALL AND ST JAMES'S PARK

Map 4, F10. ⊖ St James's Park.

The tree-lined sweep of **The Mall** – London's nearest equivalent to a Parisian boulevard – was laid out in the first decade of the twentieth century as a memorial to Queen Victoria, and runs from Trafalgar Square to Buckingham Palace. The bombastic **Admiralty Arch** was erected to mark the entrance at the Trafalgar Square end of The Mall, while at the other end stands the ludicrous **Victoria Memorial**, Edward VII's overblown tribute to his mother.

**The best time to view The Mall is on
a Sunday, when it's closed to traffic.**

St James's Park, on the south side of The Mall, is the oldest of the royal parks, having been drained and enclosed for hunting purposes by Henry VIII. It was landscaped by Nash in the 1820s, and today its tree-lined lake is a favourite picnic spot for the civil servants of Whitehall. Pelicans can still be seen at the eastern end of the lake, and there are exotic ducks, swans and geese aplenty. From the bridge across the lake there's also a fine view over to Westminster and the jumble of domes and pinnacles along Whitehall.

Buckingham Palace

Map 4, C12. Aug & Sept daily 9.30am–4.15pm; £11.50; advance booking on ⓣ 020/7321 2233, ⓦ www.royal.gov.uk ⊖ Green Park. The graceless colossus of **Buckingham Palace**, popularly known as "Buck House", has served as the monarch's permanent London residence only since the accession of Victoria. Bought by George III in 1762, the building was

CHANGING OF THE GUARD

The Queen is colonel-in-chief of the seven Household Regiments: the Life Guards (who dress in red and white) and the Blues and Royals (who dress in blue and white) are the two Household Cavalry regiments; the Grenadier, Coldstream, Scots, Irish and Welsh Guards make up the Foot Guards.

The Foot Guards can only be told apart by the plumes (or lack of them) in their busbies, and by the arrangement of their tunic buttons. The first three date back to the seventeenth century, and all these regiments still form part of the modern army as well as performing ceremonial functions such as the Changing of the Guard. If you're keen to find out more about the Foot Guards, pay a visit to the Guards' Museum (Map 4, E13; daily 10am–4pm; £2; ⓦ www.army.mod.uk/ceremonialandheritage), in the Wellington Barracks on the south side of St James's Park.

The Changing of the Guard takes place at two separate locations in London: the two Household Cavalry regiments take it in turns to stand guard at Horse Guards on Whitehall (Map 4, G10; Mon–Sat 11am, Sun 10am), with inspection daily at 4pm, while the Foot Guards take care of Buckingham Palace (April–Aug daily 11.30am; Sept–March alternate days; no ceremony if it rains). A ceremony also takes place regularly in Windsor Castle (see p.171).

THE MALL AND ST JAMES'S PARK

THE ROYAL FAMILY

Tourists may still flock to see London's royal palaces, but over the last decade the British public have become more critical of the huge tax bill that goes to support the Royal Family (ⓦwww.royal.gov.uk) in the style to which they are accustomed. This creeping republicanism can be traced back to 1992, which the Queen herself, in one of her few memorable Christmas Day speeches, accurately described as her annus horribilis. This was the year that saw the marriage break-ups of Charles and Di, and Andrew and Fergie, and the second marriage of divorcée Princess Anne.

Matters came to a head, though, over who should pay the estimated £50 million costs of repairs after the fire at Windsor Castle (p.171). Misjudging the public mood, the Conservative government offered taxpayers' money to foot the entire bill. After a furore, it was agreed that some of the cost would be raised from the astronomical admission charges to the royal palaces instead. In addition, under pressure from the media, the Queen also reduced the number of royals paid out of the civil list, and, for the first time in her life, agreed to pay taxes on her enormous personal fortune.

Given the mounting public resentment against the Royal Family, it was hardly surprising that public opinion tended to side with Princess Diana rather than Prince Charles during their various disputes. Diana's subsequent death, and the huge outpouring of grief that accompanied her funeral, further damaged the reputation of the royals, though her demise has also meant the loss of the Royal Family's most vociferous critic. Despite the Royal Family's low poll ratings, none of the political parties currently advocates abolishing the monarchy, and public appetite for stories about the princes (and their potential girlfriends), or the latest on Charles and Camilla, shows few signs of abating.

overhauled by Nash in the late 1820s, and again by Aston Webb in time for George V's coronation in 1913, producing a palace that's about as bland as it's possible to be.

For two months of the year, the hallowed portals are grudgingly nudged open; timed tickets are sold from the marquee-like box office in Green Park at the western end of The Mall. The interior, however, is a bit of an anticlimax: of the palace's 660 rooms you're permitted to see around twenty, and there's little sign of life as the Queen decamps to Scotland every summer. For the other ten months of the year there's little to do here, as the palace is closed to visitors – not that this deters the crowds who mill around the railings and gather in some force to watch the **Changing of the Guard** (see p.23), in which a detachment of the Queen's Foot Guards marches to appropriate martial music from St James's Palace (unless it rains, that is).

Queen's Gallery and Royal Mews

The public can also pay through the nose to view a small portion of the Royal Collection, at the rebuilt **Queen's Gallery** (Map 4, C13; daily 10am–5.30pm; £6.50), on the south side of the palace. Exhibitions change regularly, drawn from a collection which is three times larger than the National Gallery and includes masterpieces by Michelangelo, Reynolds, Gainsborough, Vermeer, Van Dyck, Rubens, Rembrandt and Canaletto, as well as the odd Fabergé egg and heaps of Sèvres china.

There's more pageantry on show at the Nash-built **Royal Mews** (Map 4, C14; March–July & Oct daily 11am–4pm; Aug & Sept Mon–Sat 10am–5pm; £5), to the south along Buckingham Palace Road. The horses can be viewed in their luxury stables, along with an exhibition of equine accoutrements, but it's the royal carriages that are the main attraction. The most ornate is the Gold State Coach made for George III in 1762, smothered in 22-carat gilding and

THE MALL AND ST JAMES'S PARK

weighing four tons, its axles supporting four life-size figures. The Mews also house the Royal Family's fleet of five Rolls-Royce Phantoms and three Daimlers.

WHITEHALL

Map 4, H10. ⊖ Charing Cross or Westminster.

Whitehall, the unusually broad avenue connecting Trafalgar Square to Parliament Square, is synonymous with the faceless, pinstriped bureaucracy charged with the day-to-day running of the country. Since the sixteenth century, nearly all the key governmental ministries and offices have migrated here, rehousing themselves on an ever-increasing scale. The statues dotted about Whitehall recall the days when this street stood at the centre of an empire on which the sun never set. Nowadays, with even the Scots, Welsh and Northern Irish all with their own assemblies, Whitehall's remit is somewhat diminished.

During the sixteenth and seventeenth centuries Whitehall was also synonymous with royalty, since it was the permanent residence of the kings and queens of England. The original **Whitehall Palace** was the London seat of the Archbishop of York, confiscated and greatly extended by Henry VIII after a fire at Westminster forced him to find alternative accommodation; it was here that he celebrated his marriage to Anne Boleyn in 1533, and here that he died fourteen years later.

The chief section of the old palace to survive the fire of 1698 was the **Banqueting House** (Map 4, H10; Mon–Sat 10am–5pm; £4; Ⓦ www.hrp.org.uk), begun by Inigo Jones in 1619 and the first Palladian building to be built in England. The one room now open to the public has no original furnishings, but is well worth seeing for the superlative Rubens ceiling paintings glorifying the Stuart dynasty, commissioned by Charles I in the 1630s. Charles himself walked through the room for the last time in 1649, when he stepped onto the executioner's scaffold from one of its windows.

Across the road, two mounted sentries of the Queen's Household Cavalry and two horseless colleagues, all in ceremonial uniform, are posted daily from 10am to 4pm. Ostensibly they are protecting the **Horse Guards** building, originally built as the old palace guard house, but now guarding nothing in particular. The mounted guards are changed hourly; those standing change every two hours. Try to coincide your visit with the Changing of the Guard (see p.23), when a squad of twelve mounted troops arrive in full livery. The main action takes place in the parade ground at the rear of the building overlooking Horse Guards' Parade.

Further down this west side of Whitehall is London's most famous address, **Number 10 Downing Street** (Map 4, G11; ⓦ www.number-10.gov.uk), the seventeenth-century terraced house that has been the residence of the prime minister since it was presented to Robert Walpole, Britain's first PM, by George II in 1732. Just past the Downing Street gates, in the middle of the road, stands Edwin Lutyens' **Cenotaph**, eschewing any kind of Christian imagery, and inscribed simply with the words "The Glorious Dead". The memorial remains the focus of the Remembrance Sunday ceremony held in early November (see p.343).

In 1938, in anticipation of Nazi air raids, the basement of the civil service buildings on the south side of King Charles Street were converted into the **Cabinet War Rooms** (Map 4, G12; daily: May–Sept 9.30am–6pm; Oct–April 10am–6pm; £5.80; ⓦ www.iwm.org.uk/cabinet). It was here that Winston Churchill directed operations and held cabinet meetings for the duration of World War II. The rooms have been left pretty much as they were when they were finally abandoned on VJ Day 1945, and make for an atmospheric underground trot through wartime London. The museum's free acoustophone commentary helps bring the place to life and includes various eyewitness accounts by folk who worked there.

THE HOUSES OF PARLIAMENT

Map 4, H13. Ⓦ www.parliament.uk ⊖ Westminster.

Clearly visible at the south end of Whitehall is one of London's best-known monuments, the Palace of Westminster, better known as the **Houses of Parliament**. The city's finest Victorian Gothic Revival building and symbol of a nation once confident of its place at the centre of the world, it is distinguished above all by the ornate, gilded clock tower popularly known as **Big Ben**, after the thirteen-ton main bell that strikes the hour (and is broadcast across the world by the BBC).

The original **Westminster Palace** was built by Edward the Confessor in the first half of the eleventh century, so that he could watch over the building of his abbey. It then served as the seat of all the English monarchs until a fire forced Henry VIII to decamp to Whitehall. The Lords have always convened at the palace, but it was only following Henry's death that the House of Commons moved from the abbey's Chapter House into the palace's St Stephen's Chapel, thus beginning the building's associations with parliament.

In 1834 the old palace burned down. The chief relic of the medieval palace is the bare expanse of **Westminster Hall**, on the north side of the complex. Built by William Rufus in 1099, it's one of the most magnificent secular medieval halls in Europe – you get a glimpse of the hall en route to the public galleries. The **Jewel Tower** (daily: April–Sept 10am–6pm; Oct 10am–5pm; Nov–March

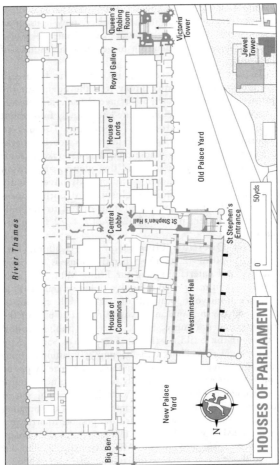

HOUSES OF PARLIAMENT

River Thames

Queen's Robing Room

Victoria Tower

Jewel Tower

Royal Gallery

House of Lords

Old Palace Yard

Central Lobby

St Stephen's Hall

St Stephen's Entrance

House of Commons

Westminster Hall

New Palace Yard

Big Ben

N

0   50yds

© crown copyright

THE HOUSES OF PARLIAMENT

29

10am–4pm; £1.60), across the road from parliament, is another remnant of the medieval palace, now housing an excellent exhibition on the history of parliament – worth visiting before you queue up to get into the Houses of Parliament.

To watch the proceedings in either the House of Commons or the Lords, simply join the queue for the **public galleries** (known as Strangers' Galleries) outside St Stephen's Gate. The public are let in slowly from about 4pm onwards on Mondays, from 1pm Tuesday to Thursday, and from 10am on Fridays; the security checks are very tight, and the whole procedure can take an hour or more. If you want to avoid the queues, turn up an hour or more later, when the crowds have usually thinned. Recesses (holiday closures) of both Houses occur at Christmas, Easter, and from August to the middle of October; phone ℡020/7219 4272 for more information.

To see **Question Time** (Mon 2.30–3.30pm, Tues –Thurs 11.30am–12.30pm) – when the House is at its most raucous and entertaining and the Prime Minister usually present – you really need to book a **ticket** several weeks in advance from your local MP (if you're a UK citizen) or your embassy in London (if you're not). For part of the summer recess (Aug & Sept), there are public **guided tours** of the building (Mon, Tues, Fri & Sat 9.15am –4.30pm, Wed & Thurs 1.15–4.30pm; £7), lasting an hour and fifteen minutes. Visitors can book in advance by phoning ℡0870/906 3773, or simply head for the ticket office on Abingdon Green, opposite Victoria Tower. The rest of the year, it's still possible to organize a tour of the building through your MP or embassy. It's also possible to arrange a free guided tour up **Big Ben** (Mon–Fri only; no under-11s; free), again through your MP or embassy. To find out more about access requirements, phone ℡020/7219 4862.

WESTMINSTER ABBEY

Map 4, G13. Mon, Tues, Thurs & Fri 9.30am–4.45pm, Wed 9.30am–7pm, Sat 9.30am–2.45pm; £6; Ⓦ www.westminster-abbey .org ⊖ Westminster.

The Houses of Parliament dwarf their much older neighbour, **Westminster Abbey**, yet this single building embodies much of the history of England: it has been the venue for all the coronations since the time of William the Conqueror, and the site of more or less every royal burial for some five hundred years between the reigns of Henry III and George II. Scores of the nation's most famous citizens are honoured here, too (though many of the stones commemorate people buried elsewhere), and the interior is crammed with hundreds of monuments, reliefs and statues.

Entry is unfortunately via the north transept, cluttered with monuments to politicians and traditionally known as **Statesmen's Aisle**, shortly after which you come to the abbey's most dazzling architectural set piece, the **Lady Chapel**, added by Henry VII in 1503 as his future resting place. With its intricately carved vaulting and fan-shaped gilded pendants, the chapel represents the final spectacular gasp of the English Perpendicular style. Unfortunately, the public are no longer admitted to the **Shrine of Edward the Confessor**, the sacred heart of the building (except on a guided verger tour; £3), though you do get to inspect Edward I's **Coronation Chair**, a decrepit oak throne dating from around 1300 and still used for coronations.

Nowadays, the abbey's royal tombs are upstaged by **Poets' Corner**, in the south transept, though the first occupant, Geoffrey Chaucer, was in fact buried here not because he was a poet but because he lived nearby. By the eighteenth century this zone had become an artistic pantheon, and since then the transept has been filled with tributes to all shades of talent. From the south transept, you can

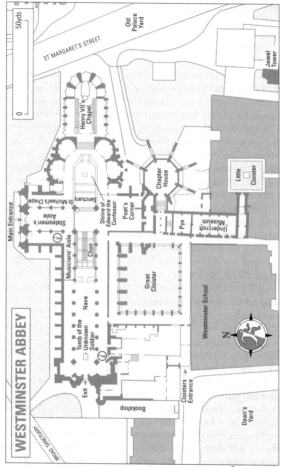

WESTMINSTER ABBEY

St Margaret's Street
Old Palace Yard
Jewel Tower
Henry VII's Chapel
Main Entrance
St Michael's Chapel
Statesmen's Aisle
Sanctuary
Shrine of Edward the Confessor
Musicians' Aisle
Poet's Corner
Chapter House
Choir
Little Cloister
Pyx
Undercroft Museum
Nave
Great Cloister
Tomb of the Unknown Soldier
Westminster School
Exit
Cloisters Entrance
Bookshop
Dean's Yard
BROAD SANCTUARY

50 yds
0

N

© crown copyright

view the central sanctuary, site of the coronations, and the wonderful **Cosmati floor mosaic**, constructed in the thirteenth century by Italian craftsmen, and often covered by a carpet to protect it.

Doors in the south choir aisle lead to the **Great Cloisters** (daily 8am–6pm), rebuilt after a fire in 1298. At the eastern end of the cloisters lies the octagonal **Chapter House** (daily: April–Sept 9.30am–5pm; Oct 10am–5pm; Nov–March 10am–4pm; £1), where the House of Commons met from 1257. The thirteenth-century decorative paving tiles and wall-paintings have survived intact. Chapter House tickets include entry to the **Abbey Museum** (daily 10.30am–4pm; £1, or free with an abbey ticket), filled with generations of bald royal death masks and wax effigies.

It's only after exploring the cloisters that you get to see the **nave** itself: narrow, light and, at over a hundred feet in height, by far the tallest in the country. The most famous monument is the **Tomb of the Unknown Soldier**, by the west door, which now serves as the main exit.

TATE BRITAIN

Map 3, H8. Daily 10am–5.50pm; free; Ⓦ www.tate.org.uk
⊖ Pimlico.

- -
The Tate offers audioguides to the displays for £3.
- -

Tate Britain, the purpose-built gallery half a mile south of parliament, founded in 1897 with money from Henry Tate, inventor of the sugar cube, is now devoted exclusively to British art. As well as displaying British art from 1500 to the present, plus a whole wing devoted to Turner, Tate Britain also showcases contemporary British artists and continues to sponsor the Turner Prize, the country's most prestigious modern-art prize.

TATE BRITAIN

The galleries are rehung more or less annually, but will always include a fair selection of works by British artists such as Hogarth, Constable, Gainsborough, Reynolds and Blake, plus foreign artists like Van Dyck who spent much of their career over here. The ever-popular **Pre-Raphaelites** are always well represented, as are established twentieth-century greats such as Stanley Spencer and Francis Bacon alongside living artists such as David Hockney and Lucian Freud. Lastly, don't miss the Tate's outstanding **Turner collection**, displayed in the Clore Gallery.

WESTMINSTER CATHEDRAL

Map 3, G7. Mon–Fri & Sun 7am–7pm, Sat 8am–7pm; free; Ⓦ www.rcdow.org.uk ⊖ Victoria.

Halfway down Victoria Street from Westminster Abbey, you'll find one of London's most surprising churches, the stripy neo-Byzantine concoction of the Roman Catholic **Westminster Cathedral**. Begun in 1895, it is one of the last and wildest monuments to the Victorian era: constructed from more than twelve million terracotta-coloured bricks and decorated with hoops of Portland stone, it culminates in a magnificent tapered **campanile** which rises to 274 feet, served by a lift (April–Nov daily 9.30am–12.30pm & 1–5pm; Dec–March Thurs–Sun 9.30am–12.30pm & 1–5pm; £2). The **interior** is only half-finished, so to get an idea of what the place will look like when it's finally completed, explore the series of **side-chapels** whose rich, multicoloured décor makes use of over one hundred different marbles from around the world. Be sure, too, to check out the low-relief **Stations of the Cross** sculpted by the controversial Eric Gill during World War I.

St James's, Piccadilly, Mayfair and Marylebone

St James's, **Mayfair** and **Marylebone** emerged in the late seventeenth century as London's first real suburbs, characterized by grid-plan streets feeding into grand, formal squares. This expansion set the westward trend for middle-class migration, and as London's wealthier consumers moved west, so too did the city's more upmarket shops and luxury hotels, which are still a feature of the area.

Aristocratic St James's, the rectangle of land to the north of St James's Park, was one of the first areas to be developed, and remains the preserve of the seriously rich. **Piccadilly**, which forms the border between St James's and Mayfair, is no longer the fashionable promenade it once was, but a whiff of exclusivity still pervades **Bond Street** and its tributaries. **Regent Street** was created as a new "Royal Mile", a tangible borderline to shore up these new fashionable suburbs against the chaotic maze of Soho and the City, where the working population still lived. Now, along with **Oxford Street**, it has become London's busiest shopping district – it's here that Londoners mean when they talk of "going shopping up the West End".

Marylebone, which lies to the north of Oxford Street, is another grid-plan Georgian development, a couple of social and property leagues below Mayfair, but a wealthy area nevertheless. It boasts a very fine art gallery, the **Wallace Collection**, and, in its northern fringes, one of London's biggest tourist attractions, **Madame Tussaud's**, the oldest and largest wax museum in the world.

ST JAMES'S

Map 4, E9. ⊖ Piccadilly Circus or Green Park.

St James's, the exclusive little enclave sandwiched between The Mall and Piccadilly, was laid out in the 1670s close to St James's Palace. Royal and aristocratic residences predominate along its southern border, gentlemen's clubs cluster along Pall Mall and St James's Street, while jacket-and-tie restaurants and expense-account gentlemen's outfitters line Jermyn Street. Hardly surprising, then, that most Londoners rarely stray into this area.

St James's does, however, contain some interesting architectural set pieces, such as **Lower Regent Street** (Map 4, E8), which was the first stage in John Nash's ambitious plan to link George IV's magnificent Carlton House with Regent's Park. Like so many of Nash's grandiose schemes, it never quite came to fruition, as George IV, soon after ascending the throne, decided that Carlton House – the most expensive palace ever to have been built in London – wasn't quite luxurious enough, and had it pulled down. Instead, Lower Regent Street now opens up into **Waterloo Place** (Map 4, F9), at the centre of which stands the Guards' Crimean Memorial, fashioned from captured

Russian cannons and featuring a statue of Florence Nightingale. Clearly visible, beyond, is the "Grand Old" **Duke of York's Column**, erected in 1833, ten years before Nelson's more famous one.

Cutting across Waterloo Place, **Pall Mall** – named after the croquet-like game of *pallo a maglio* ("ball to mallet") – leads west to **St James's Palace** (Map 4, D11), whose main red-brick gate-tower is pretty much all that remains of the Tudor palace erected here by Henry VIII. When Whitehall Palace burned down in 1698, St James's became the principal royal residence and, in keeping with tradition, an ambassador to the UK is still known as "Ambassador to the Court of St James", even though the court moved down the road to Buckingham Palace when Queen Victoria ascended the throne. The rambling complex now provides a bachelor pad for **Prince Charles** (Ⓦ www .princeofwales.gov.uk) and is off limits to the public, with the exception of the **Chapel Royal** (Oct–Good Friday Sun 8.30am & 11.15am), situated within the palace, and the **Queen's Chapel** (Map 4, E10; Easter–July Sun 8.30am & 11.15am), on the other side of Marlborough Road – both are open for services only.

One palatial St James's residence you can visit, however, is the late Princess Diana's ancestral home, **Spencer House** (Map 4, D10; Feb–July & Sept–Dec Sun 10.30am–5.45pm; £6), a superb Palladian mansion erected in the 1750s. Inside, guides take you on an hour-long tour through nine of the state rooms, the most outrageous of which is Lord Spencer's Room, with its astonishing gilded palm-tree columns.

PICCADILLY CIRCUS

Map 4, E8. ⊖ Piccadilly Circus.

Anonymous and congested it may be, but **Piccadilly Circus**, is, for many Londoners, the nearest their city comes to having a centre. A much-altered product of Nash's grand 1812 Regent Street plan, and now a major traffic bottleneck, it's by no means a picturesque place, and is probably best seen at night, when the spread of vast illuminated signs (a feature since the Edwardian era) gives it a touch of Las Vegas dazzle.

As well as being the gateway to the West End, this is also prime tourist territory, thanks mostly to Piccadilly's celebrated aluminium statue, popularly known as **Eros**. The fountain's archer is one of the city's top attractions, a status that baffles all who live here. Despite the bow and arrow, it's not the god of love at all but the Angel of Christian Charity, erected to commemorate the Earl of Shaftesbury, a Bible-thumping social reformer who campaigned, among other things, against child labour.

REGENT STREET

Map 4, D7. ⊖ Piccadilly Circus or Oxford Circus.

Regent Street, leading north off Piccadilly Circus, is like one of Haussmann's Parisian boulevards without the trees. Drawn up by John Nash in 1812 as both a luxury shopping street and a triumphal way between George IV's Carlton House and Regent's Park, it was the city's first attempt at dealing with traffic congestion, and also the first stab at slum clearance and planned social segregation, which would later be perfected by the Victorians.

Despite the subsequent destruction of much of Nash's work in the 1920s, it's still possible to admire the stately intentions of his original Regent Street plan. The increase in the purchasing power of the city's middle classes in the nineteenth century brought the tone of the street "down", and heavyweight stores catering for the masses now predominate. Among the oldest established stores are **Hamley's**, the world's largest toy shop, and **Liberty**, the department store that popularized Arts and Crafts designs at the beginning of the twentieth century.

PICCADILLY

Map 4, E8. ⊖ Piccadilly Circus or Green Park.

Piccadilly apparently got its name from the ruffs or "pickadills" worn by the dandies who used to promenade here in the late seventeenth century. Despite its fashionable pedigree, it's no place for promenading in its current state, with traffic careering down it nose to tail most of the day and night. Infinitely more pleasant places to window-shop are the various nineteenth-century arcades, originally built to protect shoppers from the mud and horse dung on the streets, but now equally useful for escaping exhaust fumes.

Piccadilly may not be the shopping heaven it once was, but there are still several old firms here that proudly display their royal warrants. One of the oldest institutions is the food emporium of **Fortnum & Mason** (Map 4, D9; ⓦ www.fortnumandmason.com) at no. 181, established in the 1770s by one of George III's footmen, Charles Fortnum, and his partner Hugh Mason. In a kitsch addition dating from 1964, the figures of Fortnum and Mason bow to each other on the hour every day as the clock over the main entrance clanks and plays the Eton school anthem.

Further along Piccadilly, with its best rooms overlooking Green Park, stands the **Ritz Hotel** (Map 4, C9; ⓦ www.theritzhotel.co.uk), a byword for decadence since it first wowed Edwardian society in 1906; the hotel's design, with its two-storey French-style mansard roof and long arcade, was based on the buildings of Paris's Rue de Rivoli. For a prolonged look inside, you'll need to be in good appetite and properly attired for the famous afternoon tea in the hotel's Palm Court (book in advance).

The Royal Academy of Arts

Map 4, D8. Daily 10am–6pm, Fri till10pm; £5–8; guided tours of the permanent collection Tues–Fri 1pm; free; ⓦ www.royalacademy .org.uk ⊖ Green Park or Piccadilly Circus.

Across the road from Fortnum & Mason, the **Royal Academy of Arts** (RA) occupies the enormous Burlington House, one of the few survivors from the ranks of aristocratic mansions that once lined the north side of Piccadilly. The Academy itself was the country's first ever formal art school, founded in 1768 by a group of English painters including Thomas Gainsborough and Joshua Reynolds. Reynolds went on to become the Academy's first president, and his statue now stands in the courtyard, palette in hand.

The Academy has always had a conservative reputation for its teaching and, until recently, most of its shows. The **Summer Exhibition**, which opens in June each year, remains a stop on the social calendar of upper middle-class England. Anyone can enter paintings in any style, and the lucky winners get hung, in rather close proximity, and sold. Supposed gravitas is added by the RA "Academicians", who are allowed to display six of their own works – no matter how awful. The result is a bewildering display, which gets annually panned by highbrow critics.

Burlington Arcade

Map 4, D8.

Running along the west side of the Royal Academy is the **Burlington Arcade**, built in 1819 for Lord Cavendish, then owner of Burlington House, to prevent commoners throwing rubbish into his garden. It's Piccadilly's longest and most expensive nineteenth-century arcade, lined with mahogany-fronted jewellers, gentlemen's outfitters and the like.

Upholding Regency decorum, it is still illegal to whistle, sing, hum, hurry or carry large packages or open umbrellas on this small stretch, and the arcade's beadles (known as Burlington Berties), in their Edwardian frock coats and gold-braided top hats, take the prevention of such criminality very seriously.

BOND STREET AND AROUND

Map 4, C7. ⊖ Green Park or Bond Street.

While Oxford Street, Regent Street and Piccadilly have all gone downmarket, **Bond Street**, which runs parallel to Regent Street, has carefully maintained its exclusivity. It is, in fact, two streets rolled into one: the southern half, laid out in the 1680s, is known as Old Bond Street; its northern extension, which followed less than fifty years later, is known as New Bond Street. They are both pretty unassuming streets architecturally, being a mixture of modest Victorian and Georgian town houses. However, the shops that line them, and those of neighbouring Conduit Street and South Molton Street, are among the flashiest in London, dominated by perfumeries, **jewellers** and designer clothing stores like Versace, Gucci, Nicole Farhi, Yves Saint-Laurent and so on.

In addition to fashion, Bond Street is also renowned for its **auction houses** and for its fine-art galleries. Despite the recent price-fixing scandal that resulted in the imprisonment of one of its former chairmen and a £12 million fine, business is still booming at Sotheby's (Map 4, C7; ⓦ www.sothebys.com), the oldest of the auction houses – its viewing galleries are open free of charge. Bond Street's **art galleries** are actually outnumbered by those on nearby Cork Street. The main difference between the two locations is that the Bond Street dealers are basically heirloom offloaders, whereas Cork Street galleries sell largely contemporary art. Both have impeccably presented and somewhat intimidating staff, but if you're interested, walk in and look around. They're only shops, after all.

Running parallel with New Bond Street and Cork Street is another classic address in sartorial matters, **Savile Row**, still the place to go for made-to-measure suits, for those with the requisite £2000 or so to spare. The number of bespoke tailors may have declined, but several venerable businesses remain. Gieves & Hawkes, at no. 1, were the first tailors to establish themselves here back in 1785, with Nelson and Wellington among their first customers, and their wares are still an exhibition of upper-class taste.

See p.302 for listings of the best shops in London.

Handel House Museum

Map 4, B6. Tues–Sat 10am–6pm, Thurs till 8pm, Sun noon–6pm; £4.50; ⊤ 020/7495 1685, ⓦ www.handelhouse.org ⊖ Bond Street

The German-born composer **George Friedrich Handel** (1685–1759) spent the best part of his life in London, producing all the work for which he is now best known at 25 Brook Street, just west of New Bond Street, now the **Handel House Museum**. The composer used the ground floor as a sort of shop where subscribers could buy scores, while the first floor was employed as a rehearsal room. Although containing few original artefacts, the house has been painstakingly reconstructed and redecorated to how it would have looked in Handel's day. Further atmosphere is provided by the harpsichord in the rehearsal room, which gets played by music students throughout the week, with more formal **performances** on Thursday evenings from 6pm (tickets are £5 and include admission to the museum). Access to the house is via the chic, cobbled yard at the back.

OXFORD STREET

Map 4, C5. Ⓦ www.oxfordstreet.co.uk ⊖ Bond Street, Oxford Circus or Tottenham Court Road.

As wealthy Londoners began to move out of the City in the eighteenth century in favour of the newly developed West End, so **Oxford Street** – the old Roman road to Oxford – gradually became London's main shopping street. Today, despite successive recessions and sky-high rents, this scruffy, two-mile hotchpotch of shops is still one of the world's busiest streets.

East of Oxford Circus, the street forms the northern border of Soho, and features two of the city's main record stores, HMV and Virgin Megastore, and the Borders megabookstore. West of Oxford Circus, the street is dominated by more upmarket stores, including one great landmark, **Selfridge's** (Map 3, E4; Ⓦ www.selfridges.co.uk), a huge Edwardian pile fronted by giant Ionic columns, with the Queen of Time riding the ship of commerce and supporting an Art Deco clock above the main entrance. The store was opened in 1909 by Chicago millionaire Gordon Selfridge, who flaunted its 130 departments under the slogan, "Why not spend a day at Selfridge's?", but was later pensioned off after running into trouble with the Inland Revenue.

THE WALLACE COLLECTION

Map 3, E4. Mon–Sat 10am–5pm, Sun noon–5pm; free; Ⓦ www.wallace-collection.org.uk ⊖ Bond Street.

Immediately north of Oxford Street, on Manchester Square, stands Hertford House, a miniature eighteenth-century French chateau which holds the splendid **Wallace Collection**, a museum-gallery best known for its eighteenth-century French paintings (especially Watteau), Frans

OXFORD STREET • THE WALLACE COLLECTION

Hals' *Laughing Cavalier*, Titian's *Perseus and Andromeda*, Velázquez's *Lady with a Fan* and Rembrandt's affectionate portrait of his teenage son, Titus. There's a modern café in the newly glassed-over courtyard, but at heart, the Wallace Collection remains an old-fashioned place, with exhibits piled high in glass cabinets, and paintings covering every inch of wall space. The fact that these exhibits are set amidst period fittings – and a bloody great armoury – makes the place even more remarkable. If you're here for the paintings, head for the Great Gallery on the first floor, where the best of the works are hung.

LANGHAM PLACE AND PORTLAND PLACE

Map 4, C3. ⊖ Oxford Circus.

Regent Street finally stops just north of Oxford Street at **Langham Place**, site of **All Souls**, Nash's simple and ingenious little Bath-stone church, built in the 1820s. The church's unusual circular Ionic portico and conical spire, which caused outrage in its day, were designed to provide a visual full stop to Regent Street and a pivot for the awkward twist in the triumphal route to Regent's Park. Behind lies the totalitarian-looking **Broadcasting House**, BBC radio headquarters since 1931. Opposite Broadcasting House stands the **Langham Hilton**, built in heavy Italianate style in the 1860s, badly bombed in the last war, but now back to its former glory.

After the chicane around All Souls, you enter **Portland Place**, laid out by the Adam brothers in the 1770s, and incorporated by Nash in his grand route. Once the widest street in London, it's still a majestic avenue, lined exclusively with Adam-style houses boasting wonderful fanlights and iron railings.

Arguably the finest of all the buildings on Portland Place, though, is the sleek **Royal Institute of British**

Architects at no. 66 (RIBA; ⓦ www.architecture.com), built in the 1930s. The highlight of the building is the interior, which you can view en route to the institute's excellent first-floor café (Mon–Fri 8am–6pm, Sat 9am–5pm), or during one of the frequent exhibitions and Tuesday-evening lectures held here. The main staircase remains a wonderful period piece, with its etched glass balustrades and walnut veneer, and with two large, fluted black–marble columns rising up on either side.

MADAME TUSSAUD'S AND THE PLANETARIUM

Map 3, E3. Mon–Fri 10am–5.30pm; Sat & Sun 9am–5.30pm; school holidays daily 9am–5.30pm; £14.95, Sat & Sun in peak season £16.95. ⊖ Baker Street.

Madame Tussaud's, just up Marylebone Road from Baker Street tube, has been pulling in the crowds ever since the good lady arrived in London from Paris in 1802 bearing the sculpted heads of guillotined aristocrats (she herself only just managed to escape the same fate – her uncle, who started the family business, was less fortunate). The entrance fee might be extortionate, the likenesses occasionally dubious and the automated dummies inept, but you can still rely on finding London's biggest queues here. The only way to avoid queuing is to pay extra and book a timed entry ticket in advance over the phone or on the Internet.

You can buy tickets for Tussaud's and the Planetarium
(or both) in advance over the phone ⓣ 0870/400 3000
or online at ⓦ www.madame-tussauds.com

As well as the usual parade of wax figures, the tour of Tussaud's ends with a manic five-minute "ride" through the history of London in a miniaturized taxi cab. Tickets for Madame Tussaud's also cover entry to the adjoining

Soho and Chinatown

When **Soho** – named for the cry that resounded through the district when it was a hunting ground – was first developed in the seventeenth century, its streets were among the most sought-after addresses in the capital. By the end of the eighteenth century, however, the party was over, the rich moved west to Mayfair, and Soho began its inexorable descent into poverty and overcrowding. Over the next hundred years, Soho became, along with the East End, the city's main dumping ground for immigrants – most recently Asians, particularly the Chinese, who took advantage of Soho's cheap rents for their workshops and restaurants. Soho has also long been a favourite haunt of the capital's creative bohos and literati. Its reputation for tolerance also made it an obvious place of refuge from dour, postwar Britain, its many clubs riding the waves of jazz and skiffle in the 1950s, folk and rock in the 1960s, and punk rock at the end of the 1970s.

Soho retains a uniquely unorthodox and slightly raffish air, and gives you the best and worst of London. It has long been the city's premier red-light district, especially to the west of Wardour Street, but in the 1990s Soho transformed itself again, this time into one of Europe's leading gay centres, with bars and cafés bursting out from the **Old Compton Street** area. Nevertheless, the area continues to boast a lively fruit and vegetable market on **Berwick Street**, and nightlife that has attracted writers and ravers since the eighteenth century. The big movie houses on **Leicester Square** always attract crowds of punters, and the tiny enclave of **Chinatown** continues to double as a focus for the Chinese community and a popular place for inexpensive Oriental restaurants.

For Soho's café, pub and restaurant
listings, see chapters 16, 17 & 18.

LEICESTER SQUARE

Map 4, G7. ⊖ Leicester Square.

By night, when the big cinemas and discos are doing good business, and the buskers are entertaining passers-by, **Leicester Square** is one of the most crowded places in London, particularly on a Friday or Saturday, when huge numbers of tourists and half the youth of the suburbs seem to congregate here. By day, queues form for half-price deals at the ticket booth at the south end of the square, while touts haggle over the price of dodgy tickets for the top shows, and clubbers hand out flyers to likely-looking punters.

For the lowdown on buying theatre tickets, see p.282.

It wasn't until the mid-nineteenth century that the square actually began to emerge as an entertainment zone, with accommodation houses (for prostitutes and their clients) and music halls such as the grandiose Empire and the

Hippodrome (just off the square), edifices which survive today as cinemas and discos. Cinema moved in during the 1930s, a golden age evoked by the sleek black lines of the Odeon on the east side, and maintains its grip on the area. The Empire, at the top end of the square, is the favourite for big premieres, and, in a rather half-hearted imitation of the Hollywood (and Cannes) tradition, there are even handprints visible in the pavement by the southwestern corner of the square.

CHINATOWN

Map 4, F7. ⊖ Leicester Square.

Chinatown, hemmed in between Leicester Square and Shaftesbury Avenue, is a self-contained jumble of shops, cafés and restaurants that makes up one of London's most distinct and popular ethnic enclaves. **Gerrard Street**, Chinatown's main drag, has been endowed with ersatz touches – fake Oriental gates and telephone kiosks rigged out as pagodas – but few of London's 60,000 Chinese actually live in the three small blocks of Chinatown. Nonetheless, it remains a focus for the community, a place to do business or the weekly shopping, celebrate a wedding, or just meet up for meals, particularly on Sundays, when the restaurants overflow with Chinese families tucking into *dim sum*.

The **Chinese New Year** celebrations, instigated here in 1973, draw in thousands of Chinese for the Sunday nearest to New Year's Day (late January or early February). Huge papier-mâché lions dance through the streets to a cacophony of firecrackers, devouring cabbages hung from the upper floors by strings pinned with money. The noise is deafening, and if you want to see anything you'll need to position yourself close to one of the cabbages around noon and stand your ground.

CHINATOWN

For Chinatown restaurant listings, see p.211.

For the rest of the year, most Londoners come to Chinatown simply to eat – easy and inexpensive enough to do, though the choice is somewhat overwhelming, especially on Gerrard Street itself. Cantonese cuisine predominates, and you're unlikely to be disappointed wherever you go.

CHARING CROSS ROAD AND SHAFTESBURY AVENUE

Map 4, G6. ⊖ Leicester Square or Tottenham Court Road.

Charing Cross Road, Soho's eastern border and a thoroughfare from Trafalgar Square to Oxford Street, boasts the highest concentration of **bookshops** anywhere in London. One of the first to open here was Foyles at no. 119, which now struggles to compete with the nearby heavyweight chain bookshops such as Borders and Blackwell's. The street retains more of its original character south of Cambridge Circus, where you'll find Alhoda, the Islamic bookshop, along with a cluster of ramshackle secondhand bookshops, such as Quinto.

One of the nicest places for secondhand book browsing is **Cecil Court** (Map 4, G7), the southernmost alleyway between Charing Cross Road and St Martin's Lane. This short, pedestrianized street boasts specialist bookshops devoted to theatre, Italy, New Age philosophies and the like, plus various antiquarian dealers. Another place you shouldn't miss, just off Charing Cross Road, is the **Photographers' Gallery** (Map 4, G7; Mon–Sat 11am–6pm, Sun noon–6pm; free; ⓦ www.photonet.org.uk) at 5 and 8 Great Newport St, which hosts temporary exhibitions that are invariably worth a browse, and has a lovely, peaceful café.

Sweeping northeast towards Bloomsbury from Piccadilly Circus, and separating Soho proper from Chinatown, the gentle curve of **Shaftesbury Avenue** is the heart of mainstream theatreland, with numerous theatres and cinemas along its length. Like Charing Cross Road, it was conceived in the late 1870s, ostensibly to relieve traffic congestion but with the dual purpose of destroying the slums that lay in its path. Ironically, it was then named after Lord Shaftesbury, whose life had been spent trying to help the likes of those dispossessed by the road scheme.

OLD COMPTON STREET AND CENTRAL SOHO

Map 4, F6. ⊖ Leicester Square or Piccadilly Circus.

If Soho has a main drag, it has to be **Old Compton Street**, which runs parallel with Shaftesbury Avenue. The corner shops, peep shows, boutiques and trendy cafés here are typical of the area and a good barometer of the latest Soho fads. Soho was a permanent fixture on the **gay scene** for much of the twentieth century, but the approach is much more upfront nowadays, with gay bars, clubs and cafés jostling for position on Old Compton Street, and round the corner in Wardour Street. And it doesn't stop there: there's now a gay travel agency, a gay financial adviser and a gay taxi service.

- -

For gay and lesbian listings, see p.253.

- -

The streets off Old Compton Street are lined with Soho institutions past and present. One of the best known is London's longest-running jazz club, *Ronnie Scott's* (ⓦ www.ronniescotts.co.uk; see listings p.245), on **Frith Street**, founded in 1958 and still capable of pulling in the big names. Opposite is the *Bar Italia*, an Italian café with a big screen for satellite TV transmissions of Italian football games, and late-night hours popular with Soho's clubbers. It was in this building, appropriately enough for such a media-saturated area, that John Logie Baird made the world's first public television transmission in 1926.

Wardour Street and beyond

Map 4, E6.

At the western end of Old Compton Street runs **Wardour Street**, a kind of dividing line between the trendier, eastern half of Soho and the seedier western zone. The street itself is largely given over to the film industry – Warner Brothers has an office here, along with numerous smaller production companies.

Immediately west of Wardour Street, the sex and prostitution rackets still have the area well staked out. However, straight prostitution in fact makes up a small proportion of what gets sold here – dodgy video shops, short con outfits and rip-off joints are more indicative of the area. Paul Raymond – one of Britain's richest men – set up his *Folies-Bergères*-style *Revue Bar* in the late 1950s, and is still hanging on in there despite the arrival of lapdancing in the West End.

In amongst the video shops and triple-X-rated cinemas is the unlikely sight of **Berwick Street Market**, one of the capital's finest (and cheapest) fruit and vegetable markets. The street itself is no beauty spot, but the market's barrow displays are works of art in themselves, while, on either side of the marketholders, are some of London's best specialist record shops.

Carnaby Street

Map 4, D6. ⊖ Oxford Circus.

Until the 1950s, **Carnaby Street** (ⓦ www.carnaby.co.uk) was a backstreet on Soho's western fringe, occupied, for the most part, by sweatshop tailors who used to make up the suits for nearby Savile Row. Then, sometime in the mid-1950s, several trendy boutiques opened catering for the new market in flamboyant men's clothing. In 1964 – the year of the official birth of the Carnaby Street myth – Mods, West Indian Rude Boys and other "switched-on people", as the *Daily Telegraph* noted, began to hang out here. The area quickly became the epicentre of Swinging Sixties London, and its street sign London's most popular postcard. A victim of its own hype, Carnaby Street declined equally quickly into an avenue of overpriced tack. More recently, the street has been smartened up, along with neighbouring Newburgh Street, and the whole area is enjoying a new lease of life, though it's never going to recapture the excitement of the 1960s.

OLD COMPTON STREET AND CENTRAL SOHO

Bloomsbury and the British Museum

Bloomsbury gets its name from its medieval landowners, the Blemunds, though nothing was built here until the 1660s. Through marriage, the Russell family (the earls and later dukes of Bedford) acquired much of the area, and established the many formal, bourgeois squares that are the main distinguishing feature of Bloomsbury today. The Russells named the grid-plan streets after their various titles and estates, and kept the pubs and shops to a minimum to maintain the tone of the neighbourhood.

In the twentieth century, Bloomsbury acquired a reputation as the city's most learned quarter, dominated by the dual institutions of the **British Museum** and **London University**, and home to many of London's chief book publishers, but perhaps best known for its literary inhabitants. Today, the British Museum is clearly the star attraction, but there are other sights, such as the **Dickens' House Museum**, that are high on many people's itineraries.

In its northern fringes, the character of the area changes dramatically, becoming steadily more seedy as you near the

THE BLOOMSBURY GROUP

The Bloomsbury Group were essentially a bevy of upper middle-class friends, who lived in and around Bloomsbury. The Group revolved around Virginia, Vanessa, Thoby and Adrian Stephen, who moved into 46 Gordon Square in 1904. Thoby's Thursday evening gatherings and Vanessa's Friday Club for painters attracted a whole host of Cambridge-educated snobs who subscribed to Oscar Wilde's theory that "aesthetics are higher than ethics". Their diet of "human intercourse and the enjoyment of beautiful things" was hardly revolutionary, but their behaviour, particularly that of the two sisters (unmarried, unchaperoned, intellectual and artistic), succeeded in shocking London society, especially through their louche sexual practices (most of the group swung both ways).

All this, though interesting, would be forgotten were it not for their individual work. In 1922 Virginia declared, without too much exaggeration, that "Everyone in Gordon Square has become famous". Lytton Strachey had been the first to make his name with *Eminent Victorians*, a series of unprecedentedly frank biographies; Vanessa, now married to the art critic Clive Bell, had become involved in Roger Fry's prolific design firm, Omega Workshop; and the economist John Maynard Keynes had become an adviser to the Treasury (he later went on to become the leading economic theorist of his day). The Group's most celebrated figure, Virginia, now married to Leonard Woolf and living in Tavistock Square, had become an established novelist; she and Leonard had also founded the Hogarth Press, which published T.S. Eliot's *The Waste Land* in 1922. Whatever their limitations, the Bloomsbury Group were Britain's most influential intellectual coterie of the interwar years, and their appeal shows little sign of waning.

two big main-line train stations of **Euston** and **King's Cross**, where cheap B&Bs and run-down council estates provide fertile territory for prostitutes and drug dealers, and an unlikely location for the new **British Library**.

THE BRITISH MUSEUM

Map 4, G3. Mon–Wed, Sat & Sun 10am–5.30pm, Thurs & Fri 10am–8.30pm; free; ⓦ www.british-museum.ac.uk ⊖ Tottenham Court Road or Russell Square.

One of the great museums of the world, the **British Museum** is Britain's most popular tourist attraction after Blackpool, drawing more than six million visitors a year. With over four million exhibits ranged over two and a half miles of galleries, the BM contains one of the most comprehensive collections of antiquities, prints, drawings and books to be housed under one roof.

The building itself, begun in 1823, is the grandest of London's Greek Revival edifices, dominated by the giant Ionian colonnade and portico that forms the main entrance. The British Library's departure to St Pancras (see p.60) has allowed the museum to open up and redevelop the building's **Great Court** (Mon–Wed, Sat & Sun 9am–6pm, Thurs & Fri 9am–11pm), which now features a remarkable, curving glass-and-steel roof, designed by Norman Foster. At the centre stands the copper-domed former **Round Reading Room**, built in the 1850s to house the British Library. It was here, at desk O7, beneath one of the largest domes in the world, that Karl Marx penned *Das Kapital*. The building is now a public study area, and features a multimedia guide to the museum's collections.

The BM's collection of **Roman and Greek antiquities** is unparalleled, and is perhaps most famous for the Parthenon sculptures, better known as the **Elgin Marbles**, after the British aristocrat who walked off with the reliefs in 1801. Amidst the plethora of Greek and Roman statuary and vases, the only other single item with a similarly high profile is the **Portland Vase**, made from cobalt-blue blown glass around the beginning of the first century, and decorated with opaque white cameos.

Great Court also houses the museum shop,
with its excellent selection of books and
periodicals as well as a café and restaurant.

The museum's **Egyptian collection** is easily the most significant outside Egypt, and ranges from monumental sculptures, such as the colossal granite head of Amenophis III, to the ever-popular mummies and their ornate outer caskets. Also on display is the **Rosetta Stone**, which finally unlocked the secret of Egyptian hieroglyphs. Close by the Egyptian Hall, you'll find a splendid series of **Assyrian reliefs** from Nineveh, depicting events such as the royal lion hunts of Ashurbanipal, in which the king slaughters one of the cats with his bare hands. Among the most extraordinary artefacts from **Mesopotamia** are the enigmatic Ram in the Thicket (a lapis lazuli and shell statuette of a goat), an equally mysterious box known as the Standard of Ur, and the remarkable hoard of goldwork known as the Oxus Treasure.

The leathery half-corpse of the 2000-year-old **Lindow Man**, discovered in a Cheshire bog, and the Anglo-Saxon treasure from the **Sutton Hoo** ship burial, are among the highlights of the prehistoric and Romano-British collection. The medieval and modern collections, meanwhile, range from the twelfth-century Lewis chessmen, carved from walrus ivory, to twentieth-century exhibits such as a copper vase by Frank Lloyd Wright. It's also worth seeking out the museum's **Money Gallery**, which begins with the

THE BRITISH MUSEUM

use of grain in Mesopotamia around 2000 BC, ends with a 1990s 500,000 million Yugoslav dinar note, and includes coins from all over the world.

The dramatically lit Mexican and North American galleries, plus the new African galleries in the basement, mark the beginning of the return of the museum's **ethnographic collection**, but lack of space means that only a fraction of the BM's enormous collection of prints and drawings can be displayed at any one time. In addition, there are fabulous **Oriental treasures** in the north wing of the museum, closest to the back entrance on Montague Place. The displays include ancient Chinese porcelain, ornate snuffboxes, miniature landscapes, a bewildering array of Buddhist and Hindu gods, and – the showpiece of the collection – dazzling limestone reliefs from the second-century stupa of Amaravati in south India.

DICKENS' HOUSE

Map 3, J3. Mon–Sat 10am–5pm, Sun 11am–5pm; £4; Ⓦ www.dickensmuseum.com ⊖ Russell Square.

Despite the plethora of blue plaques marking the residences of local luminaries, **Dickens' House**, at 48 Doughty St, in Bloomsbury's eastern fringes, is the area's only literary museum. Dickens moved here in 1837 shortly after his marriage to Catherine Hogarth, and they lived here for two years, during which time he wrote *Nicholas Nickleby* and *Oliver Twist*. This is the only one of Dickens' fifteen London addresses to survive intact, but only the drawing room, in which Dickens entertained his literary friends, has been restored to its original Regency style. Letters, manuscripts and lots of memorabilia, including first editions, the earliest known portrait and the annotated books he used during extensive lecture tours, are the rewards for those with more than a passing interest in the novelist.

THE UNIVERSITY

Map 4, G2. Ⓦ www.lon.ac.uk ↔ Russell Square or Goodge Street.

London has more students than any other city in the world (over half a million at the last count), which isn't bad going for a city that only organized its own **University** in 1826, more than six hundred years after the likes of Oxford and Cambridge. The university started life in Bloomsbury, but it wasn't until after World War I that the institution really began to take over the area.

The university's piecemeal development means that its departments are spread over a wide area, though the main focus is between the 1930s **Senate House** skyscraper, behind the British Museum, and the Neoclassical **University College** (UCL; Ⓦ www.ucl.ac.uk), near the top of Gower Street. UCL is home to London's most famous art school, the **Slade**, which puts on temporary exhibitions from its collection in the **Strang Print Room**, in the south cloister of the main quadrangle (term-time Wed–Fri 1–5pm; free). Also on display in the south cloisters is the fully clothed skeleton of philosopher **Jeremy Bentham** (1748–1832), one of the university's founders, topped by a wax head and wide-brimmed hat.

The university also runs a couple of specialist museums. On the first floor of the D.M.S. Watson building on Malet Place, off Torrington Place, the **Petrie Museum of Egyptian Archeology** (Map 4, F1; Tues–Fri 1–5pm, Sat 10am–1pm; free; Ⓦ www.petrie.ucl.ac.uk) has a couple of rooms jam-packed with antiquities, including the world's oldest dress. Further east down Torrington Place, tucked away in the southeast corner of Gordon Square, at no. 53, the **Percival David Foundation of Chinese Art** (Mon–Fri 10.30am–5pm; free; Ⓦ www.pdfmuseum.org.uk) houses two floors of top-notch Chinese ceramics. Lastly, the temporary exhibitions of photography and art at the

THE UNIVERSITY

Brunei Gallery (Map 4, G1; Mon–Fri 10.30am–5pm; free), which is part of the School of Oriental and African Studies, east of Malet Street, are usually well worth visiting.

THE BRITISH LIBRARY

Map 3, H2. Mon & Wed–Fri 9.30am–6pm, Tues 9.30am–8pm, Sat 9.30am–5pm, Sun 11am–5pm; free; ⓦ www.bl.uk ⊖ King's Cross or Euston.

The new **British Library**, located on the busy Euston Road on the northern fringes of Bloomsbury, opened to the public in 1998. As the country's most expensive public building it was hardly surprising that the place drew fierce criticism from all sides. Architecturally, the charge was led, predictably enough, by Prince Charles, who compared it to an academy for secret policemen. Yet, while it's true that the building's red-brick brutalism is horribly out of fashion, and compares unfavourably with its cathedralesque Victorian neighbour, the former *Midland Grand Hotel*, the interior of the library has met with general approval, and the hi-tech exhibition galleries are superb.

With the exception of the reading rooms, the library is open to the general public. The three exhibition galleries are to the left as you enter; straight ahead is the spiritual heart of the BL, a multistorey glass-walled tower housing the vast **King's Library**, collected by George III and donated to the museum by George IV in 1823; to the side of the King's Library are the pull-out drawers of the **philatelic collection**. If you want to explore the parts of the building not normally open to the public, you must sign up for a **guided tour** (Mon, Wed & Fri 3pm, Sat 10.30am & 3pm; £6; or Sun 11.30am & 3pm if you want to see the reading rooms; £7).

The first of the three exhibition galleries to head for is the dimly lit **John Ritblat Gallery**, where a superlative selection of the BL's ancient manuscripts, maps, documents and precious books, including the richly illustrated Lindisfarne Gospels, is displayed. One of the most appealing innovations is **"Turning the Pages"**, a small room off the main gallery, where you can turn the pages of selected texts "virtually" on a computer terminal. The **Workshop of Words, Sounds and Images** is a hands-on exhibition of more universal appeal, where you can design your own literary publication, while the **Pearson Gallery of Living Words** puts on excellent temporary exhibitions, for which there is sometimes an admission charge.

THE BRITISH LIBRARY

Covent Garden and the Strand

Covent Garden's transformation from a fruit and vegetable market into a fashion-conscious *quartier* is one of the most miraculous and enduring developments of the 1980s. More sanitized and brazenly commercial than neighbouring Soho, Covent Garden today is a far cry from its heyday when the **piazza** was the great playground (and red-light district) of eighteenth-century London. The buskers in front of St Paul's Church, the theatres round about and the **Royal Opera House** on Bow Street are survivors in this tradition, and on a balmy summer evening **Covent Garden Piazza** is still an undeniably lively place to be. Another positive side effect of the market development has been the renovation of the rundown warehouses to the north of the piazza, especially around the Neal Street area, which now boasts some of the most fashionable shops in the West End, selling everything from shoes to skateboards.

As its name suggests, the **Strand**, just to the south of Covent Garden, once lay along the riverbank: it achieved its present-day form when the Victorians shored up the banks of the Thames to create the Embankment. The Strand's most intriguing sight is **Somerset House,** the sole survivor of the street's grandiose river palaces, which now houses several museums and galleries as well as a lovely new fountain courtyard.

COVENT GARDEN PIAZZA

Map 4, I6. ⊖ Covent Garden.

London's oldest planned square, laid out in the 1630s by Inigo Jones, **Covent Garden Piazza** was initially a great success, its novelty value alone attracting a rich and aristocratic clientele. Over the next century, though, the tone of the place fell as the fruit and vegetable market expanded, and theatres and coffee houses began to take over the peripheral buildings. When the flower market closed in 1974, the piazza narrowly survived being turned into an office development. Instead, the elegant Victorian market hall and its environs were restored to house shops, restaurants and arts-and-crafts stalls. Boosted by buskers and street entertainers, the piazza has now become one of London's major tourist attractions, its success prompting a wholesale gentrification of the streets to the north of the market.

St Paul's Church

Map 4, H7.

Of Jones's original piazza, the only remaining parts are the two rebuilt sections of north-side arcading, and **St Paul's Church**, facing the west side of the market building. The proximity of so many theatres has earned it the nickname of the "Actors' Church", and it's filled with memorials to international thespians from Boris Karloff to Gracie Fields. The space in front of the church's Tuscan portico – where Eliza Doolittle was discovered selling violets by Henry

Higgins in George Bernard Shaw's *Pygmalion* – is now a legalized venue for buskers and street performers, who must audition for a slot months in advance.

The piazza's history of entertainment goes back to May 1662, when the first recorded performance of Punch and Judy in England was staged by Italian puppeteer Pietro Gimonde, and witnessed by Samuel Pepys. This historic event is commemorated every second Sunday in May by a **Punch and Judy Festival**, held in the gardens behind the church; for the rest of the year, the churchyard provides a tranquil respite from the activity outside (access is from King Street, Henrietta Street or Bedford Street).

London Transport Museum

Map 4, I6. Mon–Thurs, Sat & Sun 10am–6pm, Fri 11am–6pm; £5.95; Ⓦ www.ltmuseum.co.uk

A former flower-market shed on the piazza's east side is now home to the **London Transport Museum**. A herd of old buses, trains and trams make up the bulk of the exhibits, though there's enough interactive fun – touch-screen computers and the odd costumed conductor and vehicles to climb on – to keep most children amused. There's usually a good smattering of London Transport's stylish maps and posters on display, too, and you can buy reproductions, plus countless other LT paraphernalia, at the shop on the way out.

Theatre Museum

Map 4, I6. Tues–Sun 10am–6pm; free; Ⓦ www.theatremuseum.org

The rest of the old flower market now houses the **Theatre Museum**, displaying three centuries of memorabilia from every conceivable area of the performing arts in the West (the entrance is on Russell Street). The corridors of glass cases cluttered with props, programmes and costumes are not especially exciting, but the special exhibitions and long-term "temporary" shows tend to be a lot more fun, and usually have a performance, workshop or hands-on element to them. The museum also runs a booking service for West End shows and has an unusually good selection of cards and posters.

The Royal Opera House

Map 4, I6. ☎ 020/7304 4000, ⓦ www.royaloperahouse.org
The arcading in the northeast side of the piazza was rebuilt as part of the recent redevelopment of the **Royal Opera House** (see also listings, p.277), whose main Neoclassical facade dates from 1811 and opens onto Bow Street. Now, however, you can reach the opera house from a passageway in the corner of the arcading. The spectacular wrought-iron **Floral Hall** (daily 10am–3pm), on the first floor, serves as the opera house's main foyer, and is open to the public, as is the *Amphitheatre* bar/restaurant (open from 1hr 30min before the performance to the end of the last interval), which has a glorious terrace overlooking the piazza. **Backstage tours** of the opera house take place from Monday to Saturday (10.30am, 12.30 & 2.30pm; £7).

NORTH OF THE PIAZZA

Map 4, H6. ⊖ Covent Garden.
The area to the north of Covent Garden Piazza is, on the whole, more interesting in terms of its shops, pubs and eating places than the piazza itself. Floral Street, Long Acre, Shelton Street and especially Neal Street are all good shopping locales, with a mixture of chains, designer shops and small, trendy independent stores.

Looking east down the gentle curve of Long Acre, it's difficult to miss the austere, Pharaonic mass of the **Freemasons' Hall** (Map 4, I5; Mon–Fri 10am–5pm; free; ⓦ www.grandlodge-england.org), built as a memorial to all the masons who died in World War I. Whatever you may think of this reactionary, male-only, secretive organization, the interior is worth a peek for the Grand Temple alone, whose pompous, bombastic décor is laden with heavy symbolism. To see the Grand Temple, turn up for one of the free hourly **guided tours** (Mon–Fri 11am–4pm).

North from Long Acre runs **Neal Street**, one of the most-sought-after commercial addresses in Covent Garden, which features some fine Victorian warehouses, complete with stair towers for loading and shifting goods between floors. Today, Neal Street is dominated by big fashion stores like Mango and Diesel. A decade or so ago, though, the feel of the street was a lot less moneyed and more alternative – an ambience that only really survives in the area around **Neal's Yard**, a wholefood haven set in a tiny little courtyard off Shorts Gardens, prettily festooned with flower boxes and ivy. Round the corner at 17 Short's Gardens is Neal's Yard Dairy, the outstanding cheese emporium.

West of Neal Street is **Seven Dials** (Map 4, G6), the meeting point of seven streets which make up a little circus centred on a slender column topped by six tiny, blue sundials (the seventh dial is formed by the column itself and the surrounding road). **Earlham Street**, which runs west from Seven Dials, harbours an ironmonger's and a local butcher's alongside clubbers' shops. It was once a flourishing market street, and of the handful of stalls that remain is one of London's very best flower stalls – a visual treat at any time of year.

STRAND

Map 4, H8. ⊖ Charing Cross or Temple (Mon–Sat only).

Once famous for its riverside mansions, and later its music halls, the **Strand** – the main road connecting Westminster to the City – is a shadow of its former self. Nowadays, it's best known for the young homeless who shelter in the shop doorways at night.

One such doorway, at no. 440, belongs to what was once London's largest private bank, **Coutts & Co** (Ⓦ www.coutts.com), whose customers include the Queen herself. It was founded in 1692 by the Scottish goldsmith, John Campbell, a mock-up of whose original premises stands behind a screen in the bank's concrete and marble atrium. Today's male employees still sport anachronistic tail-coated suits, but the horse-drawn carriage which used to convey royal correspondence was sadly taken out of service in 1993.

Some way further east on the opposite side of the Strand, the blind side street of Savoy Court – the only street in the country where the traffic drives on the right – leads to **The Savoy**, London's grandest hotel, built in 1889 on the site of the medieval Savoy Palace. César Ritz was the original manager, Guccio Gucci started out as a dishwasher here, and the list of illustrious guests is endless: Monet painted the Thames from one of the south-facing rooms, Sarah Bernhardt nearly died here, and Strauss the Younger arrived with his own orchestra.

VICTORIA EMBANKMENT

Map 4, I9. ⊖ Embankment.

The **Victoria Embankment**, built between 1868 and 1874, was the inspiration of French engineer Joseph Bazalgette, whose project simultaneously relieved congestion

STRAND • VICTORIA EMBANKMENT

along the Strand, provided an extension to the underground railway and sewage systems, and created a new stretch of parkland with a riverside walk – no longer much fun due to the volume of traffic. The 1626 **York Watergate**, in the Victoria Embankment Gardens to the east of Villiers Street, gives you an idea of where the banks of the Thames used to be; the steps through the gateway once led down to the river.

London's oldest monument, **Cleopatra's Needle**, languishes little-noticed on the Thames side of the busy Victoria Embankment, guarded by two Victorian sphinxes. The 60-foot-high, 180-ton stick of granite in fact has nothing to do with Cleopatra – it's one of a pair erected in Heliopolis in 1475 BC (the other one is in New York's Central Park) and taken to Alexandria by the emperor Augustus fifteen years after Cleopatra's suicide. This obelisk was presented to Britain in 1819 by the Turkish viceroy of Egypt, but nearly sixty years passed before it finally made its way to London.

The **Benjamin Franklin House** (Map 4, H9; ⓦwww .rsa.org.uk/franklin), on the other side of Charing Cross Station at 36 Craven St, will probably attract more visitors than Cleopatra's Needle. Restored with the help of, among others, the nearby Royal Society of Arts, the museum should be open some time in 2004; for more information, phone ⓣ020/7930 9121. The tenth son of a candlemaker, Franklin (1706–1790) had "genteel lodgings" here more or less continuously from 1757 to 1775. Whilst Franklin was espousing the cause of the British colonies (as the US then was), the house served as the first de facto American Embassy; eventually, he returned to America to help draft the Declaration of Independence, negotiate the peace treaty with Britain and frame the Constitution.

ALDWYCH

Map 5, A5. ⊖ Holborn or Temple (Mon–Sat only).

The wide crescent of **Aldwych**, forming a neat "D" with the eastern part of the Strand, was driven through the slums of this zone in the last throes of the Victorian era. A confident ensemble occupies the centre, with the enormous **Australia House** and **India House** sandwiching **Bush House**, home of the BBC's World Service (ⓦ www.bbc.co.uk/worldservice) since 1940. Despite its thoroughly British associations, Bush House was actually built by the American speculator Irving T. Bush, whose planned trade-centre flopped in the 1930s. The giant figures on the north facade and the inscription, "To the Eternal Friendship of English-speaking Nations", thus refer to the friendship between the US and Britain, and are not, as many people assume, the declaratory manifesto of the current occupants.

The eastern stretch of the Strand, beyond
Aldwych, is covered in chapter 7.

Somerset House

Map 5, A6. Courtyard and terrace: daily 10am–11pm; free. Interior: daily 10am–6pm; free; ⓦ www.somerset-house.org.uk ⊖ Temple (Mon–Sat only) or Covent Garden.

Opposite the south side of Bush House stands **Somerset House**, sole survivor of the grand edifices which once lined this stretch of the riverfront, its four wings enclosing a large **courtyard** rather like a Parisian hotel. From March to October, the courtyard features a wonderful 55-jet fountain that spouts straight from the cobbles; in winter, an ice rink is set up in its place. The present building was begun in 1776 by William Chambers as a purpose-built

ALDWYCH

governmental office development, but now also houses a series of museums and galleries.

The south wing, overlooking the Thames, is home to the **Hermitage Rooms** (daily 10am–6pm; £6; Ⓦ www .hermitagerooms.com), featuring changing displays drawn from St Petersburg's Hermitage Museum, and the magnificent **Gilbert Collection** (daily 10am–6pm; £5; Ⓦ www.gilbert-collection.org.uk), a museum of decorative arts displaying European silver and gold, micro-mosaics, clocks, portrait miniatures and snuffboxes.

In the north wing are the **Courtauld Institute galleries** (daily 10am–6pm; £5; free Mon 10am–2pm; Ⓦ www.courtauld.ac.uk), chiefly known for their dazzling collection of Impressionist and Post-Impressionist paintings. Among the most celebrated works are a small-scale version of Manet's *Déjeuner sur l'herbe*, Renoir's *La Loge*, and Degas's *Two Dancers*, plus a whole heap of Cézanne's canvases, including one of his series of *Card Players*. The Courtauld also boasts a fine selection of works by the likes of Rubens, Van Dyck, Tiepolo and Cranach the Elder. The collection has recently been augmented by the long-term loan of a hundred top-notch twentieth-century paintings and sculptures by, among others, Kandinksy, Matisse, Dufy, Derain, Rodin and Henry Moore.

St Mary-le-Strand and St Clement Danes

Map 5, B5. ⊖ Temple (Mon–Sat only) or Covent Garden.

Two historic churches survived the Aldwych development, and are now stranded amid the traffic of the Strand. The first is James Gibbs' **St Mary-le-Strand** (Mon–Fri 11am–3.30pm), his first commission, completed in 1724 in Baroque style and topped by a delicately tiered tower. Even in the eighteenth century, parishioners complained of the noise from the roads, and it's incredible that recitals are still given here (Wed 1pm). The entrance is flanked by two lovely magnolia trees, and the interior has a particularly rich plastered ceiling in white and gold.

In allusion to his own St Mary's, Gibbs placed a 115-foottower on top of Christopher Wren's nearby **St Clement Danes** (daily 8.30am–4.30pm), whose bells play out the tune of the nursery rhyme "Oranges and Lemons" each day at 9am, noon, 3pm and 6pm. Reduced to a smouldering shell during the Blitz, St Clement Danes was handed over to the RAF in the 1950s and is now a very well-kept memorial to those killed in the air battles of the last war, the nave and aisles studded with more than 800 squadron and unit badges.

In front of the church are statues of the two wartime air chiefs: to the right, **Lord Dowding**, the man who oversaw the Battle of Britain; to the left, **Sir Arthur Harris** (better known as "Bomber Harris"), architect of the saturation bombing of Germany that resulted in the slaughter of thousands of civilians. Although Churchill was ultimately responsible, most of the opprobrium was left to fall on Harris, who was denied the peerage all the other service chiefs received, while his forces were refused a campaign medal.

ALDWYCH

Holborn, Clerkenwell and Hoxton

Holborn, **Clerkenwell** and **Hoxton** lie on the periphery of the financial district of the City. Holborn (pronounced "Ho-burn") has long been associated with the law, and its **Inns of Court** make for an interesting stroll, their archaic, cobbled precincts exuding the rarefied atmosphere of an Oxbridge college, and sheltering one of the city's oldest churches, the twelfth-century **Temple Church**. Close by the Inns, in Lincoln's Inn Fields, is the **Sir John Soane's Museum**, one of the most memorable and enjoyable of London's small museums, packed with architectural illusions and an eclectic array of curios.

Clerkenwell, further to the northeast, is definitely off the conventional tourist trail with just a few minor sights, including vestiges of two pre-Fire of London priories, and the **Marx Memorial Library**, where the exiled Lenin plotted revolution. Since the 1990s, however, parts of the area have been transformed and, to a certain extent, gentrified, by an influx of young, loft-living designers and media types, whose arrival has had a marked effect on the choice and style of bars and restaurants on offer.

Neighbouring Hoxton (aka Shoreditch), to the east, has also acquired a certain cachet, due to the high density of artists and architects who currently live and/or work here. Visually, Hoxton remains harsher on the eye than Clerkenwell, though it, too, has more than its fair share of trendy bars and restaurants. Several of London's contemporary art dealers now have Hoxton outlets, and there's the excellent **Geffrye Museum** of furniture design to aim for.

- -

For details of restaurants and bars in
Clerkenwell and Hoxton, see p.229 and p.231.

- -

TEMPLE AND THE LAW COURTS

Map 5, D5. ⊖ Temple (Mon–Sat only) or Covent Garden.

Temple is the largest and most complex of the Inns of Court, where every barrister in England must study before being called to the Bar. Temple itself is comprised of two Inns – **Middle Temple** (Ⓦ www.middletemple.org.uk) and **Inner Temple** (Ⓦ www.innertemple.org.uk) – both of which lie to the south of the Strand and, strictly speaking, just within the boundaries of the City of London. A few very old buildings survive here, but the overall scene is dominated by neo-Georgian reconstructions that followed the devastation of the Blitz. Still, the maze of courtyards and passageways is fun to explore – especially after dark, when Temple is gas-lit.

There are several points of access, simplest of which is Devereux Court. Medieval students ate, attended lectures and slept in the **Middle Temple Hall** (Mon–Fri 10am–noon & 3–4pm), across the courtyard, still the Inn's main dining room. The present building was constructed in the 1560s and provided the setting for many great Elizabethan masques and plays – probably including Shakespeare's *Twelfth Night*, which is believed to have been premiered here in 1602. The hall is worth a visit for its fine hammer-beam roof, wooden panelling and decorative Elizabethan screen.

The two Temple Inns share use of the complex's oldest building, **Temple Church** (Wed–Sun 11am–4pm; ⓦ www.templechurch.com), built in 1185 by the Knights Templar. An oblong chancel was added in the thirteenth century, and the whole building was damaged in the Blitz, but the original round church – modelled on the Church of the Holy Sepulchre in Jerusalem – still stands, with its striking Purbeck-marble piers, recumbent marble effigies of knights and tortured grotesques grimacing in the spandrels of the blind arcading.

Temple Bar and the Royal Courts of Justice

Map 5, C4. ⊖ Temple

If you walk to the top of Middle Temple Lane, you'll hit the Strand right at **Temple Bar**, a plinth topped by a winged dragon, the latest in a long line of structures marking the boundary between Westminster and the City of London.

On the north side of Temple Bar are the **Royal Courts of Justice** (Mon–Fri 8.30am–4.30pm; ⓦ www .courtservice.gov.uk), home to the Court of Appeal and the High Court, where the most important civil cases are tried. Appeals and libel suits are heard here – it was from here that the Guildford Four and Birmingham Six walked to freedom, and it is where countless pop and soap stars have battled it out with the tabloids. The fifty-odd court-rooms are open to the public, though you have to go through stringent security checks first (strictly no cameras allowed).

LINCOLN'S INN FIELDS

Map 5, B2. ⊖ Holborn.

North of the Law Courts lies **Lincoln's Inn Fields**, London's largest square, laid out in the early 1640s with **Lincoln's Inn** (Mon–Fri 9am–6pm; ⓦ www.lincolnsinn .org.uk), the first – and in many ways the prettiest – of the Inns of Court on its east side. The Inn's fifteenth-century **Old Hall** is open by appointment only (⊕ 020/7405 1393), but you can view the early seventeenth-century **chapel** (Mon–Fri noon–2pm), with its unusual fan-vaulted open undercroft and, on the first floor, its late Gothic nave, hit by a Zeppelin in World War I and much restored since.

The south side of Lincoln's Inn Fields is occupied by the gigantic **Royal College of Surgeons** (Map 5, B3; ⓦ www.rcseng.ac.uk), home to the **Hunterian Museum** (Mon–Fri 10am–5pm; free), a fascinating collection of pickled bits and bobs. Also on view are the skeletons of the Irish giant, O'Brien (1761–83), who was seven feet ten inches tall, and the Sicilian midget Caroline Crachami (1815–24), who was just one foot ten and a half inches when she died at the age of nine. To the southwest is one of London's few surviving timber-framed buildings, the seventeenth-century **Old Curiosity Shop** (Map 5, A3) in Portsmouth Street, which claims to be the inspiration for Dickens' cloyingly sentimental tale of the same name. This seems unlikely, but it is certainly London's oldest shop building.

LINCOLN'S INN FIELDS

Sir John Soane's Museum

Map 5, A2. Tues–Sat 10am–5pm; first Tues of the month also 6–9pm; free; ⓦ www.soane.org ⊖ Holborn

A group of buildings on the north side of Lincoln's Inn Fields house **Sir John Soane's Museum**, one of London's best-kept secrets. The chief architect of the Bank of England, Soane (1753–1837) was an avid collector who designed this house not only as a home and office, but also as a place to stash his large collection of art and antiquities. Arranged much as it was in his lifetime, the ingeniously planned house has an informal, treasure-hunt atmosphere, with surprises in every alcove; the museum has also begun to exhibit contemporary art. At 2.30pm every Saturday, a fascinating, hour-long **guided tour** (£3) takes you round the museum and the enormous research library, next door, containing architectural drawings, books and exquisitely detailed cork and wood models.

CHANCERY LANE AND GRAY'S INN

Map 5, C2. ⊖ Holborn or Chancery Lane (Mon–Sat only).

Running along the eastern edge of Lincoln's Inn is legal London's main thoroughfare, **Chancery Lane**, home of the Law Society (the solicitors' regulatory body) and lined with shops where barristers, solicitors and clerks can buy their wigs, gowns, legal tomes, stationery and champagne. Halfway up the street are the **London Silver Vaults** (Map 5, C1; Mon–Fri 9am–5.30pm, Sat 9am–1pm; free; ⓦ www.thesilvervaults.com), which began life as a safe-deposit for the rich, but now house a claustrophobic lair of subterranean shops selling every kind of silverware – mostly antique, occasionally tasteless.

The last of the four Inns of Court, **Gray's Inn** (Map 3, J3; Mon–Fri 10am–4pm; ⓦ www.graysinn.org.uk), lies hidden to the north of High Holborn, at the top of Chancery Lane; the entrance is through an anonymous cream-coloured building next door to the venerable *Cittie of Yorke* pub. Established in the fourteenth century, most of what you see today was rebuilt after the Blitz, with the exception of the hall (by appointment only; ☎020/7458 7822), with its fabulous Tudor screen and stained glass, where the premiere of Shakespeare's *Comedy of Errors* is thought to have taken place in 1594.

Heading east along High Holborn, it's worth pausing to admire **Staple Inn** (Map 5, D1) on the right, not one of the Inns of Court, but one of the now defunct Inns of Chancery, which used to provide a sort of foundation course for those aspiring to the Bar. Its overhanging half-timbered facade and gables date from the sixteenth century and are the most extensive in the whole of London. They survived the Great Fire, which stopped just short of Holborn Circus, but had to be extensively rebuilt after the Blitz.

CLERKENWELL

Map 3, K3. ⊖ Farringdon.

Poverty and overcrowding were the main features of nineteenth-century Clerkenwell, and **Clerkenwell Green** became known in the press as "the headquarters of republicanism, revolution and ultra-non-conformity". The Green's connections with **radical politics** have continued and its oldest building, built as a Welsh Charity School in 1737, is now home to the **Marx Memorial Library** (Mon, Tues & Thurs 1–6pm, Wed 1–8pm, Sat 10am–1pm; ⓦ www .marxmemoriallibrary.sageweb.co.uk), at no. 37a. One-time headquarters of the Social Democratic Federation press, this is where **Lenin** edited seventeen editions of the Bolshevik paper *Iskra* in 1902–3. The poky little back room where he worked is maintained as it was then, as a kind of shrine – you can view it along with the workerist Hastings Mural from 1935.

St John's Gate

Map 3, K3. Mon–Fri 10am–5pm, Sat 10am–4pm; free; Ⓦ www.sja.org.uk ⊖ Farringdon.

Of Clerkenwell's three medieval religious establishments, remnants of two survive, hidden away to the southeast of Clerkenwell Green. The oldest is the priory of the Order of St John of Jerusalem; the sixteenth-century **St John's Gate**, on the south side of Clerkenwell Road, is the most visible survivor of the foundation. Today, the gatehouse forms part of a **museum**, which traces the development of the order before its dissolution in this country by Henry VIII, and its reestablishment in the nineteenth century. In 1877, the St John's Ambulance was founded, to provide a voluntary first-aid service to the public. It's in this field that the order is now best known in Britain – a splendid interactive gallery is devoted to the history of the service.

To get to see the rest of the gatehouse, and to visit the Norman crypt of the Grand Priory Church over the road, you must take a **guided tour** (Tues, Fri & Sat 11am & 2.30pm; £5 donation requested).

Charterhouse

Map 3, L3. Guided tours only April–July Wed 2.15pm; £3. ⊖ Barbican.

A little to the southeast of St John's, on the edge of Smithfield, lies **Charterhouse**, founded in 1371 as a Carthusian monastery. The public school, with which the foundation is now most closely associated, moved out to Surrey in 1872, but forty-odd pensioners – known, in the monastic tradition, as "brothers" – continue to be cared for here. The only way to visit the site is to join one of the exhaustive two-hour **guided tours**, which start at the gatehouse on Charterhouse Square. Very little remains of the original monastic buildings, but there's plenty of Tudor architecture to admire, dating from after the Dissolution, when Charterhouse was rebuilt as a private residence.

HOXTON

Map 3, N2. ⊖ Old Street.

Until recently, Shoreditch, on the northeastern edge of the City, was a none-too-savoury slice of London, an unpleasant amalgam of wholesale clothes and shoe shops, striptease pubs and roaring traffic. Over the last few years, however, it has been colonized by artists, designers and architects and rebranded: what was once Shoreditch is now **Hoxton**, previously a much smaller neighbourhood confined to the north of Old Street. Whatever its real name, the area is actually rich in literary and artistic associations. It was here that James Burbage established the country's first public theatre – called simply the Theatre – in 1576 (he subsequently took it down and reassembled it on Bankside as the Globe).

The geographical focus of the area's current transformation is **Hoxton Square**, just west of Hoxton Street, a strange and not altogether happy mixture of light industrial units and artists' studios arranged around a leafy, formal square. Despite the lack of aesthetic charm, the area has become an increasingly fashionable place to live and work, and several leading West End **art galleries** have opened up premises here, among them Victoria Miro, Jay Jopling's White Cube and Sadie Coles' Hoxton House. Other than cruising the bars (listed on p.231) and art galleries (see p.299), there are no real sights as such, though you might want to take a peek at the **Prince's Foundation**

HOXTON

(Ⓦ www.princes-foundation.org), the institute of architecture set up by Prince Charles, which has its headquarters on Charlotte Road, south across Old Street from Hoxton Square; the gallery puts on temporary exhibitions of contemporary artists, photographers and designers.

Geffrye Museum

Map 3, N1. Tues–Sat 10am–5pm, Sun noon–5pm; free;
Ⓦ www.geffrye-museum.org.uk

Hoxton's one conventional tourist sight is the **Geffrye Museum**, a museum of furniture design, set back from Kingsland Road in a peaceful little enclave of eighteenth-century ironmongers' almshouses. A series of period living rooms, ranging from the oak-panelled seventeenth century through refined Georgian and cluttered Victorian, leads to the state-of-the-art New Gallery Extension, housing the excellent twentieth-century section and a pleasant café/restaurant. To get to the museum, take bus #149 or #242 from Liverpool Street tube.

The City

T he City is where London began. Long established as
the financial district, it stretches from Temple Bar in
the west to the Tower of London in the east –
administrative boundaries that are only slightly larger than
those marked by the old Roman walls and their medieval
successors. However, in this Square Mile (as the City is
sometimes called), you'll find few leftovers of London's
early days, since four-fifths of the area burned down in the
Great Fire of 1666. Rebuilt in brick and stone, the City
gradually lost its centrality as London swelled westwards,
though it has maintained its position as Britain's financial
heartland. What you see now is mostly the product of three
fairly recent phases: the Victorian construction boom of the
late nineteenth century; the postwar reconstruction following the Blitz; and the money-grabbing frenzy of the 1980s,
in which nearly fifty percent of the City's office space was
rebuilt.

When you consider what has happened here, it's amazing
that so much has survived to pay witness to the City's two-
thousand-year history. Wren's spires still punctuate the sky-
line here and there, and his masterpiece, **St Paul's
Cathedral**, remains one of London's geographical pivots.
At the eastern edge of the City, the **Tower of London** still
stands protected by some of the best-preserved medieval

THE CORPORATION OF LONDON

The one unchanging aspect of the City is its special status, conferred on it by William the Conqueror and extended and reaffirmed by successive monarchs and governments ever since. Nowadays, with its Lord Mayor, its Beadles, Sheriffs and Aldermen, its separate police force and its select electorate of freemen and liverymen, the City is an anachronism of the worst kind and pretty much a law unto itself. **The Corporation** (W www.cityoflondon.gov.uk), which runs the City like a one-party mini-state, is an unreconstructed old boys' network whose medievalist pageantry camouflages the very real power and wealth which it holds – the Corporation owns nearly a third of the Square Mile (and several tracts of land elsewhere in and around London). Its anomalous status is all the more baffling when you consider that the City was once the cradle of British democracy: it was the City that traditionally stood up to bullying sovereigns.

fortifications in Europe. Other relics, such as the City's few surviving medieval alleyways, Wren's **Monument** to the Great Fire, and London's oldest synagogue and church, are less conspicuous, and even locals have problems finding the more modern attractions such as the **Museum of London** and the **Barbican** arts complex.

Perhaps the biggest change of all, though, has been in the City's population. Up until the eighteenth century the majority of Londoners lived and worked in or around the City; nowadays over a million commuters spend the best part of **Monday to Friday** here, but only five thousand people remain at night and at weekends. The result of this demographic shift is that the City is fully alive only during office hours. This means that by far the best time to visit is during the week, since many pubs, restaurants and even some tube stations and tourist sights close down at the weekend.

FLEET STREET

Map 5, E4. ⊖ Temple (Mon–Sat only) or Blackfriars.

In 1500 a certain Wynkyn de Worde, a pupil of William Caxton, moved the Caxton presses from Westminster to **Fleet Street**, to be close to the lawyers of the Inns of Court and to the clergy of St Paul's. However, the street really boomed two hundred years later, when in 1702, the now defunct *Daily Courant*, Britain's first daily newspaper, was published from here. By the nineteenth century, all the major national and provincial dailies had their offices and printing presses in the Fleet Street district, a situation that prevailed until the 1980s, when the press barons relocated their operations elsewhere.

The best source of information about the old-style Fleet Street is the so-called "journalists' and printers' cathedral", the church of **St Bride's** (Map 5, F4; Mon–Sat 9am–5pm; Ⓦ www.stbrides.com), which boasts Wren's tallest and most exquisite spire (said to be the inspiration for the tiered wedding cake). The crypt contains a little museum of Fleet Street history, with information on the *Daily Courant* and the *Universal Daily Register*, which later became *The Times*, claiming to be "the faithful recorder of every species of intelligence … circulated for a particular set of readers only".

The western section of Fleet Street was spared the Great Fire, which stopped just short of **Prince Henry's Room** (Map 5, D4; Mon–Sat 11am–2pm; free; Ⓦ www.cityoflondon .gov.uk/phr), a fine Jacobean house with timber-framed bay windows. The first-floor room now contains material relating to the diarist **Samuel Pepys**, who was born nearby in

Salisbury Court in 1633 and baptized in St Bride's. Even if you've no interest in Pepys, the wooden-panelled room is worth a look – it contains one of the finest Jacobean plaster-work ceilings in London, and a lot of original stained glass.

Numerous narrow alleyways lead off the north side of Fleet Street, two of which – Bolt Court and Hind Court – eventually open out into Gough Square, on which stands **Dr Johnson's House** (Map 5, E3; May–Sept Mon–Sat 11am–5.30pm; Oct–April Mon–Sat 11am–5pm; £4; ⓦ www.drjh.dircon.co.uk). The great savant, writer and lexicographer lived here from 1747 to 1759 whilst compiling the 41,000 entries for the first dictionary of the English language, two first editions of which can be seen in the grey-panelled rooms of the house. You can also view the open-plan attic, in which Johnson and his six helpers put together the dictionary.

ST PAUL'S CATHEDRAL

Map 5, I4. Mon–Sat 8.30am–5pm; £6; ⓦ www.stpauls.co.uk ⊖ St Paul's.

St Paul's Cathedral, designed by Christopher Wren and topped by an enormous lead-covered dome that's second in size only to St Peter's in Rome, has been a London icon since the Blitz, when it stood defiantly unscathed amid the carnage (or so it appeared on wartime propaganda photos). It remains a dominating presence in the City, despite the encroaching tower blocks – its showpiece west facade is particularly magnificent, and is at its most impressive at night when bathed in sea-green arc lights. Westminster Abbey has the edge, however, when it comes to celebrity corpses, pre-Reformation sculpture, royal connections and sheer atmosphere. St Paul's, by contrast, is a soulless but perfectly calculated architectural set piece, a burial place for captains rather than kings, though it does contain more artists than Westminster Abbey.

The cathedral's services, featuring the
renowned St Paul's choir, are held
Mon–Sat 5pm, Sun 10.15am, 11.30am & 3.15pm.

The best place from which to appreciate the glory of St Paul's is beneath the **dome**, decorated (against Wren's wishes) by Thornhill's trompe l'oeil frescoes. The most richly decorated section of the cathedral, however, is the Quire or **chancel**, where the mosaics of birds, fish, animals and greenery, dating from the 1890s, are particularly spectacular. The intricately carved oak and limewood **choir stalls**, and the imposing organ case, are the work of Wren's master carver, Grinling Gibbons. Meanwhile, in the south-choir aisle, is the only complete effigy to have survived from Old St Paul's (see p.87), the upstanding shroud of **John Donne**, poet, preacher and one-time dean of St Paul's.

A series of stairs, beginning in the south aisle, leads to the dome's three **galleries**, the first of which is the internal **Whispering Gallery**, so called because of its acoustic properties – words whispered to the wall on one side are distinctly audible over 100ft away on the other, though the place is often so busy you can't hear much above the hubbub. The other two galleries are exterior: the wide **Stone Gallery**, around the balustrade at the base of the dome; and ultimately the tiny **Golden Gallery**, below the golden ball and cross which top the cathedral.

The City of London tourist office, to the south of
St Paul's, is open April–Sept daily 9.30am–5pm
Oct–March Mon–Fri 9.30am–5pm, Sat 9.30am–12.30pm;
☎ 020/7332 1456, Ⓦ www.cityoflondon.gov.uk

ST PAUL'S CATHEDRAL

THE BLITZ

The **Blitz** bombing of London in World War II began on September 7, 1940, and continued for 57 consecutive nights, then intermittently until the final and most devastating attack on the night of May 10, 1941, when 550 Luftwaffe planes dropped over 100,000 incendiaries and hundreds of explosive bombs in a matter of hours. The death toll that night was over 1400, bringing the total killed during the Blitz to between 20,000 and 30,000, with some 230,000 homes wrecked. Along with the East End, the City was particularly badly hit: in a single raid on December 29 (dubbed the "Second Fire of London"), 1400 fires broke out across the Square Mile.

The authorities were ready to build mass graves, but unable to provide adequate air-raid shelters. Around 180,000 made use of the tube, despite initial government reluctance, by simply buying a ticket and staying below ground. The cheery photos of singing and dancing in the Underground which the censors allowed to be published tell nothing of the stale air, rats and lice that folk had to contend with. And even the tube stations couldn't withstand a direct hit, as occurred at Bank, when over 100 died. In the end, the vast majority of Londoners – some sixty percent – simply stayed at home in their back-garden shelters or hid under the sheets and prayed.

Although the nave is crammed full of overblown monuments to military types, burials in St Paul's are confined to the **crypt**, reputedly the largest in Europe. The whitewashed walls and bright lighting, however, make this one of the least atmospheric mausoleums you could imagine. Immediately to your right you'll find Artists' Corner, which boasts as many painters and architects as Westminster Abbey has poets, including Christopher Wren himself, who was commissioned to build the cathedral after its Gothic predecessor, Old St Paul's, was destroyed in the Great Fire. The crypt's two other star tombs are those of **Nelson** and **Wellington**, both occupying centre stage and both with more fanciful monuments upstairs.

PATERNOSTER SQUARE TO SMITHFIELD

Map 5, H3. ⊖ St Paul's.

The Blitz destroyed the area immediately to the north of St Paul's. In its place, the City authorities built the brazenly modernist **Paternoster Square**, a grim pedestrianized piazza that has now been demolished to make way for a new, more restrained master plan courtesy of William Whitfield, who is seen as a compromise choice in the modernism-versus-classicism debate.

To the west along Newgate Street, you'll find the Central Criminal Court, more popularly known as the **Old Bailey**. Built on the site of the notoriously harsh Newgate Prison, where folk used to come to watch public hangings, the Old Bailey is now the venue for all the country's most serious criminal court cases; you can watch the proceedings from the visitors' gallery (Mon–Fri 10.30am–1pm & 2–4pm), but note that bags, cameras, mobiles, personal stereos and food and drink are not allowed in, and there is no cloakroom.

St Bartholomew's Hospital and church

Map 5, H1. ⊖ St Paul's or Farringdon.

North of the Old Bailey lies **St Bartholomew's Hospital**, affectionately known to Londoners as Bart's. It's the oldest hospital in London, founded in 1123 by Rahere, court jester to Henry I, on the orders of St Bartholomew, who appeared to him in a vision while he was in malarial delirium on a pilgrimage to Rome. You can visit the hospital's church, and the nearby **museum** (Tues–Fri 10am–4pm;

free), which has a short video on the history of Bart's. This also gives you a chance to glimpse the mid-eighteenth-century interior, which features murals by Hogarth. To see and learn more, you need to go on a **guided tour** (April–Nov Fri 2pm; £4), which also takes in Smithfield and the surrounding area.

St Bartholomew-the-Great (Map 7, A1; Tues–Fri 8.30am–5pm, Sat 10.30am–1.30pm, Sun 8.30am–1pm & 2.30–8pm; mid-Nov to mid-Feb Mon–Fri closes 4pm; Ⓦ www.greatstbarts.com), hidden away to the north of the hospital, is London's oldest and most exquisite parish church. Begun in 1123, it was partly demolished in the Reformation, and afterwards fell into ruins. Restoration didn't begin until 1887, though by no means the whole church was rebuilt. To get an idea of the scale of the original, approach through the half-timbered Tudor **gatehouse** on Little Britain Street, which incorporates the thirteenth-century arch that once formed the entrance to the nave. One side of the medieval cloisters survives to the south, as does the **chancel**, where stout Norman pillars separate the main body of the church from the ambulatory. There are various pre-Fire monuments to admire, the most prominent being the tomb of Rahere itself, which shelters under a fifteenth-century canopy north of the main altar.

Smithfield

Map 5, F1. ⊖ Farringdon.

Smithfield, to the north of Bart's, was for a long time a popular venue for **public executions** – in particular burnings, which reached a peak during the reign of "Bloody" Mary, when hundreds of Protestants were burned at the stake for their beliefs. These days, Smithfield is synonymous with its **meat market**, and if you want to see it in action, you'll need to get here early – the activity starts around 4am and is all over by 9am or 10am. The compensation for getting up at this ungodly hour are the early licensing laws, which mean you can get a hearty breakfast and an early-morning pint from the local pubs.

MUSEUM OF LONDON

Map 7, B1. Mon–Sat 10am–5.50pm, Sun noon–5.50pm; free; Ⓦ www.museumoflondon.org.uk ⊖ St Paul's or Barbican.

Despite London's long pedigree, very few of its ancient structures are now standing. However, numerous Roman, Saxon and Elizabethan remains have been discovered during the City's various rebuildings, and many of these finds are now displayed at the **Museum of London**, hidden above the western end of London Wall (the highway driven through the Blitz bomb sites north of the city), in the southwestern corner of the Barbican complex. The museum's permanent exhibition is basically an educational trot through London's past from prehistory to the present day; hence the large number of school groups who pass through. The displays are imaginatively set out, if a little dated, with only the new prehistory gallery having much in the way of hands-on stuff. Specific exhibits to look out for include the Bucklersbury Roman mosaic; the sarcophagus, coffin and skeleton of a wealthy Roman woman recently found in Spitalfields; and the Lord Mayor's heavily gilded coach (still used for state occasions). The real strength of the museum, though, lies in the excellent temporary exhibitions, lectures, walks and videos it organizes throughout the year.

THE BARBICAN

Map 7, D1. ⊖ Barbican or Moorgate.

The City's only large residential complex is the **Barbican**, a phenomenally ugly and expensive concrete ghetto built on the heavily bombed Cripplegate area. The zone's solitary prewar building is the heavily restored sixteenth-century church of **St Giles Cripplegate** (Map 7, C1; Mon–Fri 11am–4pm), situated across from the infamously user-repellent **Barbican Arts Centre** (Ⓦ www .barbican.org.uk), London's supposed answer to Paris's Pompidou Centre, which was formally opened in 1982. The complex, which is at least traffic-free, serves as home to the London Symphony Orchestra and the London chapter of the Royal Shakespeare Company, and holds free gigs in the foyer area.

BUNHILL FIELDS AND WESLEY'S CHAPEL

Map 3, M2. ⊖ Old Street.

A little way to the northeast of the Barbican lies **Bunhill Fields**, the main burial ground for Dissenters or Nonconformists (practising Christians who were not members of the Church of England). The three most famous graves have been relocated in the central paved area: William Blake's simple tombstone stands next to a replica of Daniel Defoe's, while opposite lies John Bunyan's recumbent statue.

Directly opposite Bunhill Fields on City Road stands the Georgian ensemble of **Wesley's Chapel and House** (Mon–Sat 10am–4pm; free). A place of pilgrimage for Methodists, the uncharacteristically ornate chapel, built in 1777, heralded the coming of age of Wesley's sect. Predictably enough, the **Museum of Methodism** in the basement has only a passing-reference mention to the insanely jealous 40-year-old widow Wesley married, and who eventually left him. Wesley himself spent his last two years in the delightful Georgian house to the right of the main gates, and inside you can see his deathbed, plus an early shock-therapy machine he was particularly keen on.

GUILDHALL

Map 7, D2. May–Sept daily 10am–5pm; Oct–April Mon–Sat 10am–5pm; free; Ⓦ www.cityoflondon.gov.uk ⊖ St Paul's or Bank.

Situated at the geographical centre of the City, **Guildhall** has been the ancient seat of the City administration for over eight hundred years. It remains the headquarters of the Corporation of London (see p.82), and is still used for many of the City's formal civic occasions. Architecturally, however, it is not quite the beauty it once was, having been badly damaged in both the Great Fire and the Blitz, and scarred by the addition of a grotesque 1970s concrete cloister and wing.

Nonetheless, the **Great Hall**, basically a postwar reconstruction of the fifteenth-century original, is worth a brief look, as is the **Clockmakers' Museum** (Mon–Fri 9.30am–4.30pm; free), a collection of over six hundred timepieces, including one of the clocks that won John Harrison the Longitude prize. Also worth a visit is the purpose-built **Guildhall Art Gallery** (Mon–Sat 10am–5pm, Sun noon–4pm; £2.50), which contains one or two exceptional works, such as Rossetti's *La Ghirlandata*, and Holman Hunt's *The Eve of St Agnes*, plus a massive painting depicting the 1782 Siege of Gibraltar, commissioned by the Corporation.

BANK AND AROUND

Map 7, F4. ⊖ Bank.

Bank is the finest architectural arena in the City. The heart of the finance sector and the busy meeting point of eight streets, it's overlooked by a handsome collection of Neoclassical buildings – among them, the Bank of England, the Royal Exchange and Mansion House (the Lord Mayor's official residence) – each one faced in Portland stone.

Sadly, only the **Bank of England** (Map 7, F3; ⓦwww
.bankofengland.co.uk), which stores the nation's vast gold
reserves in its vaults, actually encourages visitors. Established
in 1694 by William III to raise funds for the war against
France, the so-called "Grand Old Lady of Threadneedle
Street" wasn't erected on its present site until 1734. All that
remains of the building on which John Soane spent the best
part of his career from 1788 onwards is the windowless,
outer curtain wall, which wraps itself round the 3.5-acre
island site. However, you can view a reconstruction of
Soane's Bank Stock Office, with its characteristic domed
skylight, in the **museum** (Mon–Fri 10am–5pm; free),
which has its entrance on Bartholomew Lane.

Three churches worth exploring are situated to the south
of Bank. On Walbrook, behind Mansion House, stands the
church of **St Stephen Walbrook** (Map 7, E4; Mon–Thurs
10am–4pm, Fri 10am–3pm), Wren's most spectacular after
St Paul's, with dark-wood furnishings by Grinling Gibbons.
Hidden a short distance down King William Street is **St
Mary Woolnoth** (Map 7, F4; Mon–Fri 7.45am–5pm), a
typically idiosyncratic creation of Nicholas Hawksmoor,
one of Wren's pupils, featuring a striking altar canopy held
up by barley-sugar columns. A complete contrast to
Hawksmoor's church is provided by Wren's **St Mary
Abchurch** (Map 7, F5; Mon–Thurs 10am–2pm), on
Abchurch Lane, off King William Street. The interior is
dominated by a vast dome fresco painted by a local parish-
ioner and lit by oval lunettes, while the lime-wood reredos
is again by Gibbons.

LLOYD'S AND AROUND

Map 7, H4. ⊖ Bank or Monument.

East of Bank, beyond Bishopsgate, stands Richard Rogers'
glitzy **Lloyd's Building**, completed in 1984. A startling

array of glass and blue steel pipes – a vertical version of Rogers' own Pompidou Centre – this is easily the most popular of the modern City buildings, at least with the general public. Its closest rival is Norman Foster's giant "erotic gherkin" building for **Swiss Re**, just completed to the north on the site of the old Baltic Exchange, which was blown up by the IRA in the early 1990s.

Just south of the Lloyd's Building, you'll find the picturesque **Leadenhall Market**, whose cobbles and richly painted, graceful Victorian cast-ironwork dates from 1881. Inside, the traders cater mostly for the lunchtime City crowd, their barrows laden with exotic seafood and game, fine wines, champagne and caviar.

Bevis Marks Synagogue

Map 7, J3. Guided tours Mon–Wed, Fri & Sun noon; £2.
⊖ Aldgate or Liverpool Street.

Hidden away behind a modern red-brick office block in a little courtyard off Bevis Marks, north up St Mary Axe from the Lloyd's Building, the **Bevis Marks Synagogue** was built in 1701 by Sephardic Jews who had fled the Inquisition in Spain and Portugal. This is the country's oldest surviving synagogue, and its roomy, rich interior gives an idea of just how wealthy the congregation was at the time. Nowadays, the Sephardic community has dispersed across London and the congregation has dwindled, though the magnificent array of chandeliers makes it popular for candle-lit Jewish weddings.

LONDON BRIDGE AND THE MONUMENT

Map 7, F7. ⊖ Monument.

Until 1750, **London Bridge** was the only bridge across the Thames. The Romans were the first to build a permanent crossing here, but it was the medieval bridge that achieved world fame: built of stone and crowded with timber-framed houses, it became one of the great attractions of London (there's a model in the nearby church of St Magnus the Martyr, Map 7, G6; Tues–Fri 10am–4pm, Sun 10am–1pm). The houses were finally removed in the mid-eighteenth century, and a new stone bridge erected in 1831; that one now stands in the middle of the Arizona desert, having been bought for $2.4 million in the late 1960s by a gentleman who, so the story goes, was under the impression he had purchased Tower Bridge. The present concrete structure, without doubt the ugliest yet, dates from 1972.

THE GREAT FIRE OF LONDON

In the early hours of September 2, 1666, the **Great Fire** broke out at Farriner's, the king's bakery in Pudding Lane. The Lord Mayor refused to lose any sleep over it, dismissing it with the line, "Pish! A woman might piss it out." Four days and four nights later, the Lord Mayor was found crying "like a fainting woman": the Fire had destroyed some four-fifths of London, including 87 churches, 44 livery halls and 13,200 houses. The medieval city was no more.

Miraculously, there were only nine recorded fatalities, but 100,000 people were made homeless. "The hand of God upon us, a great wind and a season so very dry" was the verdict of the parliamentary report on the Fire; Londoners preferred to blame Catholics and foreigners. The poor baker eventually "confessed" to being an agent of the pope and was executed, after which the following words, "but Popish frenzy, which wrought such horrors, is not yet quenched", were added to the Latin inscription on the Monument. (The lines were erased in 1831.)

The only reason to go anywhere near London Bridge is to see the **Monument** (Map 7, G6; daily 10am–6pm; £1.50), which was designed by Wren to commemorate the Great Fire of 1666. Crowned with spiky gilded flames, this plain Doric column stands 202ft high, making it the tallest isolated stone column in the world; if it were laid out flat it would touch the bakery where the Fire started, east of Monument. The bas-relief on the base, now in very bad shape, depicts Charles II and the Duke of York in Roman garb conducting the emergency relief operation. The 311 steps to the viewing gallery once guaranteed an incredible view; nowadays it is somewhat dwarfed by the buildings around it.

THE TOWER OF LONDON

Map 7, K7. March–Oct Mon–Sat 9am–6pm, Sun 10am–6pm; Nov–Feb Mon & Sun 10am–5pm, Tues–Sat 9am–5pm; £11.50; Ⓦ www.hrp.org.uk ⊖ Tower Hill.

One of Britain's main tourist attractions, the **Tower of London** overlooks the river at the eastern boundary of the old city walls. Despite all the hype and heritage claptrap, it remains one of London's most remarkable buildings, site of some of the goriest events in the nation's history and somewhere all visitors and Londoners should explore at least once. Chiefly famous as a place of imprisonment and death, it has variously been used as a royal residence, armoury, mint, menagerie, observatory and – a function it still serves – a safe-deposit box for the Crown Jewels.

Before you set off to explore the Tower complex, it's a good idea to get your bearings by taking one of the free **guided tours**, given every thirty minutes or so by one of the Tower's **Beefeaters** (officially known as Yeoman Warders). Visitors today enter the Tower along Water Lane, but in times gone by most prisoners were delivered through

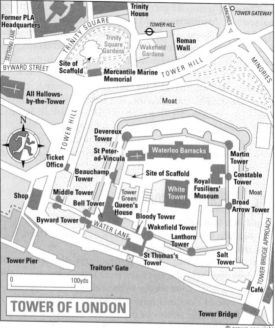

Trinity House

TOWER HILL

TOWER GATEWAY

Former PLA Headquarters

TRINITY SQUARE

Trinity Square Gardens

Wakefield Gardens

Roman Wall

MINORIES

SEETHING LANE

BYWARD STREET

Site of Scaffold

Mercantile Marine Memorial

TOWER HILL

All Hallows-by-the-Tower

Moat

N

Devereux Tower

St Peter-ad-Vincula

Waterloo Barracks

Martin Tower

Ticket Office

Beauchamp Tower

Site of Scaffold

Constable Tower

Shop

Middle Tower

White Tower

Royal Fusiliers' Museum

Moat

Bell Tower

Tower Green

Broad Arrow Tower

Byward Tower

WATER LANE

Queen's House

Bloody Tower

Wakefield Tower

Lanthorn Tower

TOWER BRIDGE APPROACH

Tower Pier

Traitors' Gate

St Thomas's Tower

Salt Tower

0   100yds

Café

TOWER OF LONDON

© crown copyright

Tower Bridge

Traitors' Gate, on the waterfront. The nearby **Bloody Tower**, which forms the main entrance to the Inner Ward, is where the 12-year-old Edward V and his 10-year-old brother were accommodated "for their own safety" in 1483 by their uncle, the future Richard III, and later murdered. It's also where **Walter Ralegh** was imprisoned on three separate occasions, including a thirteen-year stretch.

The **White Tower**, at the centre of the Inner Ward, is the original "Tower", begun in 1076, and now home to displays from the **Royal Armouries**. Even if you've no interest in military paraphernalia, you should at least pay a visit to the **Chapel of St John**, a beautiful Norman structure on the second floor that was completed in 1080 – making it the oldest intact church building in London. To the west of the White Tower is the execution spot on **Tower Green** where seven highly placed but unlucky individuals were beheaded, among them Anne Boleyn and her cousin Catherine Howard (Henry VIII's second and fifth wives).

The Waterloo Barracks, to the north of the White Tower, hold the **Crown Jewels**, perhaps the major reason so many people flock to the Tower; however, the moving walkways are disappointingly swift, allowing you just 28 seconds' viewing during peak periods. The oldest piece of regalia is the twelfth-century **Anointing Spoon**, but the vast majority of exhibits postdate the Commonwealth (1649–60), when many of the royal riches were melted down for coinage or sold off. Among the jewels are the three largest cut diamonds in the world, including the legendary **Koh-i-Noor**, set into the Queen Mother's Crown in 1937.

TOWER BRIDGE

Daily 9.30am–6pm; £4.50; Ⓦ www.towerbridge.org.uk ⊖ Tower Hill.
Tower Bridge ranks with Big Ben as the most famous of all London landmarks. Completed in 1894, its neo-Gothic towers are clad in Cornish granite and Portland stone, but conceal a steel frame, which, at the time, represented a considerable engineering achievement, allowing a road crossing that could be raised to give tall ships access to the upper reaches of the Thames. The raising of the bascules (from the French for "see-saw") remains an impressive sight – phone ahead to find out when the bridge is opening

TOWER BRIDGE

The East End and Docklands

F ew places in London have engendered as many myths as the **East End**, a catch-all title which covers just about everywhere east of the City, but has its heart closest to the latter. Its name is synonymous with slums, sweatshops and crime, as epitomized by antiheroes such as Jack the Ripper and the Kray Twins, but also with the rags-to-riches careers of the likes of Harold Pinter and Vidal Sassoon, and whole generations of Jews who were born in the most notorious of London's cholera-ridden quarters and have now moved to wealthier pastures. Old East Enders will tell you that the area's not what it was – and it's true, as it always has been. The East End is constantly changing as newly arrived immigrants assimilate and move out.

The East End's first immigrants were French Protestant Huguenots, fleeing religious persecution in the late seventeenth century. Within three generations the Huguenots were entirely assimilated, and the Irish became the new immigrant population, but it was the influx of Jews escaping pogroms in eastern Europe and Russia that defined the character of the East End in the second half of the nineteenth

SUNDAY MARKETS

Most visitors to the East End come here for the **Sunday markets**. Approaching from Liverpool Street, the first one you come to, on the east side of Bishopsgate, is **Petticoat Lane** (Map 7, J2; Sun 9am–2pm; ⊖ Liverpool Street or Aldgate East), not one of London's prettiest streets, but one of its longest-running Sunday markets, specializing in cheap (and often pretty tacky) clothing. The authorities renamed the street Middlesex Street in 1830 to avoid the mention of ladies' underwear, but the original name has stuck.

Two blocks north of Middlesex Street, down Brushfield Street, lies **Spitalfields Market** (organic market Fri & Sun 10am–5pm general market Mon–Fri 11am–3pm & Sun 10am–5pm; ⊖ Liverpool Street), once the capital's premier wholesale fruit and vegetable market, now specializing in organic food, plus clothes, crafts and jewellery. Further east lies **Brick Lane** (Map 7, M1; Sun 8am–1pm; ⊖ Aldgate East, Shoreditch or Liverpool Street), heart of the Bengali community, famous for its bric-a-brac Sunday market, wonderful curry houses and non-stop bagel bakery, and now also something of a magnet for young designers. From Brick Lane's northernmost end, it's a short walk to **Columbia Road** (Sun 8am–1pm; bus #26 from Aldwych or Liverpool Street tube), the city's best market for flowers and plants; you'll need to ask the way or head in the direction of the folk bearing plants.

century. The area's Jewish population has now dispersed throughout London, though the East End remains at the bottom of the pile; even the millions poured into the **Docklands** development have failed to make much impression on local unemployment and housing problems. Unfortunately, racism is still rife, and is directed, for the most part, against the extensive **Bengali** community, who came here from the poor rural area of Sylhet in Bangladesh in the 1960s and 1970s.

As the area is not an obvious place for sightseeing, and certainly no beauty spot – Victorian slum clearances, Hitler's bombs and postwar tower blocks have all left their mark – most visitors to the East End come for its famous **Sunday markets**. However, there's plenty more to get out of a visit, including a trio of **Hawksmoor churches**, and the vast **Canary Wharf** redevelopment, which has to be seen to be believed.

WHITECHAPEL AND SPITALFIELDS

Map 2, J4. ⊖ Liverpool Street or Aldgate East.

The districts of **Whitechapel**, and in particular **Spitalfields**, within sight of the sleek tower blocks of the financial sector, represent the old heart of the East End, where the French Huguenots settled in the seventeenth century, where the Jewish community was at its strongest in the late nineteenth century, and where today's Bengali community eats, sleeps, works and prays. If you visit just one area in the East End, it should be this zone, which preserves mementos from each wave of immigration.

The easiest approach is from Liverpool Street Station (Map 7, I1), a short stroll west of **Spitalfields Market**, the red-brick and green-gabled market hall built in 1893, half of which was recently demolished in order to make way for yet more City offices. The dominant architectural presence in Spitalfields, however, is **Christ Church** (Map 7, K1; Mon–Fri 12.30–2.30pm), built in 1714–29 to a characteristically bold design by Nicholas Hawksmoor, and now facing the market hall. Best viewed from Brushfield Street, the church's main features are its huge 225-foot-high spire and a giant Tuscan portico, raised on steps and shaped like a Venetian window (a central arched opening flanked by two smaller rectangles), a motif repeated in the tower and doors.

Whitechapel Road

Map 7, N2. ⊖ Aldgate or Aldgate East.

Whitechapel Road – as Whitechapel High Street and the
Mile End Road are collectively known – is still the East
End's main street, shared by all the many races who live in
the borough of Tower Hamlets. The East End institution
that draws in more outsiders than any other here is the
Whitechapel Art Gallery (Map 7, M2; Tues & Thurs
–Sun 11am–6pm, Wed 11am–8pm; free; ⓦwww
.whitechapel.org), housed in a beautiful crenellated 1899
Arts and Crafts building by Charles Harrison Townsend,
architect of the similarly audacious Horniman Museum
(p.150). The gallery stages some of London's most innovative exhibitions of contemporary art, as well as hosting the
biennial Whitechapel Open, a chance for local artists to get
their work shown to a wider audience.

The most visible symbol of the new Muslim presence in
the East End is the Saudi-financed **East London Mosque**,
an enormous red-brick building that's a short walk up
Whitechapel Road from the art gallery; it stands in marked
contrast to the tiny **Great Synagogue**, dating from 1899,
behind the mosque in Fieldgate Street. Neither of these
buildings is open to the public, but you can pay a visit to
the small exhibition in the nearby **Whitechapel Bell
Foundry** (Mon–Fri 9am–5pm; guided tours Sat 10am &
2pm; £8; no under-14s; book in advance on ☎020/7247
2599, ⓦwww.whitechapelbellfoundry.co.uk), on the corner
of Fieldgate Street. Big Ben, the Liberty Bell, the Bow Bells
and numerous English church bells (including those of
Westminster Abbey) all hail from the foundry, established
here in 1738.

It was on the Mile End Road – the extension of
Whitechapel Road – that Joseph Merrick, better known as
the "**Elephant Man**", was discovered in a freak show by Dr

WHITECHAPEL AND SPITALFIELDS

102

JACK THE RIPPER

In the space of just eight weeks between August and November 1888, five prostitutes were stabbed to death in and around Whitechapel; all were found with their innards removed. Few of the letters received by the press and police, which purported to come from the murderer, are thought to have been genuine, including the one which coined the nickname **Jack the Ripper**, and to this day the murderer's identity remains a mystery. At the time, it was assumed by many that he was a Jew, probably a *shochet* (a ritual slaughterman), since the mutilations were obviously carried out with some skill. The theory gained ground when the fourth victim was discovered outside the predominantly Jewish Working Men's Club in Berner Street, and for a while it was dangerous for Jews to walk the streets at night for fear of reprisals.

Ripperologists have trawled through the little evidence there is to produce numerous other suspects, none of whom can be positively proven guilty. The crime writer Patricia Cornwell has recently spent millions in an attempt to prove that the artist Walter Sickert was the Ripper, but the man who usually tops the lists is a cricket-playing barrister named Druitt, whose body was found floating in the Thames some weeks after the last murder, though there is no firm evidence linking him with any of the killings.

The one positive outcome of the murders at the time was that they focused the attention of the rest of London on the squalor of the East End. Philanthropist Samuel Barnett, for one, used the media attention to press for improved housing, street lighting and policing to combat crime and poverty in the area. Today, the murders continue to be exploited in gory, misogynistic detail by the likes of Madame Tussaud's and the London Dungeon, while guided walks retracing the Ripper's steps set off every week throughout the year (see p.14).

WHITECHAPEL AND SPITALFIELDS

Treves, and subsequently admitted as a patient to the **Royal London Hospital** on Whitechapel Road. He remained there, on show as a medical freak, until his death in 1890 at the age of just 27. There's a small section on Merrick in the **Hospital Museum** (Mon–Fri 10am–4.30pm; free), housed beside the red-brick church (now the medical college library) on Newark Street.

Just before the point where Whitechapel Road turns into Mile End Road stands the gabled entrance to the former Albion Brewery, where the first bottled brown ale was produced in 1899. Next door lies the **Blind Beggar**, the East End's most famous pub since March 8, 1966, when Ronnie Kray walked into the crowded bar and shot gangland rival George Cornell for calling him a "fat poof". This murder spelled the end of the infamous Kray Twins, Ronnie and Reggie, both of whom were sentenced to life imprisonment, though their well-publicized gifts to local charities created a Robin Hood image that still persists in these parts of town.

BETHNAL GREEN MUSEUM OF CHILDHOOD

Map 2, J4. Daily except Fri 10am–5pm; free;
ⓦ www.museumofchildhood.org.uk ⊖ Bethnal Green

North of the Whitechapel Road, the **Bethnal Green Museum of Childhood**, is conveniently situated opposite Bethnal Green tube station. The open-plan, wrought-iron hall, originally part of (and still a branch of) the V&A museum (see p.128), was transported here in the 1860s to bring art to the East End. The variety of exhibits means that there's something here for everyone from 3 to 93, but the museum's most frequent visitors are children – the displays are not very hands-on, but the workshops are popular. The ground floor is best known for its unique collection of antique dolls' houses dating back to 1673. You'll need a pile of 20p pieces with you to work the automata – Wallace the Lion gobbling up Albert is always a favourite. Elsewhere, there are puppets, a jumble of toys, a vast doll collection and excellent temporary exhibitions.

DOCKLANDS

The architectural embodiment of Thatcherism, a symbol of 1980s smash-and-grab culture according to its critics, or a blueprint for inner-city regeneration to its free-market supporters – the **Docklands** redevelopment provokes extreme reactions. Despite its catch-all name, however, Docklands is far from homogeneous. Canary Wharf, with its Manhattan-style skyscrapers, is only its most visible landmark; industrial-estate sheds and riverside flats of dubious architectural merit are more indicative of the area. **Wapping**, the westernmost district, has retained much of its old Victorian warehouse architecture, while the **Royal Docks**, further east, are only just beginning to be transformed from an industrial wasteland.

The docks were originally built from 1802 onwards to relieve congestion on the Thames quays, and eventually became the largest enclosed cargo-dock system in the world. However, competition from the railways and, later, the development of container ships, signalled the closure of the docks in the 1960s. Then, at the height of the recession in the 1980s, regeneration began in earnest. No one thought the old docks could ever be rejuvenated and, twenty-plus years on, more has been achieved than many thought possible (and less than some had hoped). Travelling through on the overhead railway, Docklands comes over as an intriguing open-air design museum, not a place one would choose to live or work – most people stationed here still see it as a bleak business-oriented outpost – but a spectacular sight nevertheless.

DOCKLANDS

DOCKLANDS TRANSPORT

Although Canary Wharf is now on the Jubilee line, the best way to view Docklands is either from one of the boats that course up and down the Thames (see p.12), or from the driverless, overhead **Docklands Light Railway** or DLR (Ⓦ www.tfl.gov.uk/dlr), which sets off from Bank, or from Tower Gateway, close to Tower Hill tube. Travelcards are valid on the DLR, or you can buy a variety of DLR-only day passes giving you unlimited travel on certain sections of the network. Tour guides give a free running commentary on DLR trains that set off on the hour from Tower Gateway (daily 10am–2pm) and Bank (Mon–Fri 11am–2pm, Sat & Sun 10am–2pm) as far as the *Cutty Sark*. If you're heading for Greenwich, and fancy taking a boat back into town, it might be worth considering a Rail River Rover ticket (£8.30), which gives you unlimited travel on the DLR and City Cruises services between Greenwich and Westminster.

Wapping to Limehouse

Map 2, K4.

From the DLR overhead railway, you get a good view of two of Hawksmoor's landmark East End churches. The first one is **St George-in-the-East**, built in 1726 and visible to the south just before you reach Shadwell station. It's easy to spot thanks to its four domed corner towers and distinctive west-end tower topped by an octagonal lantern. You're missing nothing by staying on the train, though, as the interior was devastated in the Blitz. As the DLR leaves Limehouse station and skirts Limehouse Basin marina, Hawksmoor's **St Anne's Church** is visible to the north. Begun in 1714 and dominated again by a gargantuan west tower, the church is topped by an octagonal lantern and adorned with the highest church clock in London. Again, the interior isn't worth the effort as it was badly damaged by fire in 1850.

An alternative to the DLR is to walk from Wapping to Limehouse, along the Thames Path, which sticks to, or close to, the riverbank. You begin at **St Katharine Dock** (Map 7, M7), immediately east of the Tower of London, and the first of the old docks to be renovated way back in the 1970s. St Katharine's redeeming qualities are the old swing bridges and the boats themselves, many of which are beautiful old sailing ships. Continue along **Wapping High Street**, lined with tall brick-built warehouses, most now tastefully converted into yuppie flats, and you will eventually find yourself in Limehouse, beyond which lies the Isle of Dogs. The fairly well-signposted walk is about two miles in length, and will bring you eventually to Westferry Circus – for details of riverside pubs along the way, see p.233.

The Isle of Dogs

Map 2, L5.

The Thames begins a dramatic horseshoe bend at Limehouse, thus creating the **Isle of Dogs**, the geographical and ideological heart of the new Docklands. The area reaches its apotheosis in **Canary Wharf** (ⓦ www.canarywharf.com), the strip of land in the middle of the former West India Docks, previously a destination for rum and mahogany, later tomatoes and bananas (from the Canary Islands – hence the name).

The only really busy bit of the new Docklands, Canary Wharf, is best known as the home of Britain's tallest building, Cesar Pelli's landmark tower, officially known as **One Canada Square**. The world's first skyscraper to be clad in stainless steel, it's an undeniably impressive sight, both from a distance (its flashing pinnacle is a feature of the horizon at

DOCKLANDS

numerous points in London) and close up. However, it no longer stands alone, having been joined recently by several other skyscrapers that stop just short of Pelli's stumpy peak.

The warehouses to the north of Canary Wharf have been converted into flats, bars, restaurants and a **Docklands Museum** (scheduled to open in 2003; for more information, call ☎020/7515 1162), and will also include a thirty-storey tower block and a multiplex cinema. Unless you're keen to visit the museum, there's little point in getting off the DLR as it cuts right through the middle of the Canary Wharf office buildings under a parabolic steel-and-glass canopy.

The rest of the Isle of Dogs remains surreally lifeless, an uneasy mix of drab high-rises, council estates, warehouses converted into expensive apartments, and a lot of new architecture – some of it startling, some of it crass. If you're heading for Greenwich (see p.151), you have a choice: either get off at **Island Gardens**, Christopher Wren's favourite spot from which to contemplate his masterpieces across the river (the Royal Naval College and Royal Observatory), and walk through the 1902 foot tunnel to Greenwich; alternatively, you can stay on the DLR, which now tunnels underneath the Thames, and alight at Cutty Sark station.

DOCKLANDS

The South Bank

The **South Bank** (Ⓦ www.southbanklondon.com) – the area immediately opposite Victoria Embankment – is best known for the **South Bank Centre**, London's much-unloved concrete culture bunker of theatres and galleries, built, for the most part, in the 1960s. After decades in the doldrums, the centre itself is currently under inspired artistic direction and the whole area is enjoying something of a renaissance, thanks in no small part to the towering presence of the **London Eye**, the world's largest observation wheel and one of the capital's most popular millennium projects. The wheel's success prompted a major refurbishment programme of the area, beginning with the transformation of **Hungerford Bridge**, connecting the South Bank to Embankment, into a gleaming double suspension footbridge. What's more, you can now happily explore the whole area on foot, free from the traffic noise and fumes that blight so much of central London, thanks to the well-marked **Thames Path**, which runs along the riverside.

Further afield, too, in what used to be the village of **Lambeth**, there are one or two places worth visiting, in particular the **Imperial War Museum**, which contains the most detailed exhibition on the Holocaust in Britain.

SOUTH BANK CENTRE

Map 6, B3. ⊖ Waterloo.

The modern development of the South Bank dates back to the 1951 **Festival of Britain**, when the South Bank Exhibition was held on derelict land south of the Thames. The festival was a (pretty much successful) attempt to revive postwar morale by celebrating the centenary of the Great Exhibition (when Britain really did rule over half the world). The most striking features of the site were the Royal Festival Hall (which still stands), the ferris wheel (inspiration for the current London Eye), the saucer-shaped Dome of Discovery (disastrously revisited in the guise of the Millennium Dome), and the cigar-shaped Skylon tower.

The festival's success provided the impetus for the eventual creation of the **South Bank Centre** (Ⓦ www .sbc.org.uk), now home to a variety of artistic institutions. The most attractive of the South Bank's venues is the **Royal Festival Hall** (Ⓦ www.rfh.org.uk), the only building left over from the 1951 festival and one of London's main concert venues. It's a great place to wander through during the day since there's usually a free gig or exhibition going on in the foyer. The centre's two other concert venues – the **Queen Elizabeth Hall** (QEH) and the more intimate **Purcell Room** – are its most depressing part architecturally, built in uncompromisingly brutalist 1960s style, as is the **Hayward Gallery** (Ⓦ www.hayward.org.uk), with its strange rooftop neon sculpture.

Tucked underneath Waterloo Bridge, the **National Film Theatre** (NFT) screens London's most esoteric films and has a decent café/bar, plus buskers and several secondhand bookstalls more or less permanently located outside. Behind the NFT, in amongst the skateboarders and the homeless who inhabit the roundabout at the southern end of Waterloo Bridge, is the eye-catching glass-drum of the **BFI**

London IMAX Cinema. Lastly, on the east side of the bridge, looking like a multistorey car park, is the **Royal National Theatre** (ⓦ www.nt-online.org) – popularly known as "the National" or "the NT" – which boasts three separate theatres.

For details of the venues in the
South Bank Centre, see chapters 21 & 22.

LONDON EYE

Map 6, A5. Daily: April–Sept 9.30am–10pm; Oct–March 9am–8pm; £10.50; ⓣ 0800/5000 600, ⓦ www.ba-londoneye.com ⊖ Waterloo or Westminster.

South of the South Bank Centre proper, beside County Hall, is London's most prominent new landmark, the **London Eye**, British Airways' magnificently graceful millennium wheel which spins slowly and silently over the Thames. Standing 443ft high, the wheel is the largest ever built, and it's constantly in slow motion – a full-circle "flight" in one of its 32 pods takes around thirty minutes, and lifts you high above the city. It's one of the few places (apart from a plane window) from which London looks a manageable size, as you can see right out to where the suburbs slip into the countryside. Ticket prices are outrageously high, and queues can be very bad at the weekend, so book in advance over the phone or online.

COUNTY HALL

Map 6, A6. ⊖ Westminster or Waterloo.

The colonnaded crescent of **County Hall** is the only truly monumental building in this part of town. Designed to house the LCC (London County Council), it was completed in

1933 and enjoyed its greatest moment of fame as the head-quarters of the GLC (Greater London Council), abolished by Margaret Thatcher in 1986, leaving London as the only European city without an elected authority. In 2000, the former GLC leader Ken Livingstone was elected as Mayor of London, and moved into the new GLA (Greater London Authority) building near Tower Bridge (see p.97). County Hall, meanwhile, is in the hands of a Japanese property company, and currently houses hotels, restaurants, an amusement arcade, the London Aquarium and Dalí Universe.

The London Aquarium

Daily 10am–6pm or later; £8.75; ⓦ www.londonaquarium.co.uk
⊖ Waterloo or Westminster.

So far, the most popular attraction in County Hall is the **London Aquarium**, laid out across three floors of the basement. With some super-large, multi-floor tanks, and everything from dog-face puffers to piranhas, this is somewhere that's pretty much guaranteed to please younger kids. The "**Beach**", where children can actually stroke the (non-sting) rays, is particularly popular. Though impressive in scale, the aquarium is fairly conservative in design, however, with no walk-through tanks and only the very briefest of information on any of the fish.

Dalí Universe

Daily 10am–5.30pm (later in the summer); £8.50;
ⓦ www.daliuniverse.com. ⊖ Westminster or Waterloo.

Three giant Surrealist sculptures on the river-facing side of County Hall advertise the building's latest attraction, **Dalí Universe**. There's no denying Dalí was an accomplished and prolific artist, but you'll be disappointed if you're expecting to see his "greatest hits" – those are scattered across the globe. Most of the works here are little-known bronze and glass sculptures, and various drawings from the many illustrated books which he published, ranging from Ovid to the Marquis de Sade. Aside from these, there's one of the numerous lobster telephones, which Edward James commissioned for his London home, a copy of his famous Mae West lips sofa, and the oil painting from the dream sequence in Hitchcock's movie *Spellbound*.

LAMBETH

South of Westminster Bridge, you leave the South Bank proper, and enter what used to be the village of **Lambeth** (now the name of the entire borough stretching as far south as Brixton). This stretch of the riverbank affords the best views of the Houses of Parliament, and there are a few sights worth considering, such as the **Florence Nightingale Museum**. Inland lies London's most even-handed military museum, the **Imperial War Museum**, housed in a former lunatic asylum.

Florence Nightingale Museum

Map 3, I6. Mon–Fri 10am–5pm, Sat & Sun 11.30am–4.30pm; £4.80; ⓦ www.florence-nightingale.co.uk ⊖ Westminster.

On the south side of Westminster Bridge, on Lambeth Palace Road and in the midst of St Thomas's Hospital, the **Florence Nightingale Museum** celebrates the woman who revolutionized the nursing profession by establishing the first school of nursing at St Thomas's in 1860. The exhibition hits just the right note, putting the two years she spent in the Crimea in the context of a lifetime of tireless social campaigning. Exhibits include the white lantern that earned her the nickname "The Lady with the Lamp", and a reconstruction of a Crimean military hospital ward.

LAMBETH

Museum of Garden History

Map 3, I7. March to mid-Dec daily 10.30am–5pm; free though £2.50 donation suggested; ⓦ www.cix.co.uk/~museumgh.
⊖ Westminster.

A short walk south of St Thomas's is the Kentish ragstone church of St Mary-at-Lambeth, which now contains a café and an unpretentious little **Museum of Garden History**. The graveyard has been transformed into a small seventeenth-century garden, where two interesting sarcophagi lurk among the foliage: one belongs to Captain Bligh, the commander of the *Bounty* in 1787; the other is a memorial to John Tradescant, gardener to James I and Charles I.

The Imperial War Museum

Map 3, K7. Daily 10am–6pm; free; ⓦ www.iwm.org.uk ⊖ Lambeth North or Elephant & Castle.

The domed building at the east end of Lambeth Road, formerly the infamous lunatic asylum "Bedlam", is now the **Imperial War Museum**, by far the best military museum in the capital. The treatment of the subject is impressively wide-ranging and fairly sober, with the main hall's militaristic display offset by the lower-ground-floor array of documents and images attesting to the human damage of war. The museum also has a harrowing **Holocaust Exhibition** (not recommended for children under 14), which you enter from the third floor. The exhibition pulls few punches, and has made a valiant attempt to avoid depicting the victims of the Holocaust as nameless masses by focusing on individual cases, and interspersing the archive footage with eyewitness accounts from contemporary survivors.

LAMBETH

Southwark

U ntil well into the seventeenth century, the only reason for north-bank residents to cross the Thames, to what is now **Southwark**, was to visit the infamous Bankside entertainment district around the south end of London Bridge, which lay outside the jurisdiction of the City. What started out as a red-light district under the Romans reached its peak as the pleasure quarter of Tudor and Stuart London, where disreputable institutions banned in the City – most notably theatres – continued to flourish until the Puritan purges of the 1640s.

Thanks to wholesale regeneration in the last few years, Southwark's riverfront is once more somewhere to head for. A whole cluster of sights vie for attention, most notably the **Tate Modern** art gallery, housed in a converted power station, and next to it a reconstruction of Shakespeare's **Globe Theatre**. The **Thames Path** connects the district with the South Bank to the west, and allows you to walk east along Clink Street and Tooley Street, home to a further rash of popular sights such as the **London Dungeon**. Further east still, **Butler's Wharf** is a thriving little warehouse development centred on the excellent **Design Museum**.

BANKSIDE: THE TATE AND THE GLOBE

⊖ Southwark or Blackfriars.

Bankside, which lies between Blackfriars and Southwark Bridge, was the most nefarious area in London in Elizabethan times, thanks to its brothels, bearpits and theatres. Four hundred years on, and Bankside is once more a magnet for visitors and Londoners alike, thanks to the reconstructed **Globe Theatre** (where most of Shakespeare's plays had their first performances), and the **Tate Modern** housed in the old Bankside power station. In addition, the area is now linked to St Paul's and the City by the fabulous new Norman Foster-designed **Millennium Bridge**, the first to cross the Thames for over a century, and London's first pedestrian-only bridge.

Tate Modern

Map 7, A7. Daily 10am–6pm; Fri & Sat open until 10pm; free; ☎ 020/7887 8000, ⒲ www.tate.org.uk ⊖ Southwark or Blackfriars.

Bankside is dominated by the austere power station of the same name, now transformed by the Swiss duo Herzog & de Meuron into the **Tate Modern**. The masterful conversion has left plenty of the original, industrial feel, while providing wonderfully light and spacious galleries in which to show off the Tate's vast international twentieth-century art collection. The best way to enter is down the ramp from the west, so you get the full effect of the stupendously large turbine hall. It's easy enough to find your way around the galleries, with levels 3 and 5 displaying the permanent collection, level 4 used for fee-paying temporary exhibitions, and level 7 home to a rooftop café with a great view over the Thames.

Given that Tate Modern is the largest modern art gallery in the world, you need to spend the best part of a day here to do justice to the place, or be very selective. Pick up a plan (and, for an extra £1, an audioguide), and take the escalator to level 3. The curators have eschewed the usual chronological approach through the "isms", preferring to group works together thematically: Landscape/Matter /Environment, Still Life/Object/Real Life, History /Memory/Society, and Nude/Action/Body. On the whole this works very well, though the early twentieth-century canvases in their gilded frames do struggle when made to compete with contemporary installations.

Although the displays change every six months or so, you're still pretty much guaranteed to see at least some works by **Monet** and Bonnard, Cubist pioneers **Picasso** and Braque, Surrealists such as **Dalí**, abstract artists like **Mondrian**, Bridget Riley and Pollock, and Pop supremos **Warhol** and Lichtenstein. There are seminal works such as a replica of **Duchamp**'s urinal, entitled *Fountain* and signed "R. Mutt", Yves Klein's totally blue paintings and Carl André's trademark piles of bricks. And such is the space here that several artists get whole rooms to themselves, among them the painter Francis Bacon, Joseph Beuys and his shamanistic wax and furs, and **Mark Rothko**, whose abstract "Seagram Murals", originally destined for a posh restaurant in New York, have their own shrine-like room in the heart of the collection.

Shakespeare's Globe Theatre

Map 7, B7. Box office ⓣ 020/7401 9919,
ⓦ www.shakespeares-globe.org ⊖ Southwark or Blackfriars.
Seriously dwarfed by the Tate Modern is the equally spectacular **Shakespeare's Globe Theatre**, a reconstruction of the polygonal playhouse where most of the Bard's later works were first performed, and which was originally erected on nearby Park Street in 1598. To find out more about Shakespeare and the history of Bankside, the Globe's pricey

but stylish **exhibition** (daily: May–Sept 9am–noon & 12.30–4pm; Oct–April 10am–5pm; £8) is well worth a visit. It begins by detailing the long campaign by American actor Sam Wanamaker to have the Globe rebuilt, but it's the imaginative hands-on exhibits that really hit the spot. You can have a virtual play on medieval instruments such as the crumhorn or sackbut, prepare your own edition of Shakespeare, and feel the thatch, hazelnut shell and daub used to build the theatre. Visitors also get taken on an informative **guided tour** round the theatre itself, except in the afternoons during the summer season, when you can only visit the exhibition (for a reduced entrance fee).

For more on attending performances
at the Globe, see p.286.

You can view the archeological remains of another
Elizabethan playhouse, the **Rose Theatre**, nearby at
56 Park St, by arrangement with the Globe ☎ 020/7902 1500.

CLINK STREET, SOUTHWARK CATHEDRAL AND AROUND

✚ London Bridge.

East of Bankside, beyond Southwark Bridge, lies **Vinopolis** (Map 7, D8; Mon, Fri & Sat noon–9pm, Tues–Thurs & Sun noon–6pm; £11.50; ⓦ www.vinopolis.co.uk), discreetly housed in former wine vaults under the railway arches on Clink Street. The focus of the complex is the "**Wine Odyssey**", a light-hearted trot through the world's wine regions, equipped with an audioguide. There are plenty of visual gags – you get to tour round the Italian vineyards on a Vespa – but the most appealing and educational aspect of the tour is the **wine tasting**. Visitors get five generous samples – from champagne to vintage port – with the option of buying more if you've the head for it.

Further down the suitably gloomy confines of dark and narrow Clink Street is the **Clink Prison Museum** (Map 7, D8; daily 10am–6pm; until 9pm in summer; £4; Ⓦwww.clink.co.uk), built on the site of the former Clink Prison, origin of the expression "in the clink". The prison began as a dungeon for disobedient clerics, built under the Bishop of Winchester's Palace – the rose window of the palace's Great Hall survives just east of the museum – and later became a dumping ground for heretics, prostitutes and a motley assortment of Bankside lowlife. Today's exhibition features a handful of prison-life tableaux, and dwells on the torture and grim conditions within, but, given the rich history of the place, this is a disappointingly lacklustre museum.

An exact replica of the **Golden Hinde** (Map 7, E8; phone for times ☎0870/011 8700; £2.75; Ⓦwww.goldenhinde.co.uk), the galleon in which Francis Drake sailed around the world from 1577 to 1580, nestles in St Mary Overie Dock, at the eastern end of Clink Street. The ship is surprisingly small, and its original crew of eighty plus must have been cramped to say the least. There's a refreshing lack of interpretive panels, so it's worth paying the little bit extra and getting a guided tour from one of the folk in period garb – ring ahead to check that a group hasn't booked the place up.

Southwark Cathedral

Map 7, E8. Mon–Sat 10am–6pm, Sun 11am–5pm;
Ⓦwww.dswark.org/cathedral ⊖ London Bridge.
Close by the *Golden Hinde* stands **Southwark Cathedral**, built as the medieval Augustinian priory church of St Mary

Overie, and given cathedral status only in 1905. Of the original thirteenth-century church, only the choir and retrochoir now remain, separated by a tall and beautiful stone Tudor screen, making them probably the oldest Gothic structures left in London. The nave was entirely rebuilt in the nineteenth century, but the cathedral contains numerous interesting monuments, from a thirteenth-century oak effigy of a knight to an early twentieth-century memorial to Shakespeare. If you're feeling peckish, the cathedral refectory serves tasty food, but the new multi-media **exhibition** (£3), which whizzes through Southwark's history, can be happily skipped.

Bramah Tea and Coffee Museum

Map 7, D9. Daily 10am–6pm; £4; ⓦ www.bramahmuseum.co.uk
The **Bramah Tea and Coffee Museum** in its new location at 40 Southwark St, a couple of blocks southwest of the cathedral, is endearingly ramshackle and well worth a visit. Founded in 1992 by Edward Bramah, who began his career on an African tea garden in 1950, the museum's emphasis is firmly on tea, though the café also serves a seriously good cup of coffee. There's an impressive array of teapots from Meissen to the world's largest, plus plenty of novelty ones, and coffee machines spanning the twentieth century, from huge percolator siphons to espresso machines.

The Old Operating Theatre

Map 7, F9. Daily 10.30am–5pm; £3.75; ⓦ www.thegarret.org.uk
⊖ London Bridge.
The most educational and strangest of Southwark's museums, the **Old Operating Theatre, Museum** and **Herb Garret** is located to the east of the cathedral on St Thomas Street, on the other side of Borough High Street. Built in

1821 at the top of a church tower, where the hospital apothecary's herbs were stored, this women's operating theatre dates from the pre-anaesthetic era. Despite being entirely gore-free, the museum is as stomach-churning as the London Dungeon (see below). The surgeons who used this room would have concentrated on speed and accuracy (most amputations took less than a minute), but there was still a thirty percent mortality rate, with many patients simply dying of shock, and many more from bacterial infection, about which very little was known.

TOOLEY STREET AND AROUND

Map 7, G8. ⊖ London Bridge.

The vaults beneath the railway arches of London Bridge train station, on the south side of **Tooley Street**, are now occupied by two museums. Young teenagers and the credulous probably get the most out of the ever-popular **London Dungeon** (daily: March to mid-July, Sept & Oct 10am–5.30pm; mid-July to Aug 9.30am–7.30pm; Nov–Feb 10.30am–5pm; £10.95; ⓦ www.thedungeons.com) – to avoid the inevitable queue, buy your ticket online. The life-sized waxwork tableaux inside include a man being hung, drawn and quartered, and one being boiled alive, the general hysteria being boosted by actors, dressed as top-hatted Victorian vampires, pouncing out of the darkness. Visitors are then herded into a courtroom, condemned to the "River of Death" boat ride, and forced to endure the "Jack the Ripper Experience", an exploitative trawl through postmortem photos and wax mock-ups of the victims, followed by the "Great Fire of London", in which you experience the heat and the smell of the plague-ridden city, before walking through a revolving tunnel of flames.

A little further east along Tooley Street is **Winston Churchill's Britain at War** (Map 7, H9; daily: April–Sept

10am–5.30pm; Oct–March 10am–4.30pm; £6.50; Ⓦ www.britainatwar.co.uk), an illuminating insight into the stiff-upper-lip London mentality during the Blitz. The museum contains hundreds of wartime artefacts, including an Anderson shelter, where you can hear the chilling sound of the V-1 "doodlebugs" and tune in to contemporary radio broadcasts. The final set piece is a walk through the chaos of a just-bombed street.

On the other side of Tooley Street is **Hay's Galleria** (Map 7, H8), a shopping precinct built over what used to be Hay's Dock. The idea of filling in the curvaceous dock and covering it with glass and steel barrel-vaulting, while retaining the old Victorian warehouses on three sides, is an effective one. The pastiche of phoney market barrows, gravel underfoot and red phone boxes and the gimmicky kinetic sculpture at the centre, however, is disappointing.

Permanently moored just along the riverfront from Hay's Galleria is the **HMS Belfast** (Map 7, I8; daily: March–Oct 10am–6pm; Nov–Feb 10am–5pm; £5.80; Ⓦ www .iwm.org.uk), a World War II cruiser. Armed with six torpedoes, and six-inch guns with a range of over fourteen miles, the *Belfast* spent over two years of the war in the Royal Naval shipyards after being hit by a mine in the Firth of Forth at the beginning of hostilities. It later saw action in the Barents Sea during World War II, and during the Korean War, before being decommissioned. The maze of cabins is fun to explore but if you want to find out more about the *Belfast*, head for the exhibition rooms in zone 5.

A short stroll east of the *Belfast* is Norman Foster's startling glass-encased **City Hall** (Map 7, J9; Mon–Fri 8am–8pm; Ⓦ www.london.gov.uk), the new Greater London Authority headquarters that looks like a giant car headlight. Visitors are welcome to stroll around the building and watch the London Assembly proceedings from the second floor. On certain weekends (check the website for details), access is also possible to "London's Living Room" on the ninth floor, from where there's a great view over the Thames.

BUTLER'S WHARF: THE DESIGN MUSEUM

Map 7, L9. ⊖ Tower Hill, London Bridge or Bermondsey.

In contrast to the brash offices on Tooley Street, **Butler's Wharf**, east of Tower Bridge, has retained its historical character. **Shad Thames**, the narrow street at the back of Butler's Wharf, has kept the wrought-iron overhead gangways by which the porters used to transport goods from the wharves to the warehouses further back from the river, and is one of the area's most atmospheric alleyways. The eight-storey Butler's Wharf warehouse itself, with its shops and restaurants, forms part of Terence Conran's commercial empire and caters for a moneyed clientele, but the wide promenade on the riverfront is open to the public.

The chief attraction of Butler's Wharf is Conran's superb riverside **Design Museum** (daily 10am–5.45pm; Fri until 9pm; £6; ⓦ www.designmuseum.org), a stylish, Bauhaus-like conversion of a 1950s warehouse at the eastern end of Shad Thames. The excellent temporary **exhibitions** on important designers, movements or single products are staged on the first floor, while the **galleries** on the top floor offer a brief overview of mass-produced industrial design from TVs to Tupperware. The small coffee bar in the foyer is a great place to relax, and there's a pricier Conran restaurant on the top floor.

Hyde Park, Kensington, Chelsea and Notting Hill

Hyde Park, together with its westerly extension, Kensington Gardens, covers a distance of two miles from Oxford Street in the northeast to Kensington Palace in the southwest. At the end of your journey, you've made it to one of London's most exclusive districts, the Royal Borough of **Kensington** and **Chelsea**, which makes up the bulk of this chapter. Other districts go in and out of fashion, but this area has been in vogue ever since royalty moved into **Kensington Palace** in the late seventeenth century.

Aside from the shops around Harrods in Knightsbridge, however, the popular tourist attractions lie in **South Kensington**, where three of London's top (and currently free) **museums** – the Victoria and Albert, Natural History and Science museums – stand on land bought with the proceeds of the Great Exhibition of 1851. Chelsea, to the south, has a slightly more bohemian pedigree. In the 1960s, the **King's Road** carved out its reputation as London's cat-walk, while in the late 1970s it was the epicentre of the punk explosion. Nothing so rebellious goes on in Chelsea now, though its residents like to think of themselves as rather more artistic and intellectual than the purely mon-eyed types of Kensington.

Once slummy, now swanky, **Bayswater** and **Notting Hill**, to the north of Hyde Park, were the bad boys of the borough for many years, dens of vice and crime comparable to Soho. Despite gentrification over the last 25 years, they remain the borough's most cosmopolitan districts, with a strong Arab presence and vestiges of the African-Caribbean community who initiated and still run the city's (and Europe's) largest street **carnival**, which takes place every August Bank Holiday.

HYDE PARK AND KENSINGTON GARDENS

Map 3, D5. ⊖ Marble Arch, Hyde Park Corner or Lancaster Gate.
Seized from the Church by Henry VIII to satisfy his desire for yet more hunting grounds, **Hyde Park** (Ⓦwww .royalparks.gov.uk) was first opened to the public by James I, and soon became a fashionable gathering place for the beau monde, who rode round the circular drive known as the Ring, pausing to gossip and admire each other's *équipage*. Hangings, muggings and duels, the Great Exhibition of 1851 and numerous public events have all taken place in Hyde Park – and it's still a popular gathering point or destination for political demonstrations. For most of the time, however, the park is simply a leisure ground – a wonderful open space which allows you to lose all sight of the city beyond a few persistent tower blocks.

Located at the treeless northeastern corner of the park, **Marble Arch** (Map 3, D4) was originally erected in 1828 as a triumphal entry to Buckingham Palace, but is now stranded on a ferociously busy traffic island at the west end of Oxford Street. This is the most historically charged spot in Hyde Park, as it marks the site of **Tyburn gallows**, the city's main public execution spot until 1783. It's also the location of **Speakers' Corner**, once an entertaining and peculiarly English Sunday tradition, featuring an assembly of characterful speakers and hecklers – now, sadly, a forum for soap-box religious extremists.

A better place to enter the park is at **Hyde Park Corner** (Map 3, F6), the southeast corner, where the **Wellington Arch** (Wed–Sun: April–Sept 10am–6pm; Oct 10am–5pm; Nov–March 10am–4pm; £2.50) stands in the midst of another of London's busiest traffic interchanges. Erected in 1828 to commemorate Wellington's victories in the Napoleonic Wars, the arch was originally topped by an equestrian statue of the Duke himself, later replaced by Peace driving a four-horse chariot. Inside, you can view an exhibition on London's outdoor sculpture and take a lift to the top of the monument, where the exterior balconies offer a bird's-eye view of the swirling traffic.

Close by stands **Apsley House** (Map 3, F6; Tues–Sun 11am–5pm; £4.50; ⓦ www.apsleyhouse.org.uk), Wellington's London residence and now a museum to the "Iron Duke". Unless you're a keen fan of the Duke (or the architect, Benjamin Wyatt), the highlight of the museum is the **art collection**, much of which used to belong to the King of Spain. Among the best pieces, displayed in the Waterloo Gallery on the first floor, are works by de Hooch, Van Dyck, Velázquez, Goya, Rubens and Murillo. The famous, more than twice life-size, nude statue of Napoleon by Antonio Canova stands at the foot of the main staircase.

Hyde Park is divided in two by the **Serpentine Lake**, which has a popular **Lido** (June–Aug daily 10am–6pm; £2.50) on its south bank. By far the prettiest section of the lake, though, is the upper section known as the **Long**

Water, which narrows until it reaches a group of four fountains, laid out symmetrically in front of an Italianate summerhouse designed by Wren.

The western half of the park is officially known as **Kensington Gardens** and is, strictly speaking, a separate entity, though you hardly notice the change. Its two most popular attractions are the **Serpentine Gallery** (Map 3, C6; daily 10am–6pm; free; ⓦ www.serpentinegallery.org), which has a reputation for lively, and often controversial, contemporary art exhibitions, and the richly decorated, high-Gothic **Albert Memorial** (Map 3, B6), clearly visible to the west. Erected in 1876, the monument is as much a hymn to the glorious achievements of Britain as to its subject, Queen Victoria's husband (who died of typhoid in 1861). Recently restored to his former gilded glory, Albert occupies the central canopy, clutching a catalogue for the 1851 Great Exhibition that he helped to organize.

The Exhibition's most famous feature, the gargantuan glasshouse of the Crystal Palace, no longer exists, but the profits were used to buy a large tract of land south of the park, now home to South Kensington's remarkable cluster of museums and colleges, plus the vast **Royal Albert Hall** (Map 3, C6; ⓦ www.royalalberthall.com), a splendid iron-and-glass-domed concert hall, with an exterior of red brick, terracotta and marble that became the hallmark of South Ken architecture. The hall is the venue for Europe's most democratic music festival, the Henry Wood Promenade Concerts, better known as the **Proms**, which take place from July to September, with standing-room tickets for as little as £3.

Kensington Palace

Map 3, A6. Daily: March–Oct 10am–6pm; Nov–Feb 10am–5pm; £10; ⓦ www.hrp.org.uk ⊖ High Street Kensington or Queensway.
On the western edge of Kensington Gardens stands

Kensington Palace, a modestly proportioned Jacobean brick mansion bought by William and Mary in 1689, and the chief royal residence for the next fifty years. KP, as it's fondly known in royal circles, is best known today as the place where **Princess Diana** lived until her death in 1997. It was, in fact, the official London residence of both Charles and Di until the couple formally separated. In the weeks following Diana's death, literally millions of flowers, mementos, poems and gifts were deposited at the gates to the south of the palace.

Visitors don't get to see Diana's apartments, which were on the west side of the palace, where various minor royals still live. Instead, they get to view some of the frocks worn by Diana, and also several worn by the Queen, and then the sparsely furnished state apartments. The highlights are the trompe l'oeil ceiling paintings by William Kent, in particular the Cupola Room, and the oil paintings in the King's Gallery. En route, you also get to see the tastelessly decorated rooms in which the future Queen Victoria spent her unhappy childhood. To recover from the above, take tea in the exquisite **Orangery** (times as for palace), to the north of the palace.

VICTORIA AND ALBERT MUSEUM

Map 8, E7. Daily 10am–5.45pm; Wed & last Fri of month until 10pm; free; ⓦ www.vam.ac.uk ⊖ South Kensington.

In terms of sheer variety and scale, the **Victoria and Albert Museum** (popularly known as the V&A), on Cromwell Road, is the greatest museum of applied arts in the world. The range of exhibits on display here means that, whatever your taste, there is almost bound to be something to grab your attention.

The most celebrated of the V&A's numerous exhibits are the **Raphael Cartoons**, seven vast biblical paintings that served as designs for a set of tapestries destined for the Sistine Chapel. Close by, you can view highlights from the country's largest dress collection, and the world's largest collection of Indian art outside India. In addition, there are galleries devoted to British, Chinese, Islamic, Japanese and Korean art, as well as costume jewellery, glassware, metalwork and photography. Wading through the huge collection of European sculpture, you come to the surreal **Plaster Casts** gallery, filled with copies of European art's greatest hits, from Michelangelo's *David* to Trajan's Column (sawn in half to make it fit). There's even a gallery of twentieth-century *objets d'art* – everything from Bauhaus furniture to Swatch watches – to rival that of the Design Museum (see p.123).

Over in the **Henry Cole Wing**, meanwhile, you'll find an entire office interior by Frank Lloyd Wright, a collection of sixteenth-century portrait miniatures, more Constable paintings than the Tate, and a goodly collection of sculptures by Rodin. As if all this were not enough, the V&A's temporary shows are among the best in Britain, ranging over vast areas of art, craft and technology.

Beautifully but haphazardly displayed across a sevenmile, four-storey maze of halls and corridors, the V&A's treasures are impossible to survey in a single visit. Floor plans from the information desks can help you decide which areas to concentrate on. If you're flagging, there's a restaurant in the basement of the Henry Cole Wing, or a more edifying, snacky café in the museum's period-piece **Poynter, Morris and Gamble** refreshment rooms. If you've energy left after your visit, stop by London's most flamboyant Roman Catholic church, the **Brompton Oratory** (Map 8, F6), built in neo-Baroque style in the 1880s, which lies just next door to the museum on Brompton Road.

VICTORIA AND ALBERT MUSEUM

SCIENCE MUSEUM

Map 8, D6. Daily 10am–6pm; free; ⓦ www.sciencemuseum.org.uk
⊖ South Kensington.

The **Science Museum**, on Exhibition Road, is undeniably impressive, filling seven floors with items drawn from every conceivable area of science, including space travel, telecommunications, time measurement, chemistry, computing, photography and medicine. Keen to dispel the enduring image of museums devoted to its subject as boring and full of dusty glass cabinets, the Science Museum has been busy updating its galleries with more interactive displays, and puts on daily demonstrations to show that not all science teaching has to be deathly dry.

First off, head for the **information desk** in the Power Hall and find out what events and demonstrations are taking place; you can also sign up for a guided tour on a specific subject. Most people will want to head for the new **Wellcome Wing**. To do so, go past the info desk, and through the Space gallery, to the far side of the Making of the Modern World, a display of iconic inventions from Robert Stephenson's *Rocket* of 1829 to the Ford Model T, the world's first mass-produced car. The Wellcome Wing's four floors, full of state-of-the-art interactive computers and an IMAX cinema, are geared to appeal to even the most museum-phobic teenager.

The **Launch Pad**, one of the first hands-on displays aimed at kids, remains as popular and enjoyable as ever, as do the **Garden** and **Things** galleries, all of which are in the basement. The **Materials** gallery, on the first floor, is aimed more at adults, and is an extremely stylish exhibition covering the use of materials ranging from aluminium to zerodur (used for making laser gyroscopes).

NATURAL HISTORY MUSEUM

Map 8, C7. Mon–Sat 10am–5.50pm, Sun 11am–5.50pm; free;
Ⓦwww.nhm.ac.uk ⊖ South Kensington.

Alfred Waterhouse's purpose-built mock-Romanesque colossus ensures the **Natural History Museum**'s status as London's most handsome museum. Caught up, without huge public funds, in the current enthusiasm for museum redesign and accessibility, the contents are a mishmash of truly imaginative exhibits peppered amongst others little changed since the museum's opening in 1881. The museum is caught in a genuine conundrum, for its collections are important resources for serious zoologists, while its collection of real dinosaurs is a big hit with the kids.

The **main entrance**, in the middle of the museum's 675-foot terracotta facade, leads to what are now known as the **Life Galleries**. Just off the vast Central Hall, dominated by an 85-foot-long plaster cast of a diplodocus skeleton, you'll find the Dinosaur gallery, where a team of animatronic deinonychi feast on a half-dead tenontosaurus. Other popular sections include the Creepy-Crawlies Room, the Mammals gallery with its life-size model of a blue whale, and the hi-tech Ecology gallery, plus the somewhat ancient displays of stuffed creatures.

Visitors can now view more of the museum's millions of zoological specimens in the collections store of the new **Darwin Centre**, phase one of which opened in 2002. To see the rest of the building, however, you need to sign up for a **guided tour** (free; book ahead either online or by phoning ☏020/7942 6128). These set off roughly every half an hour and last about 35 minutes, allowing visitors to get a closer look at the specimens, including the larger ones, which have to be preserved in tanks. You also get to see behind the scenes at the labs, and even talk to one of the museum's 350 scientists about their work.

If the queues for the museum are long (as they can be at weekends and during school holidays), you might be better off heading for the side entrance on Exhibition Road, which leads into the former Geology Museum, now known as the **Earth Galleries**, an expensively revamped and visually exciting romp through the earth's evolution. The most popular sections are the slightly tasteless Kobe earthquake simulator, and the spectacular display of gems and crystals in the Earth's Treasury.

KENSINGTON HIGH STREET AND AROUND

Map 3, A7 ⊖ High Street Kensington.

Shopper-thronged **Kensington High Street** is dominated architecturally by the twin presences of George Gilbert Scott's neo-Gothic church of St Mary Abbots, whose 250-foot spire makes it London's tallest parish church, and the Art Deco colossus of Barkers department store, remodelled in the 1930s.

Kensington's sights are mostly hidden away in the back-streets, the one exception being the **Commonwealth Institute** (Mon–Sat 10am–5pm, Sun 2–5pm; free, £2 donation recommended; ℡020/7603 4535, ⓦwww .commonwealth.org.uk), housed in a bold 1960s building set back from the High Street. The Institute currently puts on excellent, challenging, interactive temporary exhibitions focusing on a particular Commonwealth country – phone ahead, or visit the website to check what's on.

Two paths along the side of the Commonwealth Institute lead to densely wooded **Holland Park**, the former grounds of a Jacobean mansion (only the east wing still stands). Theatrical and opera performances are staged here throughout the summer, and several **formal gardens** surround the house, most notably the Japanese-style Kyoto Gardens, while the rest of the park is dotted with a series of abstract sculptures.

A number of wealthy Victorian artists rather self-consciously founded an artists' colony in the streets that lie between the High Street and Holland Park. It's now possible to visit one of the most remarkable of these artist pads, **Leighton House** (daily except Tues 11am–5.30pm; free), at 12 Holland Park Road. "It will be opulence, it will be sincerity," Lord Leighton opined before starting work on the house in the 1860s – he later became President of the Royal Academy and was ennobled on his deathbed. The big attraction is the domed Arab Hall, decorated with Saracen tiles, gilded mosaics and woodwork drawn from all over the Islamic world. The other rooms are less spectacular but, in compensation, are hung with paintings by Lord Leighton and his Pre-Raphaelite chums.

KNIGHTSBRIDGE

Map 3, D7. ⊖ Knightsbridge.

Knightsbridge is irredeemably snobbish, revelling in its reputation as the swankiest shopping area in London, a status epitomized by **Harrods** (Mon–Sat 10am–7pm; ⓦwww .harrods.com) on Brompton Road. London's most famous department store started out as a family-run grocery store in 1849, with a staff of two. The current 1905 terracotta building is owned by the Egyptian Mohammed Al Fayed and employs in excess of three thousand staff. Tourists flock to Harrods – it's thought to be one of the city's top-ranking tourist attractions – though if you can do without the Harrods carrier bag you can buy most of what the shop stocks more cheaply elsewhere.

The store does, however, have a few sections that are architectural sights in their own right: the Food Hall, with its exquisite Arts and Crafts tiling, and the Egyptian Hall, with its pseudo-hieroglyphs and sphinxes, are particularly striking. Now that a fountain dedicated to Di and Dodi is

KNIGHTSBRIDGE

in place, the Egyptian Escalators are an added attraction, and will whisk you to the first-floor "luxury washrooms", where you can splash on free perfume after relieving yourself. Note, too, that the store has a draconian dress code: no shorts, no vest T-shirts and backpacks must be carried in the hand.

CHELSEA

Map 3, E8. ⊖ Sloane Square.

It wasn't until the latter part of the nineteenth century that **Chelsea** began to earn its reputation as London's very own Left Bank. Its household fame, however, came through **King's Road**'s role as the unofficial catwalk of the "Swinging Sixties". The road remained a fashion parade for hippies, too, and in the Jubilee Year of 1977 it witnessed the birth of punk, masterminded from a shop called Sex, run by Vivienne Westwood and Malcolm McLaren. These days, the area is better known for its young, upper-class residents – the original Sloane Rangers – and is lined with the usual chain stores and interior design shops.

The area's other aspect, oddly enough considering its boho reputation, is a military one. For, among the most nattily attired of all those parading down the King's Road are the scarlet or navy-blue-clad Chelsea Pensioners, army veterans from the nearby **Royal Hospital** (Map 3, E8; Mon–Fri 9am–noon & 2–4.30pm, Sat & Sun 9am–noon & 2–3pm; free), founded by Charles II in 1681. The hospital's majestic red-brick wings and grassy courtyards became a blueprint for institutional and collegiate architecture all over the English-speaking world. The public are allowed to view the austere hospital chapel, and the equally grand, wood-panelled dining hall, opposite, which has a vast allegorical mural of Charles II.

The concrete bunker next door to the Royal Hospital, on Royal Hospital Road, houses the **National Army Museum** (daily 10am–5.30pm; free; ⓦ www.national-army-museum.ac.uk). The militarily obsessed are unlikely to be disappointed by the succession of uniforms and medals, but there is very little here for non-enthusiasts. The temporary exhibitions staged on the ground floor are the museum's strong point, but it's rather disappointing overall – you're better off visiting the infinitely superior Imperial War Museum (see p.114).

Cheyne Walk and Cheyne Row

Map 3, D9. Any bus heading down King's Road from ⊖ Sloane Square.

The quiet riverside locale of **Cheyne** (pronounced "chainy") drew artists and writers in great numbers during the nineteenth century. Since the building of the Embankment and the increase in the volume of traffic, however, the character of this peaceful haven has been lost. Novelist Henry James, who lived at no. 21, used to take "beguiling drives" in his wheelchair along the Embankment; today, he'd be hospitalized in the process.

The chief reason to come here nowadays is to visit the **Chelsea Physic Garden** (April–Oct Wed noon–5pm, Sun 2–6pm; £4; ⓦ www.chelseaphysicgarden.co.uk), which marks the beginning of Cheyne Walk. Founded in 1673, this small walled garden is the second oldest botanical garden in the country. At the entrance (on Swan Walk) you can pick up a map of the garden with a list of the month's most interesting flowers and shrubs, whose labels are slightly more forthcoming than the usual terse Latinate tags. The garden also has an excellent teahouse, where you can get delicious home-made cakes.

It's also worth popping into the nearby **Chelsea Old**

CHELSEA

Church (Tues–Fri 1.30–5.30pm; ⓦ www.domini.org /chelsea-old-church), halfway down Cheyne Walk, where Thomas More built his own private chapel in the south aisle. The church was badly bombed in World War II, but an impressive number of monuments were retrieved from the rubble and continue to adorn the church's interior.

A short distance inland from Cheyne Walk, at 24 Cheyne Row, is **Carlyle's House** (Map 3, D9; April–Oct Wed–Fri 2–5pm, Sat & Sun 11am–5pm; £3.60), where the historian Thomas Carlyle set up home, having moved down from his native Scotland in 1834. Now a National Trust property, the house became a museum just fifteen years after Carlyle's death and is a typically dour Victorian abode, kept much as the Carlyles would have had it – his hat still hanging in the hall, and his socks in the chest of drawers. The top floor contains the garret study where Carlyle tried in vain to escape the din of the neighbours' noisy roosters in order to complete his final magnum opus on Frederick the Great.

NOTTING HILL

Map 3, A5. ⊖ Notting Hill.

Epicentre of the country's first race riots, when busloads of whites attacked West Indian homes in the area, **Notting Hill** is now more famous for its annual Carnival (see p.339), which began life in direct response to the riots. These days, it's the world's biggest street festival outside Rio, with an estimated two million revellers turning up on the last weekend of August for the two-day extravaganza of parades, steel bands and deafening sound systems.

The rest of the year, Notting Hill is a lot quieter, though its cafés and restaurants are cool enough places to pull in folk from all over. On Saturdays, big crowds of Londoners and tourists alike descend on the mile-long **Portobello Road**

Market, lined with stalls selling everything from aʳ cheap secondhand clothes and fruit and vegetableˢ

Within easy walking distance of Portobello Roaᵈ other side of the railway tracks, gasworks and canaˡ

Kensal Green Cemetery (Ⓦ www.kensalgreen.co.uk; ⊖ Kensal Rise), opened in 1833 and still a functioning burial ground. Graves of the more famous incumbents – Thackeray, Trollope and Brunel – are less interesting architecturally than those arranged on either side of the Centre Avenue, which leads from the easternmost entrance on Harrow Road. Guided tours of the cemetery take place every Sunday at 2pm (£5); on the first and third Sunday of month, the tour includes a trip down the catacombs (bring a torch).

North London

This chapter concentrates on just a handful of the capital's satellite villages, now subsumed into the general mass of **north London**. Almost all the northern suburbs are easily accessible by tube from the centre; in fact, it was the expansion of the tube which encouraged the forward march of bricks and mortar into many of these suburbs.

The first section covers one of London's finest parks, **Regent's Park**, framed by Nash-designed architecture and home of **London Zoo**. Close by is **Camden Town**, where the weekend market is one of the city's big attractions – a warren of stalls selling street fashion, books, records and ethnic goods.

The real highlights of north London, though, for visitors and residents alike, are **Hampstead** and **Highgate**, elegant, largely eighteenth-century developments which still reflect their village origins. They have the added advantage of proximity to one of London's wildest patches of greenery, **Hampstead Heath**, where you can enjoy stupendous views, kite-flying and nude bathing, as well as outdoor concerts and high art in the setting of **Kenwood House**.

Also covered are a handful of sights in more far-flung northern suburbs. They include the **RAF Museum** at Hendon and the **Shri Swaminarayan Mandir**, the largest Hindu temple outside India.

REGENT'S PARK

Map 3, E2. ⓦ www.royalparks.org.uk ⊖ Regent's Park, Baker Street or Great Portland Street.

As with almost all of London's royal parks, Londoners have Henry VIII to thank for **Regent's Park**, which he confiscated from the Church for yet more hunting grounds. However, it wasn't until the reign of the Prince Regent (later George IV) that the park began to take its current form. According to the master plan, devised by John Nash in 1811, the park was to be girded by a continuous belt of terraces, and sprinkled with a total of 56 villas, including a magnificent pleasure palace for the Prince himself, which would be linked by Regent Street to Carlton House in St James's. The plan was never fully realized, due to lack of funds, but enough was built to create something of the idealized garden city that Nash and the Prince Regent envisaged.

To appreciate the special quality of Regent's Park, take a closer look at the architecture, starting with the Nash terraces, which form a near-unbroken horseshoe of cream-coloured stucco around the Outer Circle. Within the Inner Circle is the **Open Air Theatre** (ⓦ www.open-air-theatre .org.uk; see p.285), which puts on summer performances of Shakespeare, opera and ballet, and **Queen Mary's Gardens**, by far the prettiest section of the park. A large slice of the gardens is taken up with a glorious rose garden, featuring some four hundred varieties, surrounded by a ring of ramblers.

Clearly visible on the western edge of the park is the shiny copper dome and minaret of the **London Central Mosque** (ⓦ www.islamicculturalcentre.co.uk), an entirely appropriate addition, given the Prince Regent's taste for the Orient. Non-Muslim visitors are welcome to look in at the information centre, and glimpse inside the hall of worship, which is packed out with a diversity of communities for the lunchtime Friday prayers.

REGENT'S PARK

LONDON ZOO

Map 3, E1. Daily: March–Oct 10am–5.30pm; Nov–Feb 10am–4pm; £11; Ⓦ www.londonzoo.co.uk Ⓔ Camden Town.

The northeastern corner of the park is occupied by **London Zoo**, founded in 1826. It may not be the most uplifting place for animal lovers, but kids love the place – smaller ones are particularly taken with the children's enclosure, where they can actually handle the animals, and the regular "Animals in Action" live shows. The zoo boasts some striking architectural features, too, most notably the modernist, spiral-ramped 1930s concrete penguin pool (where Penguin Books' original colophon was sketched); it

REGENT'S CANAL BY BOAT

Three companies run **boat services** on the Regent's Canal between Camden Lock (Ⓔ Camden Town) and Little Venice (Ⓔ Warwick Avenue), passing through the Maida Hill tunnel and stopping off at London Zoo on the way. The narrowboat *Jenny Wren* (☏ 020/7485 4433) starts off at Camden Lock, at the top of Camden High Street, while Jason's narrowboats (☏ 020/7286 3428, Ⓦ www.jasons.co.uk) start off at Little Venice; the London Waterbus Company (☏ 020/7482 2660) sets off from both places. Jason's and the London Waterbus Company run all year round, though only on weekends during winter. Whichever you choose, you can board at either end; **tickets** cost around around £5–6 one way (and only a little more return) and journey time is 50 minutes one way.

Those interested in the history of the canal should head off to the **London Canal Museum** (Map 3, I1; Tues–Sun 10am –4.30pm; £2.50; Ⓦ www.canalmuseum.org.uk), on the other side of York Way, down New Wharf Road, ten minutes' walk from King's Cross Station.

was designed by the Tecton partnership, led by Russian émigré Berthold Lubetkin. Other zoo landmarks include the colossal tetrahedral aluminium-framed tent of the Snowdon Aviary, and the eco-conscious invertebrate-filled Web of Life.

CAMDEN TOWN

Map 2, H3. ⊖ Camden Town.

For all the gentrification of the last twenty years, **Camden Town** retains a gritty aspect, compounded by the various railway lines that plough through the area, the canal, and the large shelter for the homeless on Arlington Street. The market, however, gives the area a positive lift on the weekends, and is now the district's best-known attribute.

Having started out as a tiny crafts market in the cobbled courtyard by the lock, **Camden Market** has since mushroomed out of all proportion. More than 100,000 shoppers turn up here each weekend, and parts of the market now stay open all week long, alongside a similarly oriented crop of shops, cafés and bistros. The sheer variety of what's on offer – from bootleg tapes to furniture, along with a mass of street fashion and clubwear, and plenty of foodstalls – is what makes Camden so special. To avoid the crowds, which can be overpowering on a summer Sunday afternoon, you'll need to get here by 10am – by 4pm, many of the stalls will be packing up to go.

Despite having no significant Jewish associations, Camden is home to London's **Jewish Museum** (Mon –Thurs 10am–4pm, Sun 10am–5pm; £3.50; ⓦ www.jewishmuseum.org.uk), at 129 Albert St, just off Parkway. The purpose-built premises are smartly designed, but the conventional style and contents of the museum are disappointing: apart from the usual displays of Judaica, there's a video and exhibition explaining Jewish religious practices and the

CAMDEN TOWN

141

history of the Jewish community in Britain. More challenging temporary exhibitions are held in the museum's Finchley branch at 80 East End Rd, N3 (Map 2, F1; ☎ 020/8349 1143; ⊖ Finchley Central).

HAMPSTEAD

Map 2, G2. ⊖ Hampstead.

Perched on a hill above Camden Town, **Hampstead** village developed into a fashionable spa in the eighteenth century, after Dr Gibbons, a celebrated physician, declared the waters of its spring as being of great medicinal value. Its sloping site, which deterred Victorian property speculators and put off the railway companies, saved much of the Georgian village from destruction, and it's little altered to this day. Later, it became one of the city's most celebrated literary *quartiers* and even now it retains its reputation as a bolt hole of the high-profile intelligentsia. You can get some idea of its tone from the fact that the local Labour MP is currently the actress-turned-politician Glenda Jackson.

The steeply inclined High Street, lined with trendy clothes shops and arty cafés, flaunts the area's ever-increasing wealth without completely losing its picturesqueness. There are several small house museums to explore, but proximity to the Heath is the real joy of Hampstead, for this mixture of woodland, smooth pasture and landscaped garden is quite simply the most exhilarating patch of greenery in London.

Fenton House

Map 2, G2. Mid-March to Oct Wed–Fri 2–5pm, Sat & Sun 11am–5pm; £4.40. ⊖ Hampstead.

Whichever route you take north of Hampstead tube, you'll probably end up at the small triangular green on Holly Bush Hill, on the north side of which stands the late seventeenth-century **Fenton House**. As well as housing a collection of European and Oriental ceramics, this National Trust house contains the superb Benton-Fletcher collection of early musical instruments, chiefly displayed on the top floor. Among the many spinets, virginals and clavichords are the earliest extant English grand piano, and an Unverdorben lute from 1580 (one of only three in the world). For an extra £1, you can hire a tape of music played on the above instruments, to listen to while you walk round.

Freud Museum

Map 2, G3. Wed–Sun noon–5pm; £5; ⓦ www.freud.org.uk
⊖ Swiss Cottage.

One of the most poignant of London's house museums is the **Freud Museum**, hidden away in the leafy streets of south Hampstead at 20 Maresfield Gardens. Having lived in Vienna for his entire adult life, Freud, by now a semi-invalid with only a year to live, was forced to flee the Nazis, arriving in London in the summer of 1938. The ground-floor study and library look exactly as they did when Freud lived here; the collection of erotic antiquities and the famous couch, sumptuously draped in Persian carpets, were all brought here from Vienna. Upstairs, home movies of family life in Vienna are shown continually, and a small room is dedicated to his daughter, Anna, herself an influential child analyst, who lived in the house until her death in 1982.

Burgh House – the Hampstead Museum

Map 2, G3. Wed–Sun noon–5pm; free;
ⓦ www.london-northwest.com/burghhouse ⊖ Hampstead.

The Queen Anne mansion of **Burgh House**, on New End Square, dates from the halcyon spa days of Hampstead Wells – as Hampstead was briefly known – and was at one time

HAMPSTEAD

occupied by Dr Gibbons, the physician who discovered the spring's medicinal qualities. Surrounded by council housing, it now serves as the **Hampstead Museum**, an exhibition space and a modest local museum, with special emphasis on such notable locals as Constable and Keats; there's also a nice tearoom in the basement.

2 Willow Road

Map 2, G3. Tours: March Sat noon–5pm; April–Oct Thurs–Sat noon–5pm every 45min; ⓣ 020/7435 6166; £4.20. ⊖ Hampstead.

For a fascinating insight into the modernist mind-set, take a look inside **2 Willow Road**, an unassuming red-brick terraced house built in the 1930s by the Hungarian-born architect Ernö Goldfinger. When Goldfinger moved in, this was a state-of-the-art pad and, as he changed little in the house in the following sixty years, what you see is a 1930s avant-garde dwelling preserved in aspic, a house at once both modern and old-fashioned. An added bonus is that the rooms are packed with works of art by the likes of Max Ernst, Duchamp, Henry Moore and Man Ray. There are a limited number of tickets for the **guided tours**, so it's worth booking ahead. Incidentally, James Bond's adversary is indeed named after Ernö – Ian Fleming lived close by and had a deep personal dislike of both Goldfinger and his modernist abode.

Keats' House

Map 2, G3. Tues–Sun: April–Oct noon–5pm; Nov–March noon–4pm; £3; ⓦ www.keatshouse.org ⊖ Hampstead.

Hampstead's most lustrous figure is celebrated at **Keats' House**, an elegant, whitewashed Regency double villa on Keats Grove, a short walk south of Willow Road. Inspired by the peacefulness of Hampstead and by his passion for girl-next-door Fanny Brawne (whose house is also part of the museum), Keats wrote some of his most famous works here before leaving for Rome, where he died of consumption in 1821. The neat, rather staid interior contains books and letters, Fanny's engagement ring and the four-poster bed in which the poet first coughed up blood, confiding to his companion, Charles Brown, "that drop of blood is my death warrant".

Hampstead Heath

Map 2, G2. ⊖ Hampstead.

North London's "green lung", **Hampstead Heath** is the city's most enjoyable public park. It may not have much of its original heathland left, but it packs a wonderful variety of bucolic scenery into its 800 acres. At its southern end are the rolling green pastures of **Parliament Hill**, north London's premier spot for kite-flying. On either side are numerous ponds, three of which – one for men, one for women and one mixed – you can swim in for free. The thickest woodland is to be found in the **West Heath**, beyond Whitestone Pond, also the site of the most formal section, **Hill Garden**, a secretive and romantic little gem with eccentric balustraded terraces and a ruined pergola. Beyond lies **Golders Hill Park**, where you can gaze at pygmy goats and fallow deer, and inspect the impeccably maintained aviaries, home to flamingos, cranes and other exotic birds.

Finally, don't miss the landscaped grounds of Kenwood, in the north of the Heath, which are focused on the white-washed Neoclassical mansion of **Kenwood House** (daily: April–Sept 10am–6pm; Oct 10am–5pm; Nov–March 10am–4pm; free). The house is now home to the **Iveagh Bequest**, a collection of seventeenth- and eighteenth-century art, including a handful of real masterpieces by the

HAMPSTEAD

likes of Vermeer, Rembrandt, Boucher, Gainsborough and Reynolds. Of the house's period interiors, the most spectacular is Robert Adam's sky-blue-and-gold **library**, its book-filled apses separated from the central entertaining area by paired columns. To the south of the house, a grassy amphitheatre slopes down to a lake, where outdoor classical concerts are held on summer evenings.

HIGHGATE

Map 2, H2. ⊖ Highgate or bus #210 from ⊖ Archway.

Northeast of the Heath, and fractionally lower than Hampstead (appearances notwithstanding), **Highgate** lacks the literary cachet of its neighbour, but makes up for it with London's most famous cemetery, resting place of Karl Marx. It also retains more of its village origins, especially around **The Grove**, Highgate's finest row of houses, the oldest dating as far back as 1685.

To get to the cemetery, head south down Highgate High Street and **Highgate Hill**, with its amazing views towards the City. When you get to the copper dome of "Holy Joe", the Roman Catholic church which stands on Highgate Hill, pop into the pleasantly landscaped **Waterlow Park**, next door, with its fine café and restaurant.

The park provides a through-route to **Highgate Cemetery** (Map 2, H2; ⓦwww.highgate-cemetery.org), which is ranged on both sides of Swain's Lane. Highgate's most famous corpse, that of **Karl Marx**, lies in the **East Cemetery** (April–Oct Mon–Fri 10am–5pm, Sat & Sun 11am–5pm; Nov–March closes 4pm; £2). Marx himself asked for a simple grave topped by a headstone, but by 1954 the Communist movement decided to move his grave to a more prominent position and erect the vulgar bronze bust that now surmounts a granite plinth. Close by lies the much simpler grave of the author George Eliot.

What the East Cemetery lacks in atmosphere is in part compensated for by the fact that you can wander at will through its maze of circuitous paths, whereas to visit the more atmospheric and overgrown **West Cemetery**, with its spooky Egyptian Avenue and terraced catacombs, you must go round with a guided tour (March–Nov Mon–Fri noon, 2pm & 4pm, Sat & Sun hourly 11am–4pm; Dec–Feb Sat & Sun hourly 11am–3pm; £3). Among the prominent graves usually visited are those of artist Dante Gabriel Rossetti and lesbian novelist Radclyffe Hall.

HENDON: THE RAF MUSEUM

Map 2, E1. Daily 10am–6pm; free; ⓦ www.rafmuseum.org.uk ⊖ Colindale.

A world-class assembly of historic military aircraft can be seen at the **RAF Museum**, located in a godforsaken part of north London beside the M1 motorway. Enthusiasts won't be disappointed, but those looking for a balanced account of modern aerial warfare will – the overall tone is unashamedly militaristic, not to say jingoistic. Those with children should head for the hands-on Fun 'n' Flight Gallery; those without might prefer to explore the often-overlooked display galleries, ranged around the edge of the Main Aircraft Hall, which contain an art gallery and an exhibition on the history of flight, accompanied by replicas of some of the deathtraps of early aviation.

NEASDEN: THE SHRI SWAMINARAYAN TEMPLE

Map 2, D3. Daily 9am–6pm; free; ⓦ www.swaminarayan-baps .org.uk ⊖ Stonebridge Park or Neasden.

Perhaps the most remarkable building in the whole of London lies just off the North Circular, in the glum suburb of **Neasden**. Here, rising majestically above the surrounding semi-detached houses like a mirage, is the **Shri Swaminarayan Mandir**, a traditional Hindu temple topped with domes and shikharas, erected in 1995 in a style and scale unseen outside of India for more than a millennium. To reach the temple, you must enter through the adjacent Haveli, or cultural complex, with its carved wooden portico and balcony. After taking off your shoes, you can proceed to the **Mandir** (temple) itself, carved entirely out of Carrara marble, with every possible surface transformed into a honeycomb of arabesques, flowers and seated gods. Beneath the Mandir, an **exhibition** (Mon–Fri 9am–6pm, Sat & Sun 7am–7pm; £2) explains the basic tenets of Hinduism and details the life of Lord Swaminarayan, and includes a video about the history of the building.

South London

N ow largely built up into a patchwork of Victorian terraces, one area of **South London** stands head and shoulders above all the others in terms of sightseeing, and that is **Greenwich**, with its outstanding ensemble of the **Old Royal Naval College** and the Queen's House, courtesy of Christopher Wren and Inigo Jones respectively. Most visitors, it has to be said, come to see the **National Maritime Museum**, the **Royal Observatory** and the beautifully landscaped royal park, though Greenwich also pulls in an ever-increasing volume of Londoners in search of bargains at its Sunday **market**.

Greenwich is, of course, also famous as the "home of time", thanks to its status as the **Prime Meridian of the World**, from where time all over the globe is measured. It's partly for this reason that Greenwich was chosen as the centrepiece of the country's millennium celebrations, though the **Dome** is, in fact, situated in the reclaimed industrial wasteland of North Greenwich, a mile or so northeast of Greenwich town centre.

The only other suburban sights that stand out are the **Dulwich Picture Gallery**, a public art gallery even older than the National Gallery (see p.19), and the eclectic **Horniman Museum**, in neighbouring Forest Hill.

DULWICH PICTURE GALLERY

Map 2, J7. Tues–Fri 10am–5pm, Sat &Sun 11am–5pm; £4, free on Fri; Ⓦ www.dulwichpicturegallery.org.uk
West Dulwich train station, from Victoria.

Dulwich Picture Gallery, on College Road, is the nation's oldest public art gallery, designed by John Soane (see p.76) and opened in 1817. Soane created a beautifully spacious building, awash with natural light and crammed with superb paintings – elegiac landscapes by Cuyp, one of the world's finest Poussin series, and splendid works by Hogarth, Gainsborough, Van Dyck, Canaletto and Rubens, plus **Rembrandt**'s tiny *Portrait of a Young Man*, a top-class portrait of poet, playwright and Royalist, the future Earl of Bristol. At the centre of the museum is a tiny mausoleum designed by Soane for the sarcophagi of the gallery's founders.

THE HORNIMAN MUSEUM

Map 2, J7. Daily 10.30am–5.30pm; free; Ⓦ www.horniman.ac.uk
Forest Hill train station, from Victoria or London Bridge.

To the southeast of Dulwich Park, on the busy South Circular road, is the wacky **Horniman Museum**, purpose-built in 1901 by Frederick Horniman, a tea trader with a passion for collecting. The museum is principally a monument to its creator's freewheeling eclecticism: in addition to its small aquarium and its large collection of stuffed creatures, there's a wide-ranging anthropology section, and a musical department with more than 1500 instruments from Chinese gongs to electric guitars. The museum also has a lovely **park** (daily 8am–dusk), around the back, where you'll find turkeys, goats and rabbits, a sunken water garden, a bandstand and a graceful Victorian conservatory.

GREENWICH

Greenwich is one of London's most beguiling spots, and the one place in southeast London that draws large numbers of visitors. In Tudor times, Greenwich boasted a royal palace and, in neighbouring Deptford, the royal naval dockyard. Both have long since disappeared, and in place of the palace stands one of the capital's finest architectural set pieces, the former **Royal Naval College** overlooking the Thames. To the west lies Greenwich town centre, while to the south you'll find Greenwich's two prime tourist sights, the **National Maritime Museum** and the **Royal Observatory**. If you're heading straight for either of the latter pair from central London, the quickest way to get there is to take the **train** from London Bridge (every 30min) to Maze Hill, on the eastern edge of Greenwich Park. Those wanting to start with the town or the *Cutty Sark* should alight at Greenwich station.

A more scenic way of getting to Greenwich is to take a **boat** from one of the piers in central London (see p.12). A third possible option is to take the **Docklands Light Railway** (DLR) to Cutty Sark station. For the best view of the Wren buildings, though, get off the DLR at Island Gardens, and then take the Greenwich Foot Tunnel under the Thames.

The town centre

See map on p.152, B2.

Greenwich town centre, laid out in the 1820s with Nash-style terraces, is nowadays plagued with heavy traffic. To escape the busy streets, head for the original covered section of **Greenwich Market**. There are stalls here from Thursday to Sunday, but the place is at its liveliest at the weekend, when the stalls spill out up the High Road,

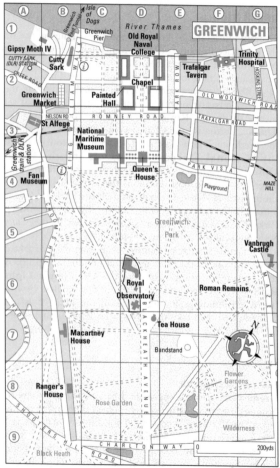

GREENWICH

River Thames

GREENWICH

Isle of Dogs

Greenwich Pier

Gipsy Moth IV

Old Royal Naval College

Trafalgar Tavern

Trinity Hospital

CUTTY SARK (DLR) STATION

Cutty Sark

CREEK ROAD

Greenwich Market

NELSON RD

St Alfege

Chapel

Painted Hall

HOSKINS STREET

OLD WOOLWICH ROAD

ROMNEY ROAD

TRAFALGAR ROAD

Greenwich train & DLR station

Fan Museum

National Maritime Museum

Queen's House

PARK VISTA

MAZE HILL

Playground

Greenwich Park

Vanbrugh Castle

Royal Observatory

Roman Remains

Tea House

Macartney House

Bandstand

N

Ranger's House

Flower Gardens

SHOOTERS HILL ROAD

Rose Garden

Wilderness

CHARLTON WAY

0   200yds

Black Heath

© crown copyright

Stockwell Road and Royal Hill. The best sections are the indoor secondhand book markets, flanking the Central Market on Stockwell Road; the antiques hall, further down on Greenwich High Road; and the flea market on Thames Street.

Greenwich **tourist office** is in Pepys House in the old Royal Naval College (daily 10am–5pm; ☎ 0870/608 2000).

A short distance in from the old covered market, on the opposite side of Greenwich Church Street, rises the Doric portico and broken pediment of Nicholas Hawksmoor's **St Alfege's Church** (see map opposite, A3; Mon–Sat 10am–4pm, Sun noon–4pm; ⓦ www .st-alfege.org). Built in 1712–18, the church was flattened in the Blitz, but it has been magnificently restored to its former glory.

Wedged in a dry dock by the Greenwich Foot Tunnel is the majestic **Cutty Sark** (see map opposite, B2; daily 10am–5pm; £3.90; ⓦ www.cuttysark.org.uk), the world's last surviving tea clipper, built in 1869. The *Cutty Sark* lasted just eight years in the China tea trade, and it was as a wool clipper that it actually made its name, returning from Australia in just 72 days. Inside, there's little to see beyond an exhibition in the main hold which tells the ship's story, from its inception to its arrival in Greenwich in 1954.

A mast's length from the *Cutty Sark*, and dwarfed by the bulk of its neighbour, is the tiny **Gipsy Moth**, the 54-foot boat in which, at the age of 66, Francis Chichester became the first person to sail solo around the world, in 1965–6 (for which he was knighted on this very spot).

GREENWICH

THE MILLENNIUM DOME

London's controversial **Millennium Dome** (⊖ North Greenwich) is clearly visible from the riverside at Greenwich and from the upper parts of Greenwich Park. Built at a cost approaching £800 million, and designed by Richard Rogers (of Lloyd's Building and Pompidou Centre fame), it is by far the world's largest dome – over half a mile in circumference and 160ft in height – held up by a dozen, 300-foot-tall yellow steel masts. In 2000, for one year only, it housed the nation's chief millennium extravaganza: an array of hi-tech themed zones set around a stage, on which a circus-style performance took place twice a day.

Like most grand projects, the Dome had a rough ride from the press right from the beginning. The hiccups and headaches continued into the new millennium, with bad reviews and over-optimistic estimates of visitor numbers. Nevertheless, millions paid up £20 each to visit the Dome, and millions went away happy. With the empty Dome eating up £28 million of public money on maintenance costs in 2001 alone, the government were no doubt relieved when entertainment giants, AEG, agreed to spend £135 million of their own money turning the Dome into a 20,000-seater venue.

Old Royal Naval College

See map on p.152, D2. Daily 10am–5pm; free;
ⓦ www.greenwichfoundation.org.uk

It's entirely appropriate that the one London building that makes the most of its riverbank location should be the **Old Royal Naval College**, Wren's beautifully symmetrical Baroque ensemble, initially built as a royal palace, but eventually converted into a hospital for disabled seamen. From 1873 until 1998 it was home to the Royal Naval College, but now houses the University of Greenwich and the Trinity College of Music.

The two grandest rooms, situated underneath Wren's twin domes, are open to the public and well worth visiting. The entrance to the college is on King William Walk, and visitors are ushered first into the **Chapel** in the east wing. The exquisite pastel-shaded plasterwork and spectacular, decorative detailing on the ceiling were designed by James "Athenian" Stuart after a fire in 1799 destroyed the original interior. From the chapel, you can take the underground Chalk Walk to gain access to the magnificent **Painted Hall** in the west wing, which is dominated by James Thornhill's gargantuan allegorical ceiling painting, and his trompe l'oeil fluted pilasters.

National Maritime Museum

See map on p.152, C3. Daily 10am–5pm; free; ⓦ www.nmm.ac.uk
The main entrance to the excellent **National Maritime Museum**, which occupies the old Naval Asylum, is on Romney Road. From here, you enter the spectacular glass-roofed central courtyard, which houses the museum's largest artefacts, among them the splendid 63-foot-long gilded **Royal Barge**, designed in Rococo style by William Kent for Prince Frederick, the much-unloved eldest son of George II.

The various themed galleries are superbly designed to appeal to visitors of all ages. In "Explorers", on level 1, you get to view some of the museum's most highly prized relics, such as **Captain Cook**'s sextant and K1 marine clock, Shackleton's compass, and **Captain Scott**'s furry sleeping bag and sledging goggles. Sponsors P&O get to display their wares in "Passengers", which traces the history of modern passenger liners, and "Cargoes", which concentrates on containerization. On level 2, there's a large maritime **art gallery**, a contemporary section on the future of the sea, and a gallery devoted to the legacy of the British Empire, warts and all.

GREENWICH

Level 3 boasts two **hands-on galleries**: "The Bridge", where you can attempt to navigate a catamaran, a paddle steamer and a rowing boat to shore; and "All Hands", where children can have a go at radio transmission, loading miniature cargo, firing a cannon and so forth. Finally, you reach the **Nelson Gallery**, which contains the museum's vast collection of Nelson-related memorabilia, including Turner's *Battle of Trafalgar, 21st October, 1805*, his largest work and only royal commission.

Inigo Jones's **Queen's House**, originally built amidst a rambling Tudor royal palace, is now the focal point of the Greenwich ensemble, and is an integral part of the Maritime Museum. As royal residences go, it's an unassuming country house, but as the first Neoclassical building in the country it has enormous architectural significance. The interior is currently used for temporary exhibitions. Nevertheless, one or two features survive (or have been reinstated) from Stuart times. Off the Great Hall, a perfect cube, lies the beautiful Tulip Staircase, Britain's earliest cantilevered spiral staircase; its name derives from the floral patterning in the wrought-iron balustrade.

Royal Observatory

See map on p.152, D6. Daily: April–Sept 10am–6pm; Oct–March 10am–5pm; free; ⓦ www.rog.nmm.ac.uk

Crowning the highest hill in Greenwich Park, behind the National Maritime Museum, the **Royal Observatory** was established in 1675 by Charles II to house the first Astronomer Royal, John Flamsteed. Flamsteed's chief task was to study the night sky in order to discover an astronomical method of finding the longitude of a ship at sea, the lack of which was causing enormous problems for the emerging British Empire. Astrologers continued to work here at Greenwich until the postwar smog forced them to

GREENWICH

decamp to Herstmonceux Castle and the clearer skies of Sussex (they've since moved to the Pacific); the old observatory, meanwhile, is now a very popular museum.

Greenwich's greatest claim to fame is, of course, as the home of **Greenwich Mean Time** (GMT) and the Prime Meridian. Since 1884, Greenwich has occupied zero longitude, which means the entire world sets its clocks by GMT. What the Royal Observatory don't tell you is that the meridian has, in fact, moved. Nowadays, longitude is calculated by a differential Global Positioning Receiver, served by several US military satellites, which places the meridian 336ft to the east of the brass strip in the courtyard that marks the Greenwich Meridian.

The oldest part of the observatory is the Wren-built **Flamsteed House**, whose northeastern turret sports a bright red time-ball that climbs the mast at 12.58pm and drops at 1pm GMT precisely; it was added in 1833, to allow ships on the Thames to set their clocks. Passing quickly through Flamsteed's restored apartments and the Octagon Room, where the king used to show off to his guests, you reach the Chronometer Gallery, which focuses on the search for the precise measurement of longitude, and displays four of the marine clocks designed by John Harrison, including "H4", which helped win the Longitude Prize in 1763.

Flamsteed's own meridian line is a brass strip in the floor of the Meridian Building. Edmond Halley, Flamsteed's successor, who charted the comings and goings of the famous comet, worked out his own meridian, and the Bradley Meridian Room reveals yet another, standard from 1750 to 1850 and still used for Ordnance Survey maps. Finally, you reach a room that's spliced in two by the present-day Greenwich Meridian, fixed by the cross hairs in Airy's "Transit Circle", the astrological instrument that dominates the room.

The exhibition ends on a soothing note in the Telescope Dome of the octagonal **Great Equatorial Building**,

GREENWICH

home to Britain's largest telescope. In addition, there are regular presentations in the Planetarium (daily 2.30pm & 3.30pm; £4), housed in the adjoining South Building.

The Ranger's House

See map on p.152, B8. Wed–Sun: April–Sept 10am–6pm; Oct 10am–5pm; Nov, Dec & March 10am–4pm; closed Christmas to Feb; £4.50.

Southwest of the observatory, and backing onto Greenwich park's rose garden, is the **Ranger's House**, a red-brick Georgian villa that houses an art collection amassed by Julius Wernher, the German-born millionaire who made his money by exploiting the diamond deposits of South Africa. His taste in art is eclectic, ranging from medieval ivory miniatures to Iznik pottery, though he was definitely a man who placed technical virtuosity above artistic merit. The high points of the collection are Memlinc's *Virgin and Child*, the pair of six-teenth-century majolica dishes decorated with mythological scenes for Isabella d'Este, both located upstairs, and the Reynolds portraits and de Hooch interior, located downstairs.

The Fan Museum

See map on p.152, A4. Tues–Sat 11am–5pm, Sun noon–5pm; £3.50; ⓦ www.fan-museum.org

Croom's Hill boasts some of Greenwich's finest Georgian buildings, one of which houses the **Fan Museum** at no. 12. It's a fascinating little place (and an extremely beautiful house), revealing the importance of the fan as a social and political document. The permanent exhibition on the ground floor traces the history of the materials employed, from peacock feathers to straw, while temporary exhibitions on the first floor explore such subjects as techniques of pro-duction and changing fashion.

GREENWICH

Chiswick to Windsor

Most people experience west London en route to or from Heathrow airport, either from the confines of the train or tube (which runs overground most of the way) or the motorway. The city and its satellites seem to continue unabated, with only fleeting glimpses of the countryside. However, in the five-mile stretch from Chiswick to Osterley there are several former country retreats, now surrounded by suburbia, which are definitely worth digging out.

The Palladian villa of **Chiswick House** is perhaps the best known of these attractions, though it draws nothing like as many visitors as **Syon House**, most of whom come for the gardening centre rather than for the house itself, a showcase for the talents of Robert Adam, who also worked at **Osterley House**, another Elizabethan conversion, now owned by the National Trust.

Running through much of the chapter is the **River Thames**, once known as the "Great Highway of London" and still the most pleasant way to travel in these parts during the summer. Boats plough up the Thames all the way

RIVER TRANSPORT

From April to October, Westminster Passenger Services Association (☎ 020/7930 2061, ⓦ www.wpsa.co.uk) run two to three **boats** daily between Westminster and Hampton Court, calling at Kew and Richmond; the full trip takes 3–4hr one way, and costs £12 one way, £18 return.

from central London, via the **Royal Botanic Gardens of Kew** and the picturesque riverside at **Richmond**, as far as **Hampton Court**, home of the country's largest and most impressive royal residence (and the famous maze). To reach the heavily touristed royal outpost of **Windsor Castle**, however, you really need to take the train.

CHISWICK HOUSE

Map 2, E6. Daily: April–Sept 10am–6pm; Oct 10am–5pm; £3.30. Chiswick train station, from Waterloo.

Chiswick House is a perfect little Neoclassical villa, designed by the third Earl of Burlington in the 1720s, and set in one of the most beautifully landscaped gardens in London. Like its Palladian prototype, the house was purpose-built as a "temple to the arts" – here, amid his fine art collection, Lord Burlington could entertain artistic friends such as Swift, Handel and Pope. Visitors enter via the lower floor, where you can pick up an audioguide, before heading up to the upper floor, a series of cleverly interconnecting rooms, each enjoying a wonderful view out onto the gardens – all, that is, except the Tribunal, the central octagonal hall, where the earl's finest paintings and sculptures would have been displayed.

To do a quick circuit of the **gardens**, head across the smooth carpet of grass, punctuated by urns and sphinxes, that sit under the shadow of two giant cedars of Lebanon. A great place from which to admire the northwest side of the house is from the stone benches of the exedra, a set of yew-hedge niches harbouring lions and copies of Roman statuary, situated beyond the cedars. Elsewhere, there's an Italian garden, a maze of high-hedge alleyways, a lake and a grassy amphitheatre, centred on an obelisk in a pond and overlooked by an Ionic temple.

HOGARTH'S HOUSE

Map 2, E5. April–Oct Tues–Fri 1–5pm, Sat & Sun 1–6pm; Nov–March Tues–Fri 1–4pm, Sat & Sun 1–5pm; closed Jan; free.

If you leave Chiswick House gardens by the northernmost exit, beyond the Italian garden, it's just a short walk along the thunderous A4 road to **Hogarth's House**, where the artist spent each summer from 1749 until his death in 1764. Nowadays it's difficult to believe Hogarth came here for "peace and quiet", but in the eighteenth century the house was almost entirely surrounded by countryside. Amongst the scores of Hogarth's engravings, you can see copies of his satirical series – *An Election, Marriage à la Mode, A Rake's Progress* and *A Harlot's Progress* – and compare the modern view from the parlour with the more idyllic scene in *Mr Ranby's House*.

THE WETLAND CENTRE

Map 2, E6. Mon–Sat: summer 9.30am–6pm; winter 9.30am–5pm; open Sun for WWT members only; £6.75; ⓣ 020/8409 4400, ⓦ www.wetlandcentre.org.uk. Bus #283 from ⊖ Hammersmith, or walk from Barnes train station.

For anyone even remotely interested in wildlife, the new **Wetland Centre** in well-to-do Barnes is an absolute must. On the site of four disused reservoirs, across the river from Hammersmith, the Wildfowl & Wetland Trust (WWT) has created a high-tech 105-acre mosaic of wetland habitats, a stone's throw from central London. The centre serves a dual function: to attract native species of bird to its watery lagoons, and to assist in the WWT's programme of breeding rare wildfowl in captivity. On arrival – unless it's raining – you might as well skip the (albeit superbly produced) introductory audiovisual in the theatre, and head straight out to the ponds. If the weather's bad, or you've children with you, however, it's definitely worth visiting the **Discovery Centre**, where kids can take part in a swan identification parade, or take a duck's-eye view of the world, while their minders check out the WWT website.

KEW BRIDGE STEAM MUSEUM

Map 2, D5. Daily 11am–5pm; Mon–Fri £3.50, Sat & Sun £4.50; ⓦ www.kbsm.org Kew Bridge train station from Waterloo, or bus #237 or #267 from ⊖ Gunnersbury.

Difficult to miss thanks to its stylish Italianate standpipe tower, **Kew Bridge Steam Museum** occupies a former pumping station, on the corner of Kew Bridge Road and Green Dragon Lane, 100yd west of the bridge itself. At the heart of the museum is the Steam Hall, which contains a triple expansion steam engine and four gigantic nineteenth-century Cornish beam engines, while two adjoining rooms house the pumping station's original beam engines, one of which is the largest in the world. The steam engines may be things of great beauty, but they are primarily of interest to enthusiasts. Not so the museum's "Water for Life" gallery in the basement, devoted to the history of the capital's water supply. The best time to visit is at weekends, when each of the museum's industrial dinosaurs is put through its paces, and the small narrow-gauge steam railway runs back and forth round the yard.

THE MUSICAL MUSEUM

Map 2, D5. Ⓦ www.musicalmuseum.co.uk Kew Bridge train station from Waterloo, or bus #237 or #267 from ⊖ Gunnersbury.

Just west of the Steam Museum along Kew Bridge Road and Brentford High Street is the superb **Musical Museum**, packed with musical automata and run by wildly enthusiastic and engaging volunteers. The museum has recently moved into new purpose-built premises and is due to reopen sometime in 2004. When it does, it will definitely be worth a visit for the noisy ninety-minute demonstrations, during which you get to hear every kind of mechanical music-making machine, from cleverly crafted music boxes to the huge orchestrions that were once a feature of London's swish cafés. The museum also boasts one of the world's finest collections of player-pianos, and an enormous Art Deco Wurlitzer cinema organ.

SYON HOUSE

Map 2, C6. April–Oct Wed, Thurs & Sun 11am–5pm; £6.95, including gardens; Ⓦ www.syonpark.co.uk Bus #237 or #267 from ⊖ Gunnersbury or Kew Bridge train station.

Syon, London seat of the Percy family (aka the Dukes of Northumberland) since Elizabethan times, is now more of a working commercial concern than a family home, embracing a garden centre, a wholefood shop, a trout fishery, an aquatic centre stocked with tropical fish, a mini-zoo and a butterfly house, as well as the old aristocratic mansion and its gardens.

From its rather plain, castellated exterior, you'd never guess that **Syon House** contains the most opulent eighteenth-century interiors in the whole of London. The splendour of Robert Adam's refurbishment is immediately revealed, however, in the pristine Great Hall, an apsed double cube with a screen of Doric columns at one end and classical statuary dotted around the edges. There are several more Adam-designed rooms to admire in the house, plus a smattering of works by Van Dyck, Lely, Gainsborough and Reynolds.

While Adam beautified Syon House, Capability Brown laid out its **gardens** (daily 10.30am–5.30pm; £3.50) around an artificial lake, surrounding the water with oaks, beeches, limes and cedars. The gardens' chief focus now, however, is the crescent-shaped **Great Conservatory**, an early nineteenth-century addition which is said to have inspired Joseph Paxton, architect of the Crystal Palace. Those with young children will be compelled to make use of the **miniature steam train** which runs through the park at weekends from April to October, and on Wednesdays during the school holidays.

Another plus point for kids is Syon's **Butterfly House** (daily: May–Sept 10am–5pm; Oct–April 10am–4pm; £4.95; ⓦ www.butterflies.org.uk), a small, mesh-covered hothouse, where you can walk amid hundreds of exotic butterflies from all over the world, as they flit about the foliage. An adjoining room houses a collection of iguanas, millipedes, tarantulas and giant hissing Tanzanian cockroaches.

If your kids show more enthusiasm for life-threatening reptiles than delicate insects, then you could skip the butterflies and go instead for the adjacent **London Aquatic Experience** (daily: April–Sept 10am–6pm; Oct–March 10am–5pm; £4; ⓦ www.aquatic-experience.org), a purpose-built centre with a mixed range of aquatic creatures from the mysterious basilisk, which can walk on water, to the perennially popular piranhas.

OSTERLEY

Map 2, B5. Park: daily 9am–7.30pm or dusk; free. House: March Sat & Sun 1–4.30pm; April–Oct Wed–Sun 1–4.30pm; £4.40.
 ⊖ Osterley.

Robert Adam redesigned another colossal Elizabethan mansion – this time for the Child family – three miles northwest of Syon at **Osterley Park**, which maintains the impression of being in the middle of the countryside, despite the presence of the M4 to the north of the house. The park itself is well worth exploring, and there's a great café in the Tudor stables, but anyone with a passing interest in Adam's work should pay a visit to **Osterley House** itself. If you arrive by public transport, you get a £1 reduction off the price of your ticket.

From the outside, Osterley bears some similarity to Syon, the big difference being Adam's grand entrance portico, with its tall, Ionic colonnade. From here, you enter a characteristically cool Entrance Hall, followed by the so-called State Rooms of the south wing. Highlights include the Drawing Room, with Reynolds portraits on the damask walls and a coffered ceiling centred on a giant marigold, and the Etruscan Dressing Room, in which every surface is covered in delicate painted trelliswork, sphinxes and urns, a style that Adam (and Wedgwood) dubbed "Etruscan", though it is in fact derived from Greek vases found at Pompeii.

KEW GARDENS

Map 2, C6. Daily 9.30am–7.30pm or dusk; £7.50; Ⓦ www.kew.org
⊖ Kew Gardens.

Established in 1759, the **Royal Botanic Gardens** have grown from their original eight acres into a 300-acre site in which more than 33,000 species are grown in plantations and glasshouses, a display that attracts over a million visitors every year, most of them with no specialist interest at all. There's always something to see, whatever the season, but to get the most out of the place come sometime between spring and autumn, bring a picnic and stay for the day. The

KEW GARDENS

only drawback to Kew is the fact that it lies on the main (and very noisy) flight path to Heathrow.

There are four entry points to the gardens, but the majority of people arrive at Kew Gardens tube and train station, a few minutes' walk east of the **Victoria Gate**. Of all the glasshouses, by far the most celebrated is the **Palm House**, a curvaceous mound of glass and wrought-iron designed by Decimus Burton in the 1840s. Its drippingly humid atmosphere nurtures most of the known palm species, while there's a small but excellent tropical aquarium in the basement. South of here is the largest of the glasshouses, the **Temperate House**, which contains plants from every continent, including one of the largest indoor palms in the world, the sixty-foot Chilean Wine Palm.

Kew's origins as an eighteenth-century royal pleasure garden are evident in the numerous follies dotted about the gardens, the most conspicuous of which is the ten-storey, 163-foot-high **Pagoda**, visible to the south of the Temperate House. The three-storey red-brick mansion of **Kew Palace**, to the northwest of the Palm House, was bought by George II as a nursery for his umpteen children (sadly, it's been closed for renovation for some years now). A sure way to lose the crowds is to head for the thickly wooded, southwestern section of the park around **Queen Charlotte's Cottage** (April–Sept Sat & Sun 10.30am –4pm; free), a tiny thatched summerhouse built in the 1770s as a royal picnic spot for George III's queen.

RICHMOND

Map 2, D7. ⊖ Richmond.

On emerging from the station at **Richmond**, you'd be forgiven for wondering why you're here, but the procession of chain stores spread out along the one-way system is only half the story. To see the area's more interesting side, take one of the narrow pedestrianized alleyways off busy George Street, which bring you to the wide, open space of **Richmond Green**, one of the finest village greens in London, and no doubt one of the most peaceful before it found itself on the main flight path into Heathrow. Handsome seventeenth- and eighteenth-century houses line the south side of the Green, where the medieval royal palace of Richmond once stood, though only the unspectacular **Tudor Gateway** survives today.

The other place to head for in Richmond is the **Riverside**, pedestrianized, terraced and redeveloped in ersatz classical style in the 1980s. The real joy of the waterfront, however, is **Richmond Bridge**, London's oldest extant bridge, an elegant span of five arches made from Purbeck stone in 1777. The old town hall, set back from the new development, houses the **tourist office** (Mon–Fri 10am–5pm; Easter–Sept also Sat & Sun 10.30am–1.30pm; ⊺020/8940 9125, ⓦwww.guidetorichmond.co.uk) and, on the second floor, the **Richmond Museum** (Tues–Sat 11am–5pm; May–Oct also Sun 1–4pm; free; ⓦwww.museumofrichmond.com), but most folk prefer to ensconce themselves in the riverside pubs, or head for the numerous boat- and bike-rental outlets.

Richmond's greatest attraction, though, is the enormous **Richmond Park** (daily: March–Sept 7am–dusk; Oct–Feb 7.30am–dusk; free; ⓦwww.royalparks.gov.uk), at the top of Richmond Hill – 2500 acres of undulating grassland and bracken, dotted with coppiced woodland and as wild as anything in London. Eight miles across at its widest point, this is Europe's largest city park, famed for its red and fallow deer, which roam freely, and for its ancient oaks. For the most part untamed, the park does have a couple of deliberately landscaped plantations which feature splendid springtime azaleas and rhododendrons, in particular the **Isabella Plantation**.

RICHMOND

HAM HOUSE

Map 2, C7. April–Oct Mon–Wed, Sat & Sun 1–5pm; £6, including gardens. Bus #371, or walk from ⊖ Richmond.

Continuing along the towpath beyond Richmond Bridge, you'll arrive at **Ham House** after a mile or so, home to the Earls of Dysart for nearly three hundred years. Expensively furnished in the seventeenth century, and little altered since then, the house boasts one of the finest Stuart interiors in the country, from the stupendously ornate Great Staircase to the Long Gallery, featuring six "Court Beauties" by Peter Lely. Elsewhere, there are several fine ceiling paintings, some exquisite parquet flooring, and works by Van Dyck and Reynolds. Another bonus are the formal seventeenth-century **gardens** (open all year Mon–Wed, Sat & Sun 10.30am–6pm; £2), especially the Cherry Garden, laid out with a pungent lavender parterre, and surrounded by yew hedges and pleached hornbeam arbours. The Orangery, overlooking the original kitchen garden, serves as a tearoom.

HAMPTON COURT PALACE

Map 2, B9. April–Oct Mon 10.15am–6pm, Tues–Sun 9.30am–6pm; Nov–March closes 4.30pm; £11; ⓦ www.hrp.org.uk Hampton Court train station from Waterloo.

Hampton Court Palace, a sprawling red-brick ensemble on the banks of the Thames, thirteen miles southwest of London, is the finest of England's royal abodes. Built in 1516 by the upwardly mobile **Cardinal Wolsey**, Henry VIII's Lord Chancellor, it was purloined by Henry himself after Wolsey fell from favour. Charles II laid out the gardens, inspired by what he had seen at Versailles, while William and Mary had large sections of the palace remodelled by Wren.

The **Royal Apartments** are divided into six thematic walking tours. There's not a lot of information in any of the rooms, but the palace staff are very knowledgeable, and guided tours, each lasting 45 minutes, are available at no extra charge for Henry VIII's and the King's apartments; all are led by period-costumed historians, who do a fine job of bringing the place to life. If your energy is lacking – and Hampton

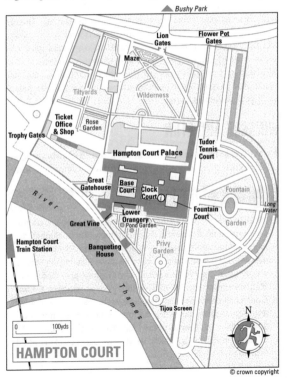

Bushy Park
Lion Gates
Flower Pot Gates
Maze
Tiltyards
Wilderness
Ticket Office & Shop
Rose Garden
Trophy Gates
Hampton Court Palace
Tudor Tennis Court
Great Gatehouse
Base Court
Clock Court
Fountain
River
Lower Orangery
Fountain Court
Long Water
Great Vine
Pond Garden
Garden
Hampton Court Train Station
Banqueting House
Privy Garden
Thames
Tijou Screen
N
0   100yds
HAMPTON COURT
© crown copyright

Court is huge – the most rewarding sections are: **Henry VIII's State Apartments**, which feature the glorious double hammer-beamed Great Hall; the **King's Apartments** (remodelled by William III); and the vast **Tudor Kitchens**. The last two are also served by audio tours.

Tickets to the Royal Apartments cover entry to the rest of the sites in the grounds. Those who don't wish to visit the apartments are free to wander around the gardens, but will have to pay extra to visit the curious **Royal Tennis Courts** (50p), the palace's famously tricky yew-hedge **Maze** (£3), and the **Privy Garden** (£3), where you can view Andrea Mantegna's colourful, heroic canvases, *The Triumphs of Caesar*, housed in the Lower Orangery, and the celebrated **Great Vine**, whose grapes are sold at the palace each year in September.

WINDSOR AND ETON

Every weekend, trains from Waterloo and Paddington are packed with people heading for **Windsor**, the royal enclave

GETTING TO WINDSOR

Windsor has two **train stations**, both very close to the centre. Direct trains from Waterloo (Mon–Sat every 30min, Sun hourly; journey time 50min) arrive at **Windsor & Eton Riverside**, five minutes' walk from the centre; trains from Paddington require a change at Slough (Mon–Fri every 20min, Sat & Sun every 30min; journey time 30–40min), and arrive at **Windsor & Eton Central**, directly opposite the castle. Note that you must arrive and depart from the same station, as tickets are not interchangeable. The **tourist office** (daily 10am–4pm; longer hours in summer; ☏ 01753/743900, ⓦ www.windsor.gov.uk) is at 24 High St.

21 miles west of London, where they join the human conveyor belt round Windsor Castle. Though almost as famous as Windsor, **Eton** (across the river from the castle) receives a mere fraction of the tourists, yet the guided tours of the school give an eye-opening glimpse of life as lived by the offspring of Britain's moneyed classes.

Windsor Castle

Daily: March–Oct 9.45am–5.15pm; Nov–Feb 9.45am–4.15pm;
£11.50; ⓦ www.royal.gov.uk

Towering above the town on a steep chalk bluff, **Windsor Castle** is an undeniably awesome sight, its chilly grey walls, punctuated by mighty medieval bastions, continuing as far as the eye can see. Once there, the small selection of state rooms open to the public are unexciting, though the magnificent St George's Chapel and the chance to see another small selection of the Queen's private art collection make the trip worthwhile. On a fine day, it pays to put aside some time for exploring **Windsor Great Park**, which stretches for several miles to the south of the castle.

Once inside the castle, it's best to head straight for **St George's Chapel** (Mon–Sat 10am–4pm), a glorious Gothic Perpendicular structure ranking with Henry VII's chapel in Westminster Abbey, and the second most important resting place for royal corpses after the Abbey – the Queen Mum and (the ashes of) Princess Margaret are buried here. Entry is via the south door and a one-way system operates, which brings you out by the **Albert Memorial Chapel**, built by Henry VII as a burial place for Henry VI, completed by Cardinal Wolsey for his own burial, but eventually converted for Queen Victoria into a high-Victorian memorial to her husband, Prince Albert.

The Changing of the Guard takes place at
Windsor April–June Mon–Sat at 11am;
alternate days the rest of the year.

Before entering the State Apartments, pay a quick visit to **Queen Mary's Dolls' House**, a palatial micro-residence designed for the amusement of the wife of George V, and the **Gallery**, where special exhibitions culled from the Royal Collection are staged. Most visitors just gape in awe at the gilded grandeur of the **State Apartments**, while the real highlights – the paintings from the Royal Collection that line the walls – are rarely given a second glance. The **King's Dressing Room**, for example, despite its small size, contains a feast of art treasures, including a dapper Rubens self-portrait, Van Dyck's famous triple portrait of Charles I, and *The Artist's Mother*, a perfectly observed portrait of old age by Rembrandt.

You'd hardly know that Windsor suffered the most devastating **fire** in its history in 1992, so thorough (and uninspired) has the restoration been in rooms such as **St George's Hall**. By contrast, the octagonal **Lantern Lobby**, beyond, is clearly an entirely new room, a safe neo-Gothic design replacing the old chapel. At this point, those visiting during the winter season (Oct–March) are given the privilege of seeing four **Semi-State Rooms**, created in the 1820s by George IV, and still used in the summer months by the Royal Family.

Most tourists are put off going to **Windsor Great Park** due to its sheer scale. With the Home Park – including Victoria and Albert's mausoleum of Frogmore – off limits to the public, except for a very few days in each year, visitors can only enter the park via the three-mile Long Walk. Another mile or so to the south is **Savill Garden** (daily: March–Oct 10am–6pm; Nov–Feb 10am–4pm; £3–5), a

35-acre patch of woodland that has one of the finest floral displays in and around London.

Eton College

College, chapel & museum: Easter, July & Aug daily
10.30am–4.30pm; after Easter to June & Sept daily 2–4.30pm;
£3.50; guided tours daily 2.15pm & 3.15pm; £4.50;
ⓦ www.etoncollege.com

Crossing the bridge at the end of Thames Avenue in Windsor town brings you to **Eton**, a one-street village lined with bookshops and antique dealers, but famous all over the world for **Eton College**, a ten-minute walk from the river. When the school was founded in 1440, its aim was to give free education to seventy poor scholars and choristers; how times have changed. The original fifteenth-century **schoolroom**, gnarled with centuries of graffiti, survives, but the real highlight is the **College Chapel**, completed in 1482, a wonderful example of English Perpendicular architecture. The self-congratulatory **Museum of Eton Life**, where you're deposited at the end of the tour, is well worth missing unless you have a fascination with flogging, fagging and bragging about the school's facilities and alumni.

LISTINGS

Accommodation

There's no getting away from the fact that **accommodation** in London is expensive. Compared with most European cities, you pay over the odds in every category. The city's hostels are among the most expensive in the world, while venerable institutions such as the *Ritz*, the *Dorchester* and the *Savoy* charge guests the very top international prices – up to £300 or more per luxurious night.

The cheapest places to stay are the dorm beds of the city's numerous independent **hostels**, followed closely behind by the official YHA hostels. Even the most basic **B&Bs** struggle to bring their tariffs down to £45 for a double with shared facilities, and you're more likely to find yourself paying £60 or more.

When choosing your **area**, bear in mind that the West End – Soho, Covent Garden, St James's, Mayfair and Marylebone – and the western districts of Knightsbridge and Kensington are dominated by expensive, upmarket hotels. For cheaper rooms, the widest choice is close to the main train termini of Victoria and Paddington, and the budget B&Bs of Earl's Court. Those close to King's Cross cater for those on welfare, or charge by the hour, although neighbouring Bloomsbury is both inexpensive and very central.

If you want to avoid the hassle of contacting individual

hotels and B&Bs, you could turn to one of the various **accommodation agencies**. All London tourist offices (see p.6 for details) operate a room-booking service, for which a small fee is levied (they also take the first night's fee in advance). In addition, **Thomas Cook** has accommodation desks at Gatwick Airport (℡01293/529372) and at the British Visitor Centre on Lower Regent Street (see p.6) and will book anything from youth hostels through to five-star hotels (£5 fee). There are also **British Hotel Reservation Centre** (BHRC; ⓦwww.bhrc.co.uk) desks at Heathrow arrivals, at both Heathrow tube stations (℡020/8564 8808 or 8564 8211), and both terminals of Gatwick Airport (℡01293/502433). Alternatively, they have four desks in and around Victoria: at the train station (℡020/7828 1027), coach station (℡020/7824 8232), tube station (℡020/7828 2262), and at 13 Grosvenor Gardens (℡020/7828 2425). Most offices are open daily from 6am till midnight and there's no booking fee.

You can also **book online** for free at ⓦwww.londontown .com; payment is made directly to the hotel on checking out. Other useful websites include ⓦwww.lastminute.com, which almost always offers discounts, and ⓦwww.hotelsengland .com.

HOSTELS

London's official **Youth Hostel Association (YHA) hostels** are generally the cleanest, most efficiently run hostels in the capital. There's no age limit, and if you're not already a member you can join on the spot. You can book a bed over the phone with a credit card by ringing individual hostels, or by logging on to their **website** at ⓦwww.yha.org.uk. **Independent hostels** are cheaper and more relaxed, but can be less reliable in terms of facilities. Typical of this laid-back brand of hostel is the Astor chain of five hostels, run exclusively for the 18-30 age group. A good website for booking independent hostels online is Ⓦ www.hostellondon.com

YHA HOSTELS

- - - - - - - - - - - - - - - - - - - -

City of London

Map 5, H4. 36 Carter Lane, EC4 Ⓣ 020/7236 4965, Ⓔ city@yha.org.uk Ⓞ St Paul's. 200-bed hostel in a great situation opposite St Paul's Cathedral; some twins at £50 a room, but mostly 4- to 8-bed dorms for £24 per person. No groups.

Earl's Court

Map 3, A8. 38 Bolton Gardens, SW5 Ⓣ 020/7373 7083, Ⓔ earlscourt@yha.org.uk Ⓞ Earl's Court.
Better than a lot of accommodation in Earl's Court, but only offering dorms of mostly 10 beds – the triple bunks take some getting used to. Kitchen, café and patio garden. No groups. £19 per person.

Hampstead Heath

Map 2, G2. 4 Wellgarth Rd, NW11 Ⓣ 020/8458 9054,
Ⓔ hampstead@yha.org.uk Ⓞ Golders Green.
One of London's biggest and best-appointed YHA hostels, with its own garden and the wilds of Hampstead Heath nearby. Rooms with 3–6 beds cost £20.40 per person; family rooms with 2–5 beds are also available, starting at £35 for one adult and one child or £45 for two adults.

Holland House

Map 2, F5. Holland Walk, W8 Ⓣ 020/7937 0748, Ⓔ hollandhouse@yha.org.uk Ⓞ Holland Park or High Street Kensington.
Idyllically situated in the wooded expanse of Holland Park, and fairly convenient for the centre of town, this extensive hostel offers a decent kitchen and an inexpensive café. Popular with school groups. Dorms only at £21 per person.

Oxford Street

Map 3, G4. 14 Noel St, W1

YHA HOSTELS

ⓣ 020/7734 1618,
ⓔ oxfordst@yha.org.uk
ⓞ Oxford Circus or Tottenham Court Road.
Its West End location and modest size (75 beds in rooms of 2, 3 and 4 beds) mean that this hostel tends to be full even out of high season. No children under 6, no groups, no café, but a large kitchen. From £22 per person.

Rotherhithe
Map 2, K5 20 Salter Rd, SE16 ⓣ 020/7232 2114, ⓔ rotherhithe @yha.org.uk ⓞ Rotherhithe or Canada Water.
London's largest purpose-built hostel is a little out of things in the Docklands area, but with good connections into central London and easy access to sights in the south and east of the city it's a viable option. Rooms have 2, 4, 6 or 10 beds and cost from £24 per person.

St Pancras
Map 3, H2. 79–81 Euston Rd, NW1 ⓣ 020/7388 9998, ⓔ stpancras@yha.org.uk ⓞ King's Cross or Euston.
Big hostel situated opposite the new British Library, on the busy Euston Road. Beds cost from £24 per person, and rooms are very clean, bright, triple-glazed and air-conditioned – some even have en-suite facilities. There are a few en-suite doubles and family rooms available with TVs for £50. No groups.

PRIVATE HOSTELS

Ashlee House
Map 3, I2. 261–265 Gray's Inn Rd, WC1 ⓣ 020/7833 9400, ⓦ www.ashleehouse.co.uk ⓞ King's Cross.
Basic, a little cramped, but clean and friendly hostel in a converted office block near King's Cross Station. Dorms (4–16 beds) from £17; private rooms with bunk beds from £24 per person. Breakfast included.

Generator
Map 3, H2. Compton Place, off Tavistock Place, WC1 ⓣ 020/7388 7666, ⓦ www .the-generator.co.uk ⓞ Russell Square or Euston.

The neon- and UV-lighting and post-industrial décor may not be to everyone's tastes, but with rates including breakfast, evening meals available and a funky residents-only bar open till 2am, this is without doubt one of the best-value deals in central London. Over 800 beds, and prices that run from £42 for a single, £26.50 each for a double, or £22.50 each for a triple, down to £17 for a bed in a shared room or £12.50 for a dorm bed.

Leinster Inn

Map 3, A5. 7–12 Leinster Square, W2 ⓣ 020/7229 9641, ⓦ www.astorhostels.com ⊖ Queensway or Notting Hill Gate.

The biggest and liveliest of the Astor hostels (under 30s only), with a party atmosphere and two bars open until the small hours. Dorm beds (4–8 per room) £14–16, singles from £32, doubles from £44.

Museum Inn

Map 3, I3. 27 Montague St, W1 ⓣ 020/7580 5360, ⓦ www.astorhostels.com ⊖ Russell Square.

In a lovely Georgian house by the British Museum, this is the quietest of the Astor hostels. There's no bar, but it's still a sociable, laid-back place, and well situated. Dorms with 4–10 beds per room from £15, including breakfast. Small kitchen, TV lounge, and baths as well as showers.

St Christopher's Village

Map 7, E9. 161–165 Borough High St, SE1 ⓣ 020/7407 1856, ⓦ www.st-christophers.co.uk ⊖ London Bridge.

Flagship of a chain of independent hostels, with no fewer than three properties on Borough High Street (and more branches in Camden and Greenwich). The décor is upbeat and cheerful, the place is efficiently run and there's a party-animal ambience, fuelled by the neighbouring bar and the rooftop sauna and pool. Beds in dorms of 4–14 for £10–18.50, twins £56.

PRIVATE HOSTELS

HOTELS AND B&BS

Most **B&Bs and hotels** are housed in former residential properties, which means that rooms tend to be on the small side, and only the more upmarket properties have lifts. That said, most rooms have TVs, tea- and coffee-making facilities and telephones, and breakfast is nearly always included in the price.

The recommendations below cover every category from budget to luxury, though you're unlikely to find anything at all for under £50 – most accommodation falls between £50 and £100 per double. Bear in mind that many of the plush hotels listed slash their advertised rates at the weekend, when the business types have gone home.

Most places take all major **credit cards**, particularly Visa and Access/MasterCard, so in the listings we've simply noted those that don't.

ST JAMES'S, MAYFAIR AND MARYLEBONE

Edward Lear Hotel
Map 3, E4. 28–30 Seymour St, W1 ⓣ 020/7402 5401, ⓦ www .edlear.com ⊖ Marble Arch. Former home of the famous poet and artist, decorated with lovely flower boxes, and boasting a plush foyer and a great location close to Oxford Street and Hyde Park. The rooms themselves are less remarkable, but the low prices reflect both this and the fact that most only have shared facilities. Kids free at weekends. ❹

Hotel La Place
Map 3, E3. 17 Nottingham Place, W1 ⓣ 020/7486 2323, ⓦ www.hotellaplace.com ⊖ Baker Street. Just off the busy Marylebone Road, this is a small, good-value place; rooms are all en suite, equipped with all the gadgets usually found in grander establishments, and comfortably furnished. ❼

ACCOMMODATION PRICES

All hotel accommodation has been graded on a scale of ❶–❾ according to the minimum nightly charge you can expect to pay for a double room in high season (breakfast is generally included in the price). The prices signified by these categories are as follows:

❶ under £40 ❹ £60–70 ❼ £110–150
❷ £40–50 ❺ £70–90 ❽ £150–200
❸ £50–60 ❻ £90–110 ❾ over £200

The Metropolitan
Map 3, F6. Old Park Lane, W1
Ⓣ 020/7447 1000,
Ⓦ www.metropolitan.co.uk
⊖ Green Park or Hyde Park Corner.
This terrifyingly trendy hotel near the *Hilton* adheres to the current fad for pared-down minimalism. The Japanese restaurant is outstanding, and the *Met* bar is members- and residents-only in the evenings. Double rooms start at £250. ❾

Wigmore Court Hotel
Map 3, E4. 23 Gloucester Place, W1 Ⓣ 020/7935 0928,
Ⓦ www.wigmore-court-hotel
.co.uk ⊖ Marble Arch or Baker Street.
The relentlessly pink décor

may not be to everyone's taste, but this Georgian town house is a better than average B&B, boasting a high tally of returning clients. Comfortable rooms with en-suite facilities, plus two doubles with shared facilities at a price code lower. Unusually, there's also a laundry and basic kitchen for guests' use. ❺

SOHO, COVENT GARDEN AND THE STRAND

The Fielding Hotel
Map 4, I6. 4 Broad Court, Bow St, WC2 Ⓣ 020/7836 8305,
Ⓦ www.the-fielding-hotel.co.uk
⊖ Covent Garden.

Quietly and perfectly situated on a traffic-free and gas-lit court, this excellent hotel is one of Covent Garden's hidden gems. Its en-suite rooms are a firm favourite with visiting performers, since it's just a few yards from the Royal Opera House. Breakfast is extra. ⑥

Hazlitt's

Map 4, F5. 6 Frith St, W1 ⓣ 020/7434 1771, ⓦ www.hazlittshotel.co.uk ⊖ Tottenham Court Road. Located off the south side of Soho Square, this early eighteenth-century building is a hotel of real character and charm, offering en-suite rooms decorated and furnished as close to period style as convenience and comfort allow. There's a small sitting room, but no dining room (although some of London's best restaurants are a stone's throw away). Continental breakfast (served in the rooms) is available, but isn't included in the rates. ⑨

Manzi's

Map 4, F7. 1–2 Leicester St, WC2 ⓣ 020/7734 0224, ⓦ www.manzis.co.uk ⊖ Leicester Square. Set over the Italian and seafood restaurant of the same name, *Manzi's* is one of very few central hotels in this price range. It's certainly right in the thick of the West End, just off Leicester Square, although noise might prove to be a nuisance. Continental breakfast is included in the price. ⑤

One Aldwych

Map 5, 6A. 1 Aldwych, WC2 ⓣ 020/7300 1000, ⓦ www.onealdwych.co.uk ⊖ Covent Garden or Temple. On the outside, this is one of London's few vaguely Art Nouveau buildings, built in 1907 for the *Morning Post* newspaper. However, little survives from those days, as the interior of this desperately fashionable luxury hotel firmly follows the minimalist mantra. The draws now are the underwater music in the hotel's vast pool, the oodles of modern art about the place, and the TVs in the bathrooms of the £360-plus rooms. ⑨

St Martin's Lane

Map 4, G7. 45 St Martin's Lane, WC2 ☏ 020/7300 5500 or 0800/634 5500,
Ⓦ www.ianschragerhotels.com
⊖ Leicester Square.

So cool you wouldn't know it was a hotel, this self-consciously chic "boutique hotel" from the New York-based Ian Schrager chain is a hit with the media crowd. From the fluorescent yellow and white minimalist lobby to the large Portuguese limestone bathrooms, the interior has been designed throughout by the mischievous Philippe Starck. The *Light Bar* and the sushi *Sea Bar* are the most startling of the hotel's numerous eating and drinking outlets. Rooms currently start at around £250 a double, but rates come down at the weekend. ⑨

Sanderson

Map 4, D4. 50 Berners St, W1 ☏ 020/7300 1400,
Ⓦ www.ianschragerhotels.com

⊖ Tottenham Court Road or Oxford Circus.

This second collaboration by Schrager and Starck is set in a listed 1960s Fitzrovia office block. The usual assemblage of *objets d'art* peppers the white and magnolia lobby, where the black-clad staff flit about like silhouettes. The *Long Bar* is all translucent back-lit onyx, but, like the restaurant, is ludicrously overpriced. 3D "space" lifts take you to the equally bright white rooms (starting at around £250 a double), decked out with light wooden floors and billowing curtains. There's a large gym, steam room, sauna and health club on site. ⑨

BLOOMSBURY

Hotel Cavendish

Map 3, H3. 75 Gower St, WC1, ☏ 020/7636 9079,
Ⓦ www.hotelcavendish.com
⊖ Goodge Street.

Gower Street is very busy with traffic, but get a room at the back of the property and you'll have a peaceful night, and a real bargain, too, with lovely owners, two beautiful overrun gardens and some quite well-preserved original features. All rooms have shared facilities, and there are some good-value family rooms, too. ❸

Crescent Hotel
Map 3, H2. 49–50 Cartwright Gardens, WC1 ⓣ 020/7387 1515, ⓦ www .crescenthoteloflondon.com ⊖ Euston or Russell Square. Very comfortable and tastefully decorated Regency B&B – definitely a cut above the rest, with a lovely blacked-up range in the breakfast room. All doubles are en suite and have TVs, but there are a few bargain singles with shared facilities; guests also have use of tennis courts in the nearby gardens. ❺

Jenkins Hotel
Map 3, H2. 45 Cartwright Gardens, WC1 ⓣ 020/7387 2067, ⓦ www.jenkinshotel .demon.co.uk ⊖ Euston or Russell Square. Smartly kept, family-run place in this fine Regency

crescent, with just fourteen fairly small but well-equipped and very clean rooms, most of which are en suite. ❹

myhotel
Map 3, H3. 11–13 Bayley St, Bedford Square, WC1 ⓣ 020/7667 6000, ⓦ www.myhotels.co.uk ⊖ Tottenham Court Road. The aquarium in the lobby is the telltale sign that this is a feng shui hotel. Despite the positive vibes, and Conran-designed look, the double-glazed, air-conditioned rooms are on the small side for the price. Still, there's a gym, a very pleasant library, a restaurant attached and the location is great for the West End. ❽

Ridgemount Hotel
Map 4, F1 65–67 Gower St, WC1 ⓣ 020/7636 1141, ⓦ www.ridgemounthotel.co.uk ⊖ Goodge Street. Old fashioned, very friendly family-run place, with small rooms, half with shared facilities, a garden, free hot-drinks machine and a laundry service. Cash only, but a

reliable, basic bargain for Bloomsbury. ❸

Hotel Russell

Map 4 H1. Russell Square, WC1 ☎ 020/7837 6470, ⓦ www.lemeridian.co.uk ⊖ Russell Square.

From its grand 1898 exterior to its opulent interiors of marble, wood and crystal, this late Victorian landmark fully retains its period atmosphere in all its public areas. Thanks to a recent takeover – and makeover – by Le Meridien chain, the rooms now live up to the grandeur of the lobby, if not necessarily to its style. Most have been given a modern, minimalist redesign, a few have a more traditional old-world elegance. Expensive, but various deals are available. Breakfast is not included. ❾

CLERKENWELL AND THE CITY

City Hotel

Map 7, M2. 12 Osborn St, E1 ☎ 020/7247 3313, ⓦ www.cityhotellondon.co.uk ⊖ Aldgate East.

Spacious, clean and modern inside, this hotel stands on the eastern edge of the City, and in the heart of the Bengali East End at the bottom of Brick Lane. The plainly decorated rooms are all en suite, and many have kitchens, too; four-person rooms are a bargain for those in a small group. ❻

Great Eastern Hotel

Map 7, I1. Liverpool St, EC2 ☎ 020/7618 5010, ⓦ www.great-eastern-hotel .co.uk ⊖ Liverpool Street.

Without doubt, one of *the* best places to stay if you need or wish to be near the City. This venerable late nineteenth-century station hotel has had a complete Conran makeover, yet manages to retain much of its clubby flavour. The *George* pub boasts a superb mock-Tudor ceiling; the fabulous old lobby is now the *Aurora* restaurant, and the rooms themselves are impeccably well appointed and tastefully furnished – to maximize your natural light, get a room facing out. Doubles start from

HOTELS AND B&Bs: CLERKENWELL AND THE CITY

around £200, but rates are cut at the weekend. **9**

Jurys Inn

Map 3, J1. 60 Pentonville Rd, N1 ⓣ 020/7282 5500, Ⓦ www.jurys.com ⊖ Angel. This modern Irish chain hotel is decorated to a high, if bland, standard, and is geared up for business folk. Located on busy Pentonville Road, close to the tube, it's equally convenient for the City and for Islington and Clerkenwell's trendy bars and restaurants. Service is very friendly, and the fixed room rate is a bargain for three adults sharing or for those with kids. **6**

The Rookery

Map 3, K3. 12 Peter's Lane, Cowcross St, EC1 ⓣ 020/7336 0931, Ⓦ www.rookeryhotel .com ⊖ Farringdon. Rambling Georgian town house on the edge of the City in trendy Clerkenwell that makes a fantastically discreet little hideaway. The rooms start at around £265 a double; each one has been individually designed in a deliciously camp, modern

take on the Baroque period, and all have super bathrooms with lots of character. Farringdon tube. **9**

SOUTH BANK & SOUTHWARK

London County Hall Travel Inn

Map 6, A6. Belvedere Rd, SE1 ⓣ 020/7902 1619, Ⓦ www .travelinn.co.uk ⊖ Waterloo or Westminster. Don't expect river views at these prices, but the location in County Hall itself is pretty good if you're up for a bit of sightseeing. Décor and ambience is functional, but for those with kids the flat-rate rooms are a bargain. **5**

Mad Hatter

Map 6, F2. 3–7 Stamford St, SE1 ⓣ 020/7401 9222, Ⓦ www.fullers.co.uk ⊖ Southwark or Blackfriars. Situated above a Fuller's pub on the corner of Blackfriars Road, and run by the Fuller's brewery. Breakfast is extra, and is served in the pub, but this is a great location, a short walk from the Tate Modern and the South Bank. Ask about the weekend deals. **6**

VICTORIA

The Goring
Map 3, F7. 15 Beeston Place, SW1 ⊕020/7396 9000, Ⓦwww.goringhotel.co.uk ⊖ Victoria.
This Edwardian hotel, owned and run by the Goring family for three generations, succeeds in creating an atmosphere of elegance and tranquillity despite its position amid busy roads. Afternoon tea is served on the delightful private garden terrace in fine weather; doubles start at £247 (breakfast not included). **9**

Melbourne House Hotel
Map 3, G8. 79 Belgrave Rd, SW1 ⊕020/7828 3516, Ⓦwww.melbournehousehotel .com ⊖ Victoria or Pimlico.
One of the best B&Bs along Belgrave Road: family-run, well furnished, offering clean and bright rooms, excellent communal areas and friendly service. All doubles have en-

suite facilities, but there are a couple of very cheap singles without. **5**

Oxford House Hotel
Map 3, F8. 92–94 Cambridge St, SW1 ⊕020/7834 6467, ⊕020/7834 0225. ⊖ Victoria.
Probably the best-value rooms you can get in the vicinity of Victoria station. Showers and toilets are shared, but kept pristine. Full English breakfast is included in the price. **2**

Sanctuary House
Map 4, F13. 33 Tothill St, SW1 ⊕020/7799 4044, Ⓦwww.fullers.co.uk ⊖ St James's Park.
Run by Fuller's Brewery, situated above a Fuller's pub, and decked out like one, too, in smart, pseudo-Victoriana. Breakfast is extra, and is served in the pub, but the location right by St James's Park is very central. Ask about the weekend deals. **6**

Topham's Hotel
Map 3, F7. 26 Ebury St, SW1 ⊕020/7730 8147, Ⓦwww .tophams.co.uk ⊖ Victoria.

HOTELS AND B&BS: VICTORIA

Charming family-owned hotel in the English country-house style, just a couple of minutes' walk from Victoria mainline and tube station. Sumptuously furnished en-suite twins or doubles from £100, including full English breakfast. ❻

Windermere Hotel

Map 3, F8. 142–144 Warwick Way, SW1 ☏ 020/7834 5163, ⓦ www.windermere-hotel.co.uk ⊖ Sloane Square, Pimlico or Victoria.

Situated at the western end of Warwick Way, this is a tastefully decorated and quietly stylish place, and most rooms are en suite. There's a tasty restaurant downstairs, too. ❻

Woodville House & Morgan House

Map 3, F7. 107 & 120 Ebury St, SW1 ☏ 020/7730 1048 & 7730 2384, ⓦ www .woodvillehouse.co.uk &, ⓦ www.morganhouse.co.uk ⊖ Victoria.

Two above-average B&Bs, run by the same vivacious couple, with great breakfasts,

patio gardens, and an iron and fridge for guests to use. All rooms at *Woodville* are with shared facilities; some at *Morgan* are en suite. ❹

PADDINGTON, BAYSWATER AND NOTTING HILL

Columbia Hotel

Map 3, C5. 95–99 Lancaster Gate, W2 ☏ 020/7402 0021, ⓦ www.columbiahotel.co.uk ⊖ Lancaster Gate.

The spacious public lounge, well-worn décor and useful 24hr bar make this large white stucco hotel a rock-band favourite. The en-suite rooms themselves are actually very sober, and retain some original Victorian fittings. ❺

Garden Court Hotel

Map 3, A4. 30–31 Kensington Gardens Square, W2 ☏ 020/7229 2553, ⓦ www.gardencourthotel.co.uk. ⊖ Bayswater or Queensway.

Presentable, family-run B&B on a quiet square close to Portobello market; half the rooms are with shared facilities, half are en suite. Full English breakfast included. ❸

The Gresham Hotel

Map 3, C4. 116 Sussex Gardens, W2 ☎ 020/7402 2920, Ⓦ www.the-gresham-hotel .co.uk ⊖ Paddington. B&B with a touch more class than many in the area. Rooms are small but tastefully kitted out, and all have TV. Continental breakfast included. ❺

Inverness Court Hotel

Map 3, A5. 1 Inverness Terrace, W2 ☎ 020/7229 1444, Ⓕ 020/7229 3666. ⊖ Bayswater or Queensway. The splendid, late Victorian facade, reception area, bar and lounges lend a charming ambience, even if most of the en-suite bedrooms are in an undistinguished modern style. Continental breakfast included. ❻

Pavilion Hotel

Map 3, C4. 34–36 Sussex Gardens, W2 ☎ 020/7262 0905, Ⓦ www.msi.com.mt/pavilion ⊖ Paddington.

The successful rock star's home from home, with outrageously over-the-top décor and every room individually themed from 1970s "Honky Tonk Afro" to Moorish "Casablanca Nights". ❻

Pembridge Court Hotel

Map 3, A5. 34 Pembridge Gardens, W2 ☎ 020/7229 9977, Ⓦ www.pemct.co.uk ⊖ Notting Hill Gate or Holland Park. Attractively converted grandiose Victorian town house close to Portobello market, with spacious, fully equipped rooms. Two resident cats add to the homely feel, as does the lively *Caps Restaurant and Bar.* ❽

KNIGHTSBRIDGE, KENSINGTON AND CHELSEA

- - - - - - - - - - - - - - - - - - - -

Abbey House

Map 3, A6. 11 Vicarage Gate, W8 ☎ 020/7721 7395, Ⓦ www.abbeyhousekensington .com ⊖ High Street Kensington or Notting Hill. Inexpensive Victorian B&B in a quiet street just north of

HOTELS AND B&Bs: KNIGHTSBRIDGE, KENSINGTON AND CHELSEA

191

Kensington High Street, maintained to a very high standard by its attentive owners. Rooms are large and bright – prices are kept down by sharing facilities rather than fitting the usual cramped bathroom unit. Full English breakfast, with free tea and coffee available all day. Cash only. ⑤

Aster House

Map 3, C8. 3 Sumner Place, SW7 ⓣ 020/7581 5888, ⓦ www.asterhouse.com
⊖ South Kensington.
Pleasant, non-smoking B&B in a luxurious white-stuccoed South Ken street; there's a lovely garden at the back and a large conservatory, where breakfast is served. Singles with shared facilities start at around £90 a night. ⑦

Blakes Hotel

Map 3, B8. 33 Roland Gardens, SW7 ⓣ 020/7370 6701, ⓦ www.blakeshotel.com
⊖ Gloucester Road.
Blakes' dramatic interior – designed by Anoushka Hempel – and glamorous suites have long attracted

visiting celebs. A faintly *Raffles*-esque flavour pervades, with bamboo furniture and old travelling trunks mixing with unusual objects, tapestries and prints. Doubles from £250 are smart but small; fully equipped suites are spectacular, as they should be for £545. The restaurant and bar are excellent, and service is of a very high standard. ⑨

Five Sumner Place

Map 3, C8. 5 Sumner Place, SW7 ⓣ 020/7584 7586, ⓦ www.sumnerplace.com
⊖ South Kensington.
Another discreetly luxurious B&B (see *Aster House* above) on this attractive white-stuccoed terrace. As at *Aster House*, all rooms are en suite and breakfast is served in the house's lovely conservatory.

The Gore

Map 3, B7. 189 Queen's Gate, SW7 ⓣ 020/7584 6601, ⓦ www.gorehotel.com
⊖ South Kensington, Gloucester Road or High Street Kensington.
Popular, privately owned century-old hotel, awash with

Oriental rugs, rich mahogany, walnut panelling and other Victoriana. A pricey, but excellent bistro restaurant adds to its allure, and it's only a step away from Hyde Park. Rooms, some with four-poster beds, from £200. ⑨

The Hempel

Map 3, B5. 31–35 Craven Hill Gardens, W2 ⓣ 020/7298 9000, Ⓦ www.the-hempel.co.uk ⊖ Lancaster Gate or Queensway.
Deeply fashionable minimalist hotel, designed by the actress turned designer Anoushka Hempel, with a huge and very empty atrium entrance. White-on-white rooms start at around £200 a double, and there's an excellent postmodern Italian/Thai restaurant called *I-Thai*. ⑨

Hotel 167

Map 3, B8. 167 Old Brompton Rd, SW5 ⓣ 020/7373 3221, Ⓦ www.hotel167.com ⊖ Gloucester Road.
Small, stylishly furnished B&B with en-suite facilities, double glazing and a fridge in all rooms. Continental buffet-style breakfast is served in the attractive morning room/reception. ⑦

Vicarage Hotel

Map 3, A6. 10 Vicarage Gate, W8 ⓣ 020/7229 4030, Ⓦ www.londonvicaragehotel .com ⊖ High Street Kensington or Notting Hill.
Ideally located B&B a step away from Hyde Park. Clean rooms with shared facilities and a full English breakfast served. Cash/travellers' cheques only. ⑤

HAMPSTEAD

Hampstead Village Guesthouse

Map G3. 2 Kemplay Rd, NW3 ⓣ 020/7435 8679, Ⓦ www.HampsteadGuesthouse .com ⊖ Hampstead.
Lovely B&B in an old house set in a quiet backstreet between Hampstead village and the Heath. Rooms (some en suite, all non-smoking) have "lived-in" clutter, which makes a pleasant change from anodyne hotels and spartan B&Bs. Meals to order. ⑤

HOTELS AND B&BS: HAMPSTEAD

La Gaffe

Map 2, G3. 107–111 Heath St, NW3 ⓣ 020/7435 8965, ⓦ www.lagaffe.co.uk ⊖ Hampstead.

Small and warren-like, but a characterful hotel, situated over an Italian restaurant and bar in the heart of Hampstead village. All rooms are en suite and there's a roof terrace for use in fine weather. ❻

EARL'S COURT

Philbeach Hotel

Map 3, A8. 30–31 Philbeach Gardens, SW5 ⓣ 020/7373 1244, ⓦ www.philbeachhotel .freeserve.co.uk ⊖ Earl's Court.

Friendly, long-running gay/transvestite hotel, with basic and en-suite rooms, a pleasant TV lounge area, late bar and popular *Wilde About Oscar* garden restaurant. ❺

Rushmore Hotel

Map 3, A8. 11 Trebovir Rd, SW5 ⓣ 020/7370 3839, ⓕ 7370 0274 ⊖ Earl's Court.

A cut above the average, with its colourful murals, imaginative Italianate room décor and conservatory in this often dreary area. The attic rooms are especially spacious and comfortable. Full continental breakfast is included in the rates. ❺

Cafés and snacks

This chapter covers the full range of **cafés** from unre-constructed "greasy spoons", where you can get traditional fried egg, sausage and bacon English break-fasts, fish and chips, pies and other calorific treats, to the refined salons of London's top hotels, where you can enjoy an afternoon tea blowout. In between, you'll find bakeries, brasseries, sandwich bars, coffee shops and ice-cream par-lours, all of which are open during the day for light meals, snacks or just a drink. We've also included several **ethnic eating** places where speedy service and low prices are the priority – places perfect for an inexpensive or quick bite before going out to a theatre, cinema or club. Wherever you go, you should be able to fill yourself up for under £10.

If you want to surf while you slurp, you'll find that London has nothing like the number and variety of **inter-net cafés** as other capital cities. Your best bet is to head for a branch of *easyInternetcafe* (ⓦ www.easy.everything.com), the no-frills internet café chain – there's a 24hr branch just up the Strand, off Trafalgar Square (see Directory, p.357 for other branches). Alternatively, there's the more congenial 24hr *Be the Reds!* (ⓣ 020/7209 0984) at 39 Whitfield St, just off Tottenham Court Road (Goodge Street tube) – a Korean-run place serving *kimbab* and coffee, with billiards in the basement.

MAYFAIR AND MARYLEBONE

Apostrophe

Map 4, A5. 23 Barrett St, W1 ⓣ 020/7355 1001. ⊖ Bond Street. Mon–Sat 7.30am –8.30pm, Sun 9.30am–8.30pm. Modern take on the French boulangerie/patisserie, with tables looking out onto pedestrianized St Christopher's Place, just off Oxford Street. Serves up delicious sandwiches and coffee, and sells the legendary Poilâne bread.

Mô

Map 4, D7. 25 Heddon St, W1 ⓣ 020/7434 4040. ⊖ Piccadilly Circus. Mon–Wed 11am–11pm, Thurs–Sat noon–midnight. The ultimate Arabic pastiche but a successful one. The adjacent restaurant (*Momo*) is expensive, but the tearoom serves more reasonably priced, yet equally delicious snacks. Moreover, it's a great place to hang out, with tables and hookahs spilling out onto the pavement of this little Mayfair alleyway behind Regent Street.

Patisserie Valerie at Sagne

Map 3, E3. 105 Marylebone High St, W1 ⓣ 020/7935 6240, ⓦ www.patisserie-valerie.co.uk ⊖ Bond Street or Baker Street. Mon–Fri 7.30am–7pm, Sat 8am–7pm, Sun 9am–6pm. Founded as *Maison Sagne* in the 1920s, and preserving its wonderful décor from those days, the café is now run by Soho's fab patisserie makers, and is, without doubt, Marylebone's finest.

Paul

Map 3, E3. 116 Marylebone High St, W1 ⓣ 020/7226 5615. ⊖ Bond Street or Baker Street. Mon–Fri 7.30am–7pm, Sat & Sun 9am–7pm. Seriously French, upmarket boulangerie with a small wood-panelled café at the back. Try one of the chewy *fougasses*, quiches or tarts, before launching into the exquisite patisserie. There's also a more central branch at 29 Bedford St, Covent Garden.

SOHO

Bar du Marché

Map 4, E6. 19 Berwick St, W1
☎ 020/7734 4606.
⊖ Tottenham Court Road,
Piccadilly Circus or Leicester
Square. Mon–Sat noon–11pm.
A weird find in the middle of
raucous Berwick Street
market: a licensed French café
serving quick snacks, brasserie
staples and set meals for
around £10.

Bar Italia

Map 4, F6. 22 Frith St, W1
☎ 020/7437 4520.
⊖ Leicester Square. Open 24hr
except Sun 3–6am.
Tiny café that's a Soho
institution, serving coffee,
croissants and sandwiches
more or less around the clock
– as it has been since 1949.
Popular with late-night
clubbers and those here to
watch the Italian-league
soccer on the giant screen.

Beatroot

Map 4, E6. 92 Berwick St, W1
☎ 020/7437 8591. ⊖ Piccadilly
Circus. Mon–Fri 9am–7pm, Sat

11am–7pm.
Great little veggie café by the
market, doling out hot
savoury bakes, stews and
salads (plus delicious cakes) in
boxes of varying sizes – all
under £5.

Bread Shop

Map 4, E7. 17 Brewer St, W1
☎ 020/7434 3408. ⊖ Leicester
Square or Piccadilly Circus.
Mon–Fri 8am–7.30pm, Sat
8am–8pm.
Tiny, takeaway bakery
producing a fantastic array of
organic breads, pastries and
little pizzas, plus coffee and
tea. Try the divine sourdough
bread or spelt croissants.

Centrale

Map 4, G6. 16 Moor St, W1
☎ 020/7437 5513. ⊖ Leicester
Square or Tottenham Court
Road. Mon–Sat noon–9.30pm.
Tiny, friendly Italian café that
serves up huge plates of
steaming, garlicky pasta, as
well as omelettes, chicken and
chops for around £5. You'll
almost certainly have to wait
for – or share – a Formica-
topped table. Bring your own
booze (corkage 50p) but

SOHO

don't drink too much, as there are no toilets.

Maison Bertaux
Map 4, F6. 28 Greek St, W1 ⓣ020/7437 6007. ⊖ Leicester Square. Daily 8.30am–8pm. Long-standing, old-fashioned Soho patisserie, with tables on two floors (and one or two outside). The wonderful patisseries here are among the best in the West End and a loyal clientele keeps the place busy all day long.

Patisserie Valerie
Map 4, F6. 44 Old Compton St, W1 ⓣ020/7437 3466, ⓦwww.patisserie-valerie.co.uk ⊖ Leicester Square or Piccadilly Circus. Mon–Fri 7.30am–8pm, Sat 8am–8pm, Sun 9.30am–7pm. Popular coffee, croissant and cake emporium dating from the 1950s and attracting a loud-talking, arty Soho crowd. The same outfit runs *Patisserie Valerie at Sagne* in Marylebone (see p.198) and *Café Valerie* at 8 Russell Street, Covent Garden.

Red Veg
Map 4, F5. 95 Dean St, W1 ⓣ020/7437 3109, ⓦwww.redveg.com ⊖ Tottenham Court Road. Mon–Sat noon–10pm. There's only a faint whiff of 1980s Soviet chic about this minimalist veggie junk-food outlet, which doles out a short list of cheap, classic munchie-fodder: veggie burgers, noodles and falafel.

CHINATOWN
- - - - - - - - - - - - - - - - - - - -

Kopi-Tiam
Map 4, F7. 9 Wardour St, W1 ⊖ Leicester Square. Daily noon–11pm. Bright, cheap Malaysian café serving up curries, coconut rice, juices and "herbal soups" to local Malays, all for around a fiver.

Lee Ho Fook
Map 4, F7. 4 Macclesfield St, W1. ⊖ Leicester Square. Daily 11.30am–11pm. A genuine Chinese barbecue house – small, spartan and cheap – that's very difficult to find. So here are the directions:

on the west side of the street is Dansey Place, and on the corner is a red-and-gold sign in Chinese and a host of ducks hanging on a rack.

Misato

Map 4, F7. 11 Wardour St, W1 ⊖ Leicester Square. Daily noon–2.45pm & 5.30–10.30pm. Modern, canteen-style Japanese café serving stomach-filling rice and noodle dishes for around a fiver, plus miso soup, sushi and bento boxes.

Tokyo Diner

Map 4, G7. 2 Newport Place, WC2 ☎ 020/7287 8777. ⊖ Leicester Square. Daily noon–midnight. Conclusive proof that you don't need to take out a second mortgage to enjoy Japanese food in London, this friendly eatery on the edge of Chinatown shuns elaboration

LONDON FOR VEGGIES

Most restaurants in London will make some attempt to cater for vegetarians. Below is a list of exclusively vegetarian places recommended in this chapter and the "Restaurants" chapter.

Beatroot
92 Berwick St, W1 (see p.199)

Food for Thought
31 Neal St, WC2 (see p.202)

The Gate 2
72 Belsize Lane, NW3 (see p.222)

Manna
4 Erskine Rd, NW3 (see p.222)

Mildred's
45 Lexington St, W1 (see p.214)

The Place Below
Church of St Mary-le-Bow, Cheapside, EC2 (see p.204)

Rasa
6 Dering St, W1 (see p.216)

Red Veg
95 Dean St, W1 (see p.200)

CHINATOWN

for fast food, Tokyo style. Minimalist décor lets the sushi and sumo do the talking, which – if the number of Japanese who frequent the place is anything to go by – it does fluently.

COVENT GARDEN AND THE STRAND

Café in the Crypt

Map 4, H8. St Martin-in-the-Fields, Duncannon St, WC2 ☎ 020/7839 4342. ⊖ Charing Cross. Mon–Wed 10am–8pm, Thurs–Sat 10am–11pm, Sun noon–8pm.

The self-service buffet, which has regular veggie dishes, usually hits the spot and the handy and atmospheric location – below the church in the crypt – makes this an ideal spot to fill up before hitting the West End.

Food for Thought

Map 4, H5. 31 Neal St, WC2 ☎ 020/7836 9072. ⊖ Covent Garden. Mon–Sat 9.30am–8.30pm, Sun noon–5pm.

Long-established, minuscule

bargain veggie restaurant with takeaway counter – the food is good, with the menu changing twice daily, plus regular vegan and wheat-free options. Expect to queue and don't expect to linger at peak times.

Gaby's

Map 4, G7. 30 Charing Cross Rd, WC2 ☎ 020/7836 4233. ⊖ Leicester Square. Daily 9am–midnight.

Busy café and takeaway joint serving a wide range of home-cooked veggie and Middle Eastern specialities. Hard to beat for value, choice, location or long hours – it's licensed, too. The takeaway falafel is a central London bargain.

Mode

Map 4, H5. 57 Endell St, WC2 ☎ 020/7240 8085. ⊖ Covent Garden. Mon–Fri 8am–11pm, Sat 9am–10pm.

The best things about this stylish Covent Garden café are the Italian sandwiches, the cheeses from nearby Neal's Yard Dairy, the big puddings, and the laid-back, funky atmosphere.

Monmouth Coffee Company

Map 4, G5. 27 Monmouth St, WC2 ⓣ 020/7836 5272. ⊖ Covent Garden or Leicester Square. Mon–Sat 9am–6pm. The marvellous aroma is the first thing you notice here, while the cramped wooden booths and daily newspapers on hand evoke an eighteenth-century coffee-house atmosphere – pick and mix your coffee from a fine selection (or buy the beans to take home). No smoking.

Rock & Sole Plaice

Map 4, H5. 47 Endell St, WC2 ⓣ 020/7836 3785. ⊖ Covent Garden. Daily 11.30am–10pm. A rare survivor: a no-nonsense traditional fish and chip shop in central London. Takeaway, eat in or out at one of the pavement tables.

BLOOMSBURY

- - - - - - - - - - - - - - - - - - - -

Coffee Gallery

Map 4, H4. 23 Museum St, WC1 ⓣ 020/7436 0455. ⊖ Tottenham Court Road. Mon–Fri 8.30am–5.30pm, Sat

10am–7pm, Sun noon–7pm. An excellent, small café close to the British Museum, serving mouthwatering Italian sandwiches and a few more substantial dishes at lunchtime. Get there early to grab a seat.

Wagamama

Map 4, G4. 4 Streatham St, WC1 ⓣ 020/7323 9223, ⓦ www.wagamama.com ⊖ Tottenham Court Road. Mon–Sat noon–11pm, Sun 12.30–10pm. Much copied since, *Wagamama* was the pioneer when it comes to austere, minimalist, canteen-style noodle bars. Diners share long benches and slurp from huge bowls of noodle soup or stir-fried plates. Don't be put off if there's a queue, as the rapid turnover means it moves pretty fast, even at peak times.

CLERKENWELL AND HOXTON

- - - - - - - - - - - - - - - - - - - -

Al's Café Bar

Map 3, J2. 11–13 Exmouth Market, EC1 ⓣ 020/7837 4821. ⊖ Angel or Farringdon tube.

Mon–Fri 8am–2am, Sat 10am–2am, Sun 10am–11pm. This is a trendy little spot – a greasy spoon with designer Formica tables and a local media-luvvie clientele, who lap up the Italian breads, Mediterranean dishes, nachos, decent coffee and good soups alongside the chips and grills. In the evening, it's more club-bar than café.

Feast

Map 3, K3. 86 St John St, EC1 ⓣ 020/7253 7007, ⓦ www.feastwraps.com ⊖ Farringdon or Barbican. Mon–Fri 7.30am–3.30pm. Delicious tortilla-wrapped sandwiches made to order; take away or eat in this small, trendy, designer Clerkenwell café.

Ktchn

Map 2, N2. 35 Charlotte Rd, EC2 ⓣ 020/7739 5345, ⓦ www.ktchn.com ⊖ Old Street. Mon–Fri 8.30am–3.30pm. Tiny, vowel-free Hoxton/Shoreditch café with just four stools. Serves delicious upmarket lunch

options: big soups, grilled tuna, rare-roast beef, exotic salads and great pastries, all freshly prepared.

THE CITY

De Gustibus

Map 5, H5. 53–55 Carter Lane, EC2 ⓣ 020/7236 0056, ⓦ www.degustibus.co.uk ⊖ St Paul's or Blackfriars. Mon–Fri 7am–5pm. Award-winning bakery that constructs a wide variety of sandwiches, bruschetta, croque monsieur and quiches to eat in perched on stools or take away.

K10

Map 7, F2. 20 Copthall Ave, EC2 ⓣ 020/7562 8510. ⊖ Moorgate. Mon–Fri 11.30am–3pm & 5–9.30pm. Remarkably good, inexpensive City sushi outlet, with busy takeaway upstairs, and a *kaiten* (conveyor-belt) restaurant downstairs.

The Place Below

Map 7, D4. Church of St Mary-le-Bow, Cheapside, EC2 ⓣ 020/7329 0789,

Ⓦ www.theplacebelow.co.uk
Ⓔ St Paul's or Bank. Mon–Fri
7.30am–3.30pm.
Something of a find in the
midst of the City – a café
serving imaginative vegetarian
dishes. Added to that, the
wonderful Norman crypt
makes for a very pleasant place
in which to sample them.

Yokoso Sushi

Map 5, E4. 40 Whitefriars St,
EC4 Ⓣ 020/7583 9656.
Ⓔ Blackfriars. Mon–Fri
10am–8pm.
Top-notch sushi place just off
Fleet Street, serving really
fresh fish at very affordable
prices; dishes are mostly under
£3 and set meals under £10.

THE EAST END

Arkansas Café

Map 3, N3. Unit 12, Old
Spitalfields Market, E1
Ⓣ 020/7377 6999. Ⓔ Liverpool
Street. Mon–Fri noon–2.30pm,
Sun noon–4pm.
American barbecue fuel stop,
using only the very best free-
range ingredients. Try chef
Bubb's own smoked beef

brisket and ribs, and be sure
to taste his home-made
barbie sauce (made to a secret
formula).

Brick Lane Beigel Bake

Map 2, J4. 159 Brick Lane, E1
Ⓣ 020/7729 0616.
Ⓔ Shoreditch or Aldgate East.
Daily 24hr.
The bagels at this no-frills
takeaway in the heart of the
East End are freshly made and
unbelievably cheap, even
when stuffed with smoked
salmon and cream cheese.

Sweet & Spicy

Map 2, J4. 40 Brick Lane, E1
Ⓣ 020/7247 1081. Ⓔ Aldgate
East or Whitechapel. Daily
8am–10pm.
The Pakistani equivalent of a
greasy spoon, with fixed seats
and Formica tables. No
smoking, no alcohol, just
incredibly cheap curries and
the like.

LAMBETH AND SOUTHWARK

El Vergel

Map 3, L6. 8 Lant Rd, SE1

AFTERNOON TEA

The classic English afternoon tea – assorted sandwiches, scones and cream, cakes and tarts and, of course, lashings of tea – is available all over London. The best venues are the capital's top hotels and most fashionable department stores; a selection of the best is picked out below. To avoid disappointment it's best to book ahead. Expect to spend £15–25 a head, and leave your jeans and trainers at home – most hotels will expect men to wear a jacket of some sort, though only the Ritz insists on jacket and tie.

Brown's
Map 4, C8. 33–34 Albemarle St, W1
ⓣ 020/7493 6020,
ⓦ www.brownshotel.com
⊖ Green Park. Daily 2–6pm.

Claridge's
Map 3, A5. Brook Street, W1 ⓣ 020/7629 8860,
ⓦ www.savoy-group.co.uk
⊖ Bond Street. Daily 3–5.30pm.

The Dorchester
Map 3, E5. 54 Park Lane, W1 ⓣ 020/7629 8888,
ⓦ www.dorchesterhotel.co.uk ⊖ Hyde Park Corner. Daily 3–6pm.

Fortnum & Mason
Map 4, D9. 181 Piccadilly, W1 ⓣ 020/7734 8040,
ⓦ www.fortnumandmason.com ⊖ Green Park or Piccadilly Circus. Daily 3–5.45pm.

Lanesborough
Map 3, E6. Hyde Park Corner, SW1 ⓣ 020/7259 5599, ⓦ www.lanesborough.com
⊖ Green Park. Daily 3.30–6pm.

The Ritz
Map 4, C9. Piccadilly, W1
ⓣ 020/7493 8181,
ⓦ www.theritzhotel.co.uk
⊖ Green Park. Daily 1.30, 3.30 & 5.30pm.

The Savoy
Map 4, I8. Strand, WC2
ⓣ 020/7836 4343,
ⓦ www.savoy-group.co.uk
⊖ Charing Cross. Daily 3–5.30pm.

ⓣ 020/7357 0057,
ⓦ www.elvergel.co.uk
ⓔ Borough. Mon–Fri
8.30am–3pm, Sat 8.30am–4pm.
Small, very busy weekday
café at the west end of Lant
Street, worth the quick stroll
from Borough tube. They do
all the usual lunchtime
takeaways, but you're really
here to sample the Latin
American specialities.

Konditor & Cook
Map 6, D4. 22 Cornwall Rd,
SE1 ⓣ 020/7261 0456.
ⓔ Waterloo. Mon–Fri
7.30am–6pm, Sat 8.30am–4pm.
A cut above your average
bakery, *Konditor & Cook* make
wonderful cakes and biscuits,
as well as offering a choice of
sandwiches and coffee and
tea. With only a few tables
inside, most folk take away.
There are branches elsewhere
on the south side of the
Thames at 10 Stoney St by
Borough Market, in the
Design Museum and in the
Young Vic Theatre.

Monmouth Café
Map 7, E8. 2 Park St, SE1
ⓣ 020/7645 3585. ⓔ London

Bridge. Mon–Fri 7.30am–6pm,
Sat 8.30am–4pm.
In the foodie heart of
Borough Market, the
Monmouth Café (sister of the
Covent Garden outlet) spills
out onto the pavement,
offering delicious croissants,
bread and jam, and excelling
in serving up single-estate
coffee.

KENSINGTON, CHELSEA AND NOTTING HILL

Books for Cooks
Map 2, F4. 4 Blenheim
Crescent, W11 ⓣ 020/7221
1992, ⓦ www.booksforcooks
.com ⓔ Ladbroke Grove or
Notting Hill Gate. Tues–Sat
10am–6pm.
Tiny café/restaurant within
London's top cookery
bookshop. Conditions are
cramped, but this is an
experience not to be missed.
Just wander in and have a
coffee while browsing, or get
there in time to grab a table
for the set-menu lunch. No
smoking.

Chelsea Kitchen

Map 3, E8. 98 King's Rd, SW3 ⓣ 020/7589 1330. ⊖ Sloane Square. Daily noon–11pm.
A useful, cheap café in Chelsea (now part of the no-nonsense *Stockpot* chain). Don't expect anything remarkable – just budget stomach-fillers in the form of steaks, spag bol and the like.

Daquise

Map 8, D8. 20 Thurloe St, SW7 ⓣ 020/7589 6117. ⊖ South Kensington. Daily 11.30am–11pm.
This cosy, old-fashioned Polish café right by the tube is something of a South Ken institution, serving Polish home cooking or simple coffee, tea and cakes depending on the time of day.

Gloriette

Map 8, G6. 128 Brompton Rd, SW7 ⓣ 020/7589 4635. ⊖ South Kensington or Knightsbridge. Mon–Fri 7am–8pm, Sat 8am–8pm, Sun 9am–6pm.
Long-established Viennese café that makes a perfect post-museum halt for coffee and outrageous cakes; also serves sandwiches, Wiener schnitzel, pasta dishes, goulash and fish and chips.

Lisboa Patisserie

Map 2, F4. 57 Golborne Rd, W10 ⓣ 020/8968 5242. ⊖ Ladbroke Grove. Daily 8am–8pm.
Authentic and friendly Portuguese *pastelaria*, with coffee and cakes, including the best custard tarts this side of Lisbon. The *Oporto*, at 62a Golborne Rd, is a good fallback if this place is full.

NORTH LONDON

Café Delancey

Map 2, H3. 3 Delancey St, NW1 ⓣ 020/7387 1985. ⊖ Camden Town or Mornington Crescent. Mon–Sat 9am–11.30pm, Sun 9am–10pm.
Still probably the best brasserie-style café in Camden, tucked away down a side road off Camden High Street – coffee, croissants, snacks and full meals.

NORTH LONDON

Café Mozart

Map 2, H2. 17 Swains Lane, N6 ☎ 020/8348 1384. Gospel Oak train station. Daily 9am–10pm.
Conveniently located on the southeast side of Hampstead Heath, the best thing about this café is the Viennese cake selection and the soothing classical music.

Louis Patisserie

Map 2, G2. 32 Heath St, NW3 ☎ 020/7435 9908.
⊖ Hampstead. Daily 7am–6pm.
Popular Hungarian tearoom in Hampstead village serving sticky cakes to a mix of Heath-bound hordes and elderly locals.

Marine Ices

Map 2, G3. 8 Haverstock Hill, NW3 ☎ 020/7482 9003.
⊖ Chalk Farm. Mon–Sat 10am–11pm, Sun 11am–10pm.
Situated halfway between Camden and Hampstead, this is a splendid and justly famous old-fashioned Italian ice-cream parlour; pizza and pasta are served in the adjacent restaurant.

GREENWICH

Pistachio's Café

See p.152, B3. 15 Nelson Rd, SE10 ☎ 020/8853 0602. Cutty Sark DLR, or Greenwich DLR and train station. Daily 10am–6pm.
Just about the only good sandwich café in the centre of Greenwich, serving excellent coffee, and with a small garden out back.

Tai Won Mein

See p.152, B2. 39 Greenwich Church St, SE10 ☎ 020/8858 1668. Cutty Sark DLR, or Greenwich DLR and train station. Daily 11.30am–11.30pm.
Good-quality fast-food noodle bar that gets very busy at weekends. Décor is functional and minimalist; choose between rice, soup or various fried noodles, all for under a fiver.

KEW AND RICHMOND

Hothouse Café

Map 2, D6. 9 Station

GREENWICH • KEW AND RICHMOND

Approach, Kew ⓣ 020/8332 1923. ⊖ Kew Gardens. Mon–Sat 8am–7pm, Sun 8.30am–6pm.

This smart, bright airy café is the best refuelling spot en route to or from Kew Gardens, with everything from croissants and sandwiches to a full breakfast fry-up.

Maison Blanc

Map 2, C7. 27b The Quadrant, Richmond ⓣ 020/8332 7041, ⓦ www.maisonblanc.co.uk ⊖ Richmond. Mon–Sat 8am–7pm, Sun 9am–6pm.

The cakes, croissants and bread at this French patisserie are absolutely fabulous, so either pop in on arrival in Richmond or take some away and eat them down by the river. Other branches in St John's Wood, Holland Park, Hampstead and Chelsea.

Restaurants

London is a great place in which to **eat out**. You can sample more or less any kind of cuisine here, and, wherever you come from, you should find something new and quite possibly unique. Home to some of the best Cantonese restaurants in the whole of Europe, London is also a noted centre for Indian and Bangladeshi food, and has numerous French, Greek, Italian, Japanese, Spanish and Thai restaurants; and within all these cuisines, you can choose anything from simple meals to gourmet spreads. Traditional and modern British food is available all over town, and some of the best venues are reviewed below.

Another bonus is that there are plenty of places to eat around the main tourist drags of the West End: **Soho** has long been renowned for its eclectic and fashionable restaurants – new eateries appear here every month – while **Chinatown**, on the other side of Shaftesbury Avenue, offers value-for-money eating right in the centre of town.

Many of the restaurants we've listed will be busy on most nights of the week, particularly on Thursday, Friday and Saturday, and you're best advised to **reserve a table** wherever you're headed. The majority of places take major credit cards, such as Visa, MasterCard and Amex; in the listings, we've simply noted those that don't.

As for **prices**, you can pay an awful lot for a meal in London and, if you're used to North American portions, you're not going to be particularly impressed by the volume in most places. In the listings, we've quoted the minimum you can get away with spending (assuming you don't tip and don't drink) and the amount you can expect to pay for a full blowout. For really cheap eats, see the previous chapter.

Service is discretionary at most restaurants, but many tend to take no chances, emblazoning their bills with reminders that "Service is NOT included", or even including a ten to fifteen percent service charge on the bill (which they have to announce on the menu, by law). Normally you should, of course, pay service – it's how most of the staff make up their wages – but make sure you check you're not paying twice.

ST JAMES'S, MAYFAIR AND MARYLEBONE

Fairuz

Map 3, E4. 3 Blandford St, W1 ⓣ 020/7486 8108. ⊖ Bond Street. Daily noon–11pm. Cash or cheque only. £15–35.
One of London's more accessible Middle Eastern restaurants, with an epic list of mezze, a selection of charcoal grills and one or two oven-baked dishes. Get here early and secure one of the nook-and-crannyish, tent-like tables.

La Galette

Map 3, E3. 56 Paddington St, W1 ⓣ 020/7935 1554, ⓦ www.lagalette.com ⊖ Baker Street. Daily 10am–11pm. £7–22.
Bright and modern pancake place, which even serves breakfast between 10am and 4pm. The hors d'oeuvres are very simple and very French, and the savoury and sweet buckwheat galettes are generous. Be sure to sample the range of Breton ciders, too.

Mandalay

Map 3, D4. 444 Edgware Rd,

W2 ⓣ 020/7258 3696, ⓦ www.bcity.com/mandalay ⊖ Edgware Road. Mon–Sat noon–2.30pm & 6–10.30pm. £6–16.

Small non-smoking restaurant that serves pure, freshly cooked and unexpurgated Burmese cuisine – a melange of Thai, Malaysian, a lot of Indian and a few things that are unique. The portions are huge, flavours hit the mark, the service friendly and the prices low.

The Providores

Map 3, E3. 109 Marylebone High St, W1 ⓣ 020/7935 6175, ⓦ www.theprovidores.co.uk ⊖ Baker Street or Bond Street. Mon–Fri noon–3pm & 6–11pm, Sat & Sun brunch noon–3pm & dinner 6–11pm. £7–22. Outstanding fusion restaurant run by amiable New Zealander and split into two: snacky tapas bar downstairs and full-on restaurant upstairs. At both the food, which may sound like an untidy assemblage on paper, is original and wholly satisfying.

Truc Vert

Map 3, E4. 42 North Audley St, W1 ⓣ 020/7491 9988. ⊖ Bond Street. Mon–Fri 7.30am–9pm, Sat noon–4pm, Sun 1–3pm. £12–40.

A very upmarket restaurant serving excellent modern British cuisine. The menu changes daily and begins early with breakfast; you can assemble your own cheese platter and pay by weight, and corkage is £4.50. There's also a takeaway deli where you can order quiche, salads, rotisserie chicken, patés, cakes and pastries.

SOHO AND CHINATOWN

- - - - - - - - - - - - - - - - - - - -

China City

Map 4, F7. White Bear Yard, WC2 ⓣ 020/7734 3388. ⊖ Leicester Square. Mon–Sat noon–midnight, Sun 11.30am–10.30pm. £10–25. Large restaurant tucked into a little courtyard off Lisle Street; fresh and bright, with *dim sum* that's up there with the best, service that's "Chinatown brusque", and prices that are eminently reasonable.

SOHO AND CHINATOWN

Chowki

Map 4, E7. 2–3 Denman St, W1 ⓣ 020/7439 1330. ⊖ Piccadilly Circus. Daily noon–midnight. £6–15.

Large, cheap Indian restaurant serving authentic home-style food in stylish surroundings. The menu changes every month in order to feature three different regions of India – the regional feast for around £10 is great value.

La Trouvaille

Map 4, D6. 12a Newburgh St, W1 ⓣ 020/7287 8488. ⊖ Oxford Circus. Mon–Sat noon–3pm & 6–10.30pm, Sat 6–10.30pm. £20–50.

Here, they understand the English need for really French Frenchness and, if you hanker after a "dangerously French" dish, try the tripe terrine.

Mildred's

Map 4, E6. 45 Lexington St, W1 ⓣ 020/7494 1634. ⊖ Oxford Circus or Piccadilly Circus. Mon–Sat noon–11pm. £8–15.

Long-established veggie restaurant, *Mildred's* has moved to this much larger, more modern location in a Soho backstreet, but the stir-fries, pasta dishes and burgers are as wholesome, delicious and inexpensive as ever.

Mr Kong

Map 4, F7. 21 Lisle St, WC2 ⓣ 020/7437 7923. ⊖ Leicester Square. Daily noon–3am. £8–22.

One of Chinatown's finest, with a chef/owner who pioneered many of the modern Cantonese dishes now on menus all over town. To sample the restaurant's more unusual dishes – order from the "Today's" and "Chef's Specials" menu, and don't miss the mussels in black-bean sauce. If you want to avoid the rather grungey basement, book ahead.

New World

Map 4, F6. 1 Gerrard Place, W1 ⓣ 020/7734 0396. ⊖ Leicester Square. Daily 11am–midnight. £6–18.

Another reasonable stab at an overblown Hong Kong dining palace – all red, gold and dragons. The best deal here is the lunchtime *dim sum*, served by indefatigable trolley-pushers.

Spiga

Map 4, E6. 84–86 Wardour St, W1 ⓣ 020/7734 3444.
⊖ Leicester Square. Mon, Tues & Sun noon–3pm & 6–11pm, Wed–Sat noon–3pm & 6pm–midnight. £14–30.
A pleasantly casual Italian affair, with a lively atmosphere, a serious wood-fired oven and a cool look about it. *Spiga* may have cut the prices, but they haven't cut corners – the tableware is the latest in Italian chic.

COVENT GARDEN

Belgo Centraal

Map 4, H6. 50 Earlham St, WC2 ⓣ 020/7813 2233,
ⓦ www.belgorestaurants.com
⊖ Covent Garden. Mon–Thurs noon–11.30pm, Fri & Sat noon–midnight, Sun noon–10.30pm. £6–30.
Massive metal-minimalist cavern off Neal Street, serving excellent kilo buckets of *moules marinières*, with *frites* and mayonnaise, a

bewildering array of Belgian beers to choose from, and waffles for dessert. The £6 lunchtime specials are a bargain for central London.

Café des Amis

Map 4, H6. 11–14 Hanover Place, off Long Acre, WC2 ⓣ 020/7379 3444,
ⓦ www.cafedesamis.co.uk
⊖ Covent Garden. Mon–Sat 11.30am–11.30pm. £12–35.
Modern, clean and bright French restaurant whose menu darts from influence to influence: salmon terrine with guacamole meets *confit* of halibut and pumpkin gnocchi. The pre- and post-theatre set menus (£12.50–15) are a real bargain.

J. Sheekey

Map 4, G7. 28–32 St Martin's Court, WC2 ⓣ 020/7240 2565,
ⓦ www. caprice-holdings.co.uk
⊖ Leicester Square. Mon–Sat noon–3pm & 5.30pm–midnight, Sun noon–3.30pm & 5.30pm–midnight. £18–70.
J. Sheekey's pedigree goes back to World War I, but the place has recently been totally

COVENT GARDEN

redesigned and refurbished. The menu is still focused on fish, but in addition to traditional fare such as grilled Dover sole you're just as likely to find modernist dishes like grilled cuttlefish with creamed *brandade*. The weekend lunches (costing around £15) are the best value.

BLOOMSBURY

Cigala

Map 3, I3. 54 Lamb's Conduit St, WC1 ☏ 020/7405 1717, ⓦ www.cigala.co.uk ⊖ Russell Square. Mon–Fri 12.30–2.30pm & 6–10.45pm, Sat & Sun noon–12.30pm. £18–60.
Simple dishes, strong flavours, fresh ingredients and real passion are evident at this Iberian restaurant. The menu changes daily and is market-led, which makes for excellent seasonal dishes. Try the rabbit, ox tongue, *patatas bravas* and poached meats, as well as old favourites like *cigalas na brasa*.

Ikkyu

Map 4, E2. 67a Tottenham Court Rd, W1 ☏ 020/7636 9280. ⊖ Goodge Street. Mon–Fri noon–2.30pm & 6–10.30pm, Sun 6–10.30pm. £10–40.
Busy, basic basement Japanese restaurant, good enough for a quick lunch or a more elaborate dinner. Either way, prices are infinitely more reasonable than elsewhere in the capital, and the food is tasty and authentic. Be warned, however: it's hard to find and, when you do, shockingly popular.

Rasa Samudra

Map 4, E4. 5 Charlotte St, W1 ☏ 020/7637 0222. ⊖ Goodge Street. Mon–Sat noon–3pm & 6–11pm. £18–40.
The food served at *Rasa Samudra* would be more at home in Bombay than in London – the sophisticated southern Indian fish dishes are a million miles from the usual London curry-house staples. *Rasa* also has an exclusively vegetarian branch at 6 Dering St, W1 ☏ 020/7629 1346 (⊖ Bond Street).

CLERKENWELL AND HOXTON

Cicada

Map 3, K3. 132 St John St, EC1 ℡ 020/7608 1550. ⊖ Farringdon. Mon–Fri noon–11pm, Sat 6–11pm. £15–35.

Part bar, part restaurant, *Cicada* is set back from the street and, when the weather's fine, it's a great place for eating alfresco. The unusual Thai-based menu allows you to mix and match from small, large and side dishes ranging from hot, lemony, fishy *tom yum* soup, to sweet ginger noodles, fresh clams, white miso or kinome leaves.

St John

Map 3, K3. 26 St John St, EC1 ℡ 020/7251 0848. ⊖ Farringdon. Mon–Fri noon–3pm & 6–11pm, Sat 6–11pm. £20–35.

A genuinely English restaurant, only a stone's throw from Smithfield meat market and specializing in offal. All those strange and unfashionable cuts of meat that were once commonplace in rural England – brains, bone marrow, meat from a cow's sternum – are on offer at this white-painted former smokehouse.

Viet Hoa Café

Map 3, N2. 72 Kingsland Rd, E2 ℡ 020/7729 8293. ⊖ Old Street. Daily noon–4pm & 5.30–11.30pm. £8–18.

Large, light and airy Vietnamese café with a golden parquet floor, situated not far from the Geffrye Museum in Hoxton/Shoreditch, and serving splendid "meals in a bowl" – soups and noodle dishes with everything from spring rolls to tofu. Be sure to try the *pho* soup, a Vietnamese staple that's eaten at any and every meal.

CITY AND EAST END

Café Spice Namaste

Map 7, M5. 16 Prescot St, E1 ℡ 020/7488 9242, ⓦ www.cafespice.org ⊖ Aldgate East or Tower Hill. Mon–Fri noon–3pm &

6.15–10.30pm, Sat
6.15–10.30pm. £20–50.

Very popular Indian on the fringe of the City that is definitely not your average curry house. Parsee delicacies rub shoulders with dishes from Goa, Hyderabad and Kashmir, and the tandoori specialities are awesome. Be sure to check out the speciality menu, which changes weekly.

New Tayyab

Map 2, J4. 83 Fieldgate St, E1
Ⓣ 020/7247 9543,
Ⓦ www.tayyabs.co.uk
Ⓔ Aldgate East or Whitechapel. Daily 5pm–midnight. Cash or cheque only. £4–15.

Opened in 1974, the *Tayyab* has recently been converted into a smart, designer restaurant. Miraculously, the food remains straightforward Pakistani fare: good, freshly cooked and served without pretension. Prices have remained low, booking is essential and service is speedy and slick – not a place to um and ah over the menu.

1 Lombard Street

Map 7, F4. 1 Lombard St, EC3
Ⓣ 020/7929 6611,
Ⓦ www.1lombardstreet.com
Ⓔ Bank. Mon–Fri 11.30am–3pm & 6–10pm. £25–65.

This is a brasserie in the City, of the City, by the City and for the City. A large but straightforward spread of dishes – salads, soups, pasta, fish, seafood, meat puddings – deliver on pretty much every front, and the buzzy circular bar sits under the suitably imposing glass dome of this former banking hall.

LAMBETH AND SOUTHWARK

- - - - - - - - - - - - - - - -

Fina Estampa

Map 7, I9. 150 Tooley St, SE1
Ⓣ 020/7403 1342. Ⓔ London Bridge. Mon–Fri noon–2.30pm & 6.30–10.30pm, Sat 6.30–10.30pm. £15–30.

This may be London's only Peruvian restaurant, but it also happens to be the very best, bringing a little of downtown Lima to London Bridge. The menu is traditional Peruvian, with a big emphasis on seafood. Meat options include *Lomo saltado*, strips of rump steak stir-fried with red onions and tomatoes, and *carapulcra*, a spicy mix of dried potatoes, pork, chicken and cassava.

RSJ

Map 6, D3. 13a Coin St, SE1
ⓣ 020/7928 4554,
ⓦ www.rsj.uk.com
ⓔ Waterloo. Mon–Fri noon–2.30pm & 5.30–11pm, Sat 5.30–11pm. £19–55.
Those who know what an RSJ is won't be disappointed (there's one holding up the first floor), nor will those in search of high-standard Anglo-French cooking. Its position near the South Bank makes it an excellent spot for a meal after or before a show or concert. The set meals for around £16–17 are particularly popular.

Tentazione

Map 2, J5. 2 Mill St, SE1
ⓣ 020/7237 1100,
ⓦ www.tentazione.co.uk
ⓔ Bermondsey or Tower Hill.

Mon–Fri noon–2.30pm & 7–10.45pm, Sat 7–10.45pm. £10–26.
Small, busy Italian restaurant round the corner from the Design Museum, serving high-quality peasant fare with strong, rich flavours; try the splendid four-course Regional Menu (£26), or the daily-changing set lunch (£15–19).

KENSINGTON AND CHELSEA

Bibendum Oyster House

Map 8, F8. Michelin House, 81 Fulham Rd, SW3 ⓣ 020/7589 1480, ⓦ www.bibendum.co.uk
ⓔ South Kensington. Mon–Sat noon–10.30pm, Sun noon–10pm £12–30.
A glorious tiled affair built in 1911, this former garage is the best place to eat shellfish in London. There are three types of rock oysters, but if you're really hungry, try the "Plateau de Fruits de Mer", which also has crab, clams, langoustine, prawns, shrimps, whelks and winkles.

KENSINGTON AND CHELSEA

Boisdale

Map 3, F7. 15 Ecclestone St, SW1 ⓣ 020/7730 6922.
ⴲ Victoria. Mon–Fri noon–1am, Sat 7.30pm–1am. £15–50.
Owned by Ranald MacDonald, son of the Chief of Clanranald, this is a very Scottish place, strong on hospitality, and with a befuddlingly large range of rare malt whiskies. Fresh Scottish produce rules wherever possible, including MacSween's haggis (sheep's innards and oatmeal), venison and salmon.

Hunan

Map 3, E8. 51 Pimlico Rd, SW1 ⓣ 020/7730 5712.
ⴲ Sloane Square. Mon–Sat noon–2.30pm & 6–11.30pm. £28–50.
Probably England's only restaurant serving Hunan food, a relative of Sichuan cuisine, with the same spicy kick to most dishes and a fair wallop of pepper in those that aren't actively riddled with chillis. Most people opt for the £28 "Hunan's special leave-it-to-us feast", a multi-course extravaganza which

lets the maître d', Mr Peng, show what he can do.

NOTTING HILL

Al Waha

Map 3, A4. 75 Westbourne Grove, W2 ⓣ 020/7229 0806.
ⴲ Queensway or Bayswater. Daily noon–midnight. £10–35.
Arguably London's best Lebanese restaurant; mezze-obsessed, but also painstaking in its preparation of the main-course dishes, where spanking fresh and accurately cooked grills predominate.

Galicia

Map 2, F4. 323 Portobello Rd, W10 ⓣ 020/8969 3539.
ⴲ Ladbroke Grove or Westbourne Park. Tues–Sat noon–3pm & 7–11.30pm, Sun noon–3pm & 7–10.30pm. £14–35.
Galicia is a pleasant Spanish restaurant without pretension. The tapas at the bar are straightforward and good, so it's no surprise that quite a lot of customers never make it as far as the grilled meat and fish main courses.

The Mandola

Map 3, A4. 139 Westbourne Grove, W11 ☎ 020/7229 4734, ⓦ www.mandolacafe.co.uk ⊖ Notting Hill Gate. Mon 6–11pm, Tues–Sun noon–11pm. £12–22.

Small, seriously informal, unlicensed neighbourhood restaurant serving strikingly delicious "urban Sudanese" food at sensible prices. The place is so popular they've had to institute two sittings a night, yet the staff remain supremely laid-back. Be sure to check out the Sudanese spiced coffee at the end.

Rodizio Rico

Map 3, A4. 111 Westbourne Grove, W11 ☎ 020/7792 4035. ⊖ Notting Hill Gate or Queensway. Mon–Fri 6.30pm–midnight, Sat 12.30–4.30pm & 6.30pm–midnight, Sun 1–11pm. £18–25.

Eat as much as you like for around £18 a head at this Brazilian *churrascaria*. Carvers come round – "*rodizio*" means "rotating" – and lop off chunks of freshly grilled smoky meats from whichever skewers they are holding, while you prime your plate from the salad bar and hot buffet.

NORTH LONDON

Almeida

Map 2, I3. Almeida St, N1 ☎ 020/7354 4777, ⓦ www.conran-restaurants .co.uk ⊖ Angel or Highbury & Islington. Mon–Sat noon–2.30pm & 6–11pm, Sun noon–3pm & 6–10pm. £18–80.

A Conran restaurant, opposite the theatre of the same name, that is a distillation of all that is good about a wonderful, old-fashioned, gently familiar kind of French cooking and eating. Overdose on nostalgia with *soupe à l'oignon, escargots, jambon cru, coq au vin, steack au poivre, confit de canard…*

Cucina

Map 2, G3. 45a South End Rd, NW3 ☎ 020/7435 7814. ⊖ Belsize Park. Mon–Thurs noon–2.30pm & 7–10.30pm, Fri & Sat noon–2.30pm & 7–11pm, Sun noon–3pm. £18–40.

Brightly painted, wooden-floored, roof-lit, first-floor restaurant that's very contemporary, very fashionable and very Hampstead. The Modern British menu changes every two weeks or so, and darts about a bit from cuisine to cuisine, but wherever you alight each dish is well presented.

The Gate 2

Map 2, G3. 72 Belsize Lane, NW3 ⓣ 020/7435 7733, ⓦ www.gateveg.co.uk

 ⊖ Belsize Park. Mon & Tues 6–11pm, Wed–Sun noon–3pm & 6–11pm. £15–35.

There are ghetto-like vegetarian restaurants and then there are restaurants in a completely different class that, for one reason or another, happen not to use meat or fish in their cooking. The modern, minimalist *Gate 2* is one of the latter, serving excellent and original dishes with intense and satisfying tastes and textures, ranging from wild mushroom terrine to root vegetable *tajine*.

Jin Kichi

Map 2, G2. 73 Heath St, NW3 ⓣ 020/7794 6158.

 ⊖ Hampstead. Tues–Fri 6–11pm, Sat 12.30–2pm & 6–11pm, Sun 12.30–2pm & 6–10pm. £12–30.

Eschewing the slick minimalism and sushi-led cuisine of most Japanese restaurants, *Jin Kichi* is cramped, rather shabby, very busy (so book ahead) and specializes in grilled skewers of meat.

Manna

Map 2, G3. 4 Erskine Rd, NW3 ⓣ 020/7722 8028, ⓦ www.manna-veg.com

 ⊖ Chalk Farm. Mon–Fri 6.30–11pm, Sat & Sun 12.30–3pm. £15–45.

Old-fashioned, casual vegetarian restaurant with 1970s décor, serving large portions of very good veggie food. Don't pitch up here in a hurry or without a serious appetite.

CHISWICK TO RICHMOND

Chez Lindsay

Map 2, C7. 11 Hill Rise, Richmond, Surrey Ⓣ 020/8948 7473. ⊖ Richmond. Mon–Sat 11am–11pm, Sun noon–10pm. £7–27.

Small, bright, authentic Breton creperie, with a loyal local following, and fixed-price lunchtime menus for under £10. Choose between *galettes*, crepes or more formal French main courses, including lots of fresh fish and shellfish, and wash it all down with Breton cider in traditional earthenware *bolées*.

Fish Hoek

Map 2, E5. 6–8 Elliot St, W4 Ⓣ 020/8742 3374. ⊖ Turnham Green. Tues–Sat noon–2.30pm & 6.30–11pm. £16–45.

Light and airy South African fish restaurant in leafy Chiswick with an impressive menu that changes daily: 25 or so fish to choose from, and most dishes are available in half- or full portions.

The Gate

Map 2, F5. 51 Queen Caroline St, W4 Ⓣ 020/8748 6932, Ⓦ www.gateveg.co.uk ⊖ Hammersmith. Mon–Fri noon–2.45pm & 6–10.45pm, Sat 6–11pm. £16–35.

Tucked away behind the Hammersmith Apollo, this is a vegetarian restaurant that eschews healthy, wholefood eating. It's as rich, colourful, calorific and naughty as anywhere in town – just without meat.

Pubs and bars

L ondon's drinking establishments run the whole gamut from traditional old English alehouses to funky modern bars with resident DJs catering to a pre-club crowd. **Pubs** are one of England's most enduring social institutions, and have outlived the church and marketplace as the focal points of communities, with London's fringe theatre, alternative-comedy and live-music scenes still largely pub-based. At their best, pubs can be as welcoming as their full name, "public house", suggests, offering a fine range of drinks and filling food. At their worst, they're dismal rooms with surly bar staff and rotten snacks. One thing you can be sure of, however, is that most pubs and bars remain smoke-filled places where drinking alcohol is the prime activity.

London's great period of pub building took place in the Victorian era, to which many pubs still pay homage; genuine Victorian interiors, however, are increasingly difficult to find, as indeed are genuinely individual pubs. **Chain pubs** can now be found all over the capital: branches of All Bar One, Pitcher & Piano and Slug & Lettuce are the most obvious, as they all share the chain name, whereas Fuller's, Nicholson and J.D. Wetherspoon pubs and the Firkin chain do at least vary theirs.

Pub food, on the whole, is a lunchtime affair, although

"gastropubs", which put more effort into (and charge a lot more for) their cooking, tend to offer meals in the evening, too. The traditional image of London pub food is justifiably dire – a pseudo "ploughman's lunch" of bread and cheese, or a murky-looking pie and chips – but the last couple of decades have seen plenty of improvements. You can get a palatable lunchtime meal at many of the pubs listed in this chapter, and at a few of them you're looking at cooking worthy of high restaurant-standard praise.

Standard pub opening hours are Mon–Sat 11am–11pm, Sun noon–10.30pm, though the licensing laws are set to change. Our listings only specify the exceptions.

Though pubs may be constantly changing hands (and names), the quickest turnover is in **bars**, which go in and out of fashion with incredible speed. These are very different places to your average pub, catering to a somewhat cliquey, often youngish crowd, with designer interiors and drinks, and they also tend to be more expensive. We've included a fair few **club-bars**, places which cater for a clubby crowd, and often have resident DJs, along with late opening hours.

For gay and lesbian pubs and bars, see Chapter 20.

England's **licensing laws** are likely to have changed by the time you read this, as after more than a century of draconian restrictions, the government has finally committed itself to liberalizing English opening hours. This should allow many more pubs and bars to stay open way beyond the standard 11pm last orders, so the times listed below may well have changed significantly since this book went to press.

ENGLISH BEER

Bitter, the classic English beer, is an uncarbonated and dark-ish beverage that should be pumped by hand from the cellar and served at room temperature. Some of the beer you'll see touted as good English ale is nothing of the sort (if the stuff comes out of an electric pump, it isn't the real thing), but these days even the big breweries distribute some very good brews – Directors, for example, produced by Courage, is a very classy strong bitter.

Smaller brewers whose beers are available across London include Young's and Fuller's – the two main London breweries – and Adnams, Greene King, Flowers and Samuel Smith's. Additionally, regional concoctions from other independent breweries are often available at free houses (pubs not tied to one particular brewery). London also has a number of brew-pubs, which produce their own peculiar brand on the premises, the most famous being the one-joke Firkin chain, and one of the more recent being the Freedom Brewing Company.

Guinness, a very dark, creamy Irish stout, is also on sale virtually everywhere, and is an exception to the high-minded objection to electrically pumped beers.

WHITEHALL AND WESTMINSTER

- - - - - - - - - - - - - - - - - -

Albert

Map 3, G7. 52 Victoria St, SW1 ☏ 020/7222 5577. ⊖ St James's Park or Victoria. Roomy High Victorian pub, situated halfway between Parliament Square and Victoria, with big bay windows and glass partitions; good bar food, too, and an excellent carvery upstairs.

ICA Bar

Map 4, F10. 94 The Mall, SW1 ☏ 020/7930 3647, Ⓦ www.ica.org.uk ⊖ Piccadilly

Circus or Charing Cross. Mon noon–11pm, Tues–Sat noon–1am, Sun noon–10.30pm. You have to be a member (or be visiting an exhibition or cinema/theatre/talk event) to drink here – but anyone can join on the door (Mon–Fri £1.50, Sat & Sun £2.50). It's a cool drinking venue, with a noir dress code observed by the arty crowd and staff. Beware the weekend DJ nights.

Paviour's Arms
Map 3, H7. 75 Page St, SW1 ⓣ 020/7834 2150. ⊖ Pimlico, St James's Park or Westminster. Mon–Fri only.
A unique survivor, this large, stylish 1930s Art Deco pub, in the backstreets close to the Tate Gallery, has much of its original décor intact; you can also get decent Thai food with your beer. Be warned, though: the place is heaving with civil servants and locals at lunchtime, but is much, *much* quieter in the evenings.

ST JAMES'S, MAYFAIR AND MARYLEBONE

Dover Castle
Map 3, F3. 43 Weymouth Mews, W1 ⓣ 020/7580 4412. ⊖ Regent's Park. Mon–Fri 11.30am–11pm, Sat noon–11pm.
A really nice, quiet, traditional boozer hidden away in a Marylebone mews off Devonshire Street Restful, racing-green upholstery, dark wood, a nicotine-stained lincrusta ceiling and cheap Sam Smith's beer on tap.

O'Conor Don
Map 3, F4. 88 Marylebone Lane, W1 ⓣ 020/7935 9311. ⊖ Bond Street. Mon–Fri only.
A stripped-bare, stout-loving pub that's a cut above the average, with excellent Guinness, a pleasantly measured pace and Irish food on offer.

Red Lion
Map 4, E10. 2 Duke of York St, SW1 ⓣ 020/7321 0782.

ST JAMES'S, MAYFAIR AND MARYLEBONE

Piccadilly Circus. Mon–Sat 11.30am–11pm.

Popular little gin palace that has preserved its classic Victorian décor of dark wood and mirrors. The clientele are more often than not besuited, as you'd expect in St James's, and the malt whisky selection is impressive.

Ye Grapes

Map 4, B10. 16 Shepherd Market, W1 (no phone). Green Park or Hyde Park Corner.

Busy Victorian free house, with a good selection of real ales (including Young's and Fuller's) and an open fire – a great local in the heart of Mayfair.

SOHO

Argyll Arms

Map 4, C5. 18 Argyll St, W1 020/7734 6117. Oxford Circus. Mon–Sat 11am–11pm, Sun noon–9pm.

A stone's throw from Oxford Circus, this is a serious find: a great Victorian pub, which has preserved many of its

original features and serves good real ales.

Dog & Duck

Map 4, F5. 18 Bateman St, W1 020/7494 0697. Tottenham Court Road. Mon–Fri noon–11pm, Sat 5–11pm, Sun 6–10.30pm.

Tiny and very ancient Soho pub that retains much of its old character, a beautiful set of Victorian tiles and mosaics, a good range of real ales and a loyal clientele that often includes jazz musicians from nearby *Ronnie Scott's* club.

Dog House

Map 4, E6. 187 Wardour St, W1 020/7434 2118, www.doghouse.co.uk Oxford Circus or Piccadilly Circus. Mon–Fri 5–11pm, Sat 6–11pm.

Colourful basement DJ bar, popular for hip-hop, funk and acid-jazz, which draws a friendly mix of office types, students and film runners.

French House

Map 4, F6. 49 Dean St, W1 020/7437 2799. Leicester Square. Mon–Sat noon–11pm,

Sun noon–10.30pm.

This tiny French pub has been a Soho institution since before World War I, and boasts Free French and literary associations galore. Don't expect to get a seat, or order a pint (they only serve half pints and no real ale); instead, stand at the bar and order some wine.

Lab

Map 4, F6. 12 Old Compton St, W1 ⓣ 020/7437 7820, ⓦ www.lab-bar.co.uk ⊖ Tottenham Court Road. Mon–Sat 4pm–midnight, Sun 4–10.30pm.

Chic, multicoloured former strip joint that stirs up some of the best cocktails in town to its style-conscious crowd of beautiful Soho-ites.

Two Floors

Map 4, D6. 3 Kingly St, W1 ⓣ 020/7439 1007. ⊖ Oxford Circus or Piccadilly Circus. Mon–Sat 11am–11pm.

Relaxed, modern Soho bar, laid out, unsurprisingly, on two floors, attracting a mixed media crowd, and pumping out drum'n'bass in the evenings – quite a find in a part of Soho short of decent drinking holes.

COVENT GARDEN

- - - - - - - - - - - - - - - - - - -

Denim

Map 4, G6. 4a Upper St Martin's Lane, WC2 ⓣ 020/7497 0376. ⊖ Leicester Square. Mon–Sat 5pm–2am, Sun 5–11.30pm.

Very style-conscious bar on the Soho/Covent Garden border. The retro orange and purple décor, complete with fish tanks and funky soundtrack goes down a treat with the young after-work punters, who don't seem to flinch at the outrageous bar prices. Thurs–Sat £10 entry after 9pm.

Detroit

Map 4, G6. 35 Earlham St, WC2 ⓣ 020/7240 2662, ⓦ www.detroit-bar.com ⊖ Covent Garden. Mon–Sat 5pm–midnight.

Cavernous underground venue with an open-plan bar area, secluded, Gaudíesque booths and a huge range of

COVENT GARDEN

spirits. DJs take over at the weekends, with underground house on Saturdays.

Freedom Brewing Company

Map 4, H5. 41 Earlham St, WC2 ⓣ 020/7240 0606, ⓦ www.freedombrewery.com ⊖ Covent Garden.

Busy, brick-vaulted basement brewery bar with wrought-iron pillars, lots of brushed steel and pricey, strong brews, made on the premises – in particular, there's a very fine organic honey wheat beer.

Lamb & Flag

Map 4, H7. 33 Rose St, WC2 ⓣ 020/7497 9504. ⊖ Leicester Square or Covent Garden. Busy, tiny and highly atmospheric pub, well and truly hidden away down an alley between Garrick Street and Floral Street, where John Dryden was attacked in 1679 after scurrilous verses had been written about one of Charles II's mistresses (by someone else, as it turned out).

Punch & Judy

Map 4, H7. 40 The Market, WC2 ⓣ 020/7379 0923. ⊖ Covent Garden.

Horribly mobbed and loud, but this Covent Garden Market pub does boast an unbeatable location with a very popular balcony overlooking the Piazza – and a stone-flagged cellar.

Salisbury

Map 4, G7. 90 St Martin's Lane, WC2 ⓣ 020/7836 5863. ⊖ Leicester Square.

Easily one of the most beautifully preserved Victorian pubs in the capital – and certainly the most central – with cut, etched and engraved windows, bronze figures, red-velvet seating and a fine lincrusta ceiling.

BLOOMSBURY AND FITZROVIA

The Hope

Map 4, E2. 15 Tottenham St, W1 ⓣ 020/7637 0896. ⊖ Goodge Street.

Small pub west of Tottenham Court Road, chiefly

remarkable for its superb meat and veggie sausages, supplied by Simply Sausages, served with beans and mash, and washed down with real ales.

Jerusalem

Map 4, E4. 33–34 Rathbone Place, W1 ⓣ 020/7255 1120. ⊖ Tottenham Court Road. Mon noon–11pm, Tue & Wed noon–midnight, Thu & Fri noon–1am, Sat 7pm-1am.
The décor at the DJ-pub/bar is all chandeliers and velvet drapes, the music is especially good on Thursday nights, though it does attract a large proportion of office workers.

Lamb

Map 3, I3. 94 Lamb's Conduit St, WC1 ⓣ 020/7405 0713. ⊖ Russell Square.
Pleasant, traditional pub with a loyal clientele and a marvellously well-preserved Victorian interior of mirrors, leather seats, and old wood and "snob" screens.

Museum Tavern

Map 3, H3. 49 Great Russell St, WC1 ⓣ 020/7242 8987. ⊖ Tottenham Court Road or Russell Square.
Large and surprisingly characterful old pub conveniently situated opposite the main entrance to the British Museum. The pub (though not the name) predates the BM, serves real ales and has the honour of being an erstwhile drinking hole of Karl Marx.

The Social

Map 4, D4. 5 Little Portland St, W1 ⓣ 020/7636 4992, ⓦ www.thesocial.com ⊖ Oxford Circus. Mon–Fri noon–midnight, Sat 1pm–midnight.
Bacchanalian, industrial club-bar with great DJs playing everything from rock to rap, a truly hedonistic–cum-alcoholic crowd and the ultimate snacks – beans on toast and cosy soup in a mug – for when you get an attack of the munchies. Fab music on the upstairs jukebox, too.

CLERKENWELL

Café Kick

Map 3, J2. 43 Exmouth

Market, EC1 ☏ 020/7837 8077.
⊖ Farringdon or Angel.
Mon–Sat noon–11pm.
Stylish take on a smoky, local French-style café/bar in the heart of fashionable Exmouth Market, with three busy table-football games to complete the retro theme.

Clerkenwell House
Map 3, K3. 23–27 Hatton Wall, EC1 ☏ 020/7404 1113.
⊖ Farringdon. Mon–Fri noon–11pm, Sat 5–11pm, Sun 1–5pm.
Classic Clerkenwell bar with retro 1970s furniture including some wickedly comfy semicircular sofas. The Med food is good, if a tad pricey, and there are four American pool tables in the basement bar.

Eagle
Map 3, J3. 159 Farringdon Rd, EC1 ☏ 020/7837 1353.
⊖ Farringdon. Mon–Sat noon–11pm, Sun noon–5pm.
The first (and still one of the best) of London's pubs to go foody, this place is heaving and hearty at lunch and dinnertimes, as *Guardian* and *Observer* journos tuck into the excellent Mediterranean dishes, but you should be able to find a seat at other times.

Fox & Anchor
Map 3, K3. 115 Charterhouse St, EC1 ☏ 020/7253 5075.
⊖ Farringdon or Barbican. Mon–Fri 7am–11pm.
A handsome Smithfield market pub, complete with original Art Deco tiling, but most famous for its early opening hours and huge fried breakfasts, enjoyed by a strange mix of market workers and clubbers.

Jerusalem Tavern
Map 3, K3. 55 Britton St, EC1 ☏ 020/7490 4281.
⊖ Farringdon. Mon–Fri 11am–11pm.
Cosy little converted Georgian parlour, stripped bare and slightly "distressed", serving tasty food at lunchtimes, along with an excellent range of draught beers from St Peter's Brewery in Suffolk.

Lifthouse
Map 3, K3. 85 Charterhouse St, EC1 ☏ 020/7251 8787,

Ⓦ www.lifthouse.co.uk

⊖ Farringdon. Mon, Tues & Sun noon–midnight, Wed & Thurs noon–1am, Fri & Sat noon–2.30am.

Next door to the club *Fabric*, this three-floored New-York-style DJ-bar/restaurant houses a cocktail bar and club space upstairs. In the week it's home to office workers and young things in equal measure, but gets especially lively on Friday and Saturday nights.

HOXTON

Bricklayer's Arms
Map 3, N2. 63 Charlotte Rd, EC2 Ⓣ 020/7739 5245. ⊖ Old Street. Mon–Fri 11am–11pm, Sat noon–11pm.

One of the few real pubs (as opposed to DJ bars) in Hoxton: scruffy, slightly boho, serving Thai food, and very, very popular with the new, young residents.

Bridge & Tunnel
Map 3, N2. 4 Calvert Ave, E2 Ⓣ 020/7729 6533, Ⓦ www.nuphonic.co.uk ⊖ Old Street. Mon–Fri & Sun

noon–midnight, Sat 6pm–midnight.

This is the pre-club bar for dance music. For a few pounds (free before 9pm) you can catch top DJs playing varied, beguiling cross-sections of their favourite tunes. There's a 150-capacity club downstairs (open until 2am), complete with state-of-the-art sound system, while upstairs there's great food and choice snacks at the swish, metallic bar.

Dragon
Map 3, M2. 5 Leonard St, EC2 Ⓣ 020/7490 7110. ⊖ Old Street.

Trendy two-floored place, with bare-brick walls and crumbling leather sofas, that attracts a camouflage-trouser-wearing mix of locals and pre-clubbers at weekends. The DJ plays whatever takes his fancy, which normally includes house, breakbeat and the odd hip-hop classic.

Shoreditch Electricity Showrooms
Map 3, N2. 39a Hoxton Square, N1 Ⓣ 020/7739 6934.

HOXTON

⊖ Old Street.

One of the many trendy haunts in and around Hoxton Square, the two-floored *Electricity Showrooms* (yes, it was converted) is better value than most. Free to enter, the upstairs bar mixes kitsch artwork with digital boards flashing ironic weather and text messages, while the intimate club downstairs hosts weekend parties. Good Modern European food is available too, although the choice is limited.

THE CITY: FLEET STREET TO ST PAUL'S

The Black Friar

Map 5, G5. 174 Queen Victoria St, EC4 ⓣ 020/7236 5474. ⊖ Blackfriars. Mon–Fri 11.30am–11pm.

A gorgeous, utterly original pub, with Art Nouveau marble friezes of boozy monks, cautionary homilies, and a wonderful, highly decorated alcove – all original fittings, dating back to 1905.

Old Bank of England

Map 5, E4. 194 Fleet St, EC4 ⓣ 020/7430 2255. ⊖ Temple or Chancery Lane. Mon–Fri 11am–11pm.

Not the actual Bank of England, but the former Law Courts' branch, this imposing High Victorian banking hall is now a magnificently opulent Fuller's pub.

Old Cheshire Cheese

Map 5, E4. Wine Office Court, 145 Fleet St, EC4 ⓣ 020/7353 6170. ⊖ Temple or Blackfriars. Mon–Fri 11.30am–11pm, Sat noon–3pm & 6–11pm, Sun noon–2.30pm.

A famous seventeenth-century watering hole, where Dickens and countless other journos once supped. The tiny, snug, dark-panelled front bar has a real fire and bags of atmosphere.

THE CITY: BANK TO BISHOPSGATE

Counting House

Map 7, G4. 50 Cornhill St, EC3 ⓣ 020/7283 7123. ⊖ Bank. Mon–Fri 11am–11pm.

Another ornate bank conversion, with fantastic high ceilings, a glass dome, chandeliers and a central oval bar. Naturally enough, given the location, it's wall-to-wall suits, but the space is great. The beer and food are Fuller's usual fare.

Hamilton Hall

Map 7, I1. Liverpool Street Station, EC2 ⓣ 020/7247 3579. ⊖ Liverpool Street.
Cavernous, gilded former ballroom of the *Great Eastern* hotel, adorned with neo-Baroque nudes and chandeliers. Packed out with City commuters tanking up before the train home, but an awesome place nonetheless.

Lamb

Map 7, H4. Leadenhall Market, EC3 ⓣ 020/7626 2454. ⊖ Monument or Bank. Mon–Fri 11am–9pm.
A great Young's pub right in the middle of the beautiful Leadenhall Market, serving pricey but excellent hot salt-beef sandwiches at lunchtime.

EAST END AND DOCKLANDS

Dickens Inn

Map 7, M7. St Katharine's Way, E1 ⓣ 020/7488 2208. ⊖ Tower Hill or Tower Gateway DLR.
Eighteenth-century timber-framed warehouse transported on wheels from its original site, and then much altered. Still, it's a remarkable building, with a great view, but very firmly on the tourist trail.

The Gun

Map 2, L5. 27 Cold Harbour, E14 ⓣ 020/7987 1692. South Quay or Blackwall DLR, or ⊖ Canary Wharf.
Inexpensive old dockers' pub with lots of maritime memorabilia, and – the chief attraction – an unrivalled view of the Millennium Dome from its riverside terrace.

Prospect of Whitby

Map 2, K4. 57 Wapping Wall, E1 ⓣ 020/7481 1095. ⊖ Wapping. Mon–Sat 11.30am–11pm, Sun noon–10.30pm.

EAST END AND DOCKLANDS

233

London's most famous riverside pub has been here since 1520, and, with a flagstone floor, a cobbled courtyard and great views, it's still got bags of character and atmosphere. It's no secret, however, so expect to share the riverside terrace and balcony with others.

Town of Ramsgate

Map 2, K4. 62 Wapping High St, E1 ⊕ 020/7264 0001. ⊖ Wapping. Mon–Sat noon–11pm, Sun noon–10.30pm.

Dark, narrow medieval pub located by Wapping Old Stairs, which once led down to Execution Dock. Captain Blood was discovered here with the crown jewels under his cloak, and Admiral Bligh and Fletcher Christian were regular drinking partners in pre-mutiny days.

LAMBETH AND SOUTHWARK

Anchor Bankside

Map 7, C7. 34 Park St, SE1 ⊕ 020/7407 1577. ⊖ London Bridge, Southwark or Blackfriars.

While the rest of Bankside has changed almost beyond recognition, this pub, near the Tate Modern, still looks much as it did when first built in 1770 (on the inside, at least). Probably the best – and most mobbed – spot for alfresco drinking by the river.

George Inn

Map 7, E9. 77 Borough High St, SE1 ⊕ 020/7407 2056. ⊖ Borough or London Bridge.

Tucked away off Borough High Street, this is London's only surviving coaching inn, with a rich historical pedigree stretching back to the seventeenth century, and now owned by the National Trust. The food isn't great, service can be slow, but it serves a good range of real ales.

Market Porter

Map 7, E9. 9 Stoney St, SE1 ⊕ 020/7407 2495. ⊖ London Bridge. Mon–Sat 6–8.30am & 11am–11pm, Sun noon–10.30pm.

Handsome semicircular pub with early opening hours for

workers at the nearby Borough Market, and a seriously huge range of real ales.

KENSINGTON, CHELSEA AND NOTTING HILL

Bed Bar

Map 2, F4. 310 Portobello Rd, W10 ☎ 020/8969 4500.
⊖ Ladbroke Grove. Mon–Sat noon–11pm, Sun noon–10.30pm.

Don't let the Moroccan-theme, low-level lighting and lush, cushioned seating deceive you. This is no chill-out haven: locals cram at the bar or stand on the sofas, arms aloft while the DJs spin funky house and Latin-tinged beats.

Bunch of Grapes

Map 8, G6. 207 Brompton Rd, SW3 ☎ 020/7589 4944.
⊖ South Kensington.

This popular High Victorian pub, complete with snob screens, is the perfect place for a post-V&A (or post-Harrods) pint, pie and chips.

Cherry Jam

Map 2, F4. 52 Porchester Rd, W2 ☎ 020/7727 9950,
ⓦ www.cherryjam.net
⊖ Royal Oak. Mon–Sat 6pm–2am, Sun 4pm–midnight.

Owned by Ben Watt (house DJ and half of pop group Everything But The Girl), this smart intimate basement spot mixes a decadent cocktail bar with top-end West London DJs from the broken beat and deep house scenes.

The Cow

Map 3 A4. 89 Westbourne Park Rd, W2 ☎ 020/7221 5400.
⊖ Westbourne Park or Royal Oak. Mon–Sat noon–11pm, Sun noon–10.30pm.

Sort of vaguely Irish-themed pub owned by Tom Conran, son of gastro-magnate Terence, which pulls in the beautiful W11 types thanks to its spectacular seafoody food, including a daily supply of fresh oysters, and excellent Guinness.

Front Page

Map 3, C9. 35 Old Church St, SW3 ☎ 020/7352 2908.

KENSINGTON, CHELSEA AND NOTTING HILL

⊖ Sloane Square, then any bus down the King's Road. Tucked away in the centre of villagey, boho Chelsea and infinitely preferable to anything on offer on the King's Road, the *Front Page* is part of a posh chain, but it's small and snug, and serves good Mediterranean food.

Market Bar
Map 2, F4. 240a Portobello Rd, W11 ⊕ 020/7229 6472. ⊖ Ladbroke Grove. Mon–Sat noon–11pm, Sun noon–10.30pm.
Self-consciously bohemian pub divided by gilded mirrors and ruched curtains and scattered with weird *objets* – all very Portobello Road. Occasional live music and DJs.

Prince Bonaparte
Map 3, A4. 80 Chepstow Rd, W2 ⊕ 020/7313 9491. ⊖ Notting Hill Gate or Royal Oak. Mon–Sat noon–11pm, Sun noon–10.30pm.
Very popular pared-down, trendy, minimalist pub, with acres of space for sitting and supping while enjoying the bar snacks or the excellent Brit or Med food in the restaurant area.

ST JOHN'S WOOD AND MAIDA VALE

Prince Alfred
Map 3, B3. 5a Formosa St, W9 ⊕ 020/7286 3287. ⊖ Warwick Avenue.
A fantastic period-piece Victorian pub with all its original 1862 fittings intact, right down to the glazed snob screens that divide the bar into a series of "snugs". Despite the heritage, the pub manages to pull in a young and funky crowd.

Warrington Hotel
Map 3, B2. 93 Warrington Crescent, W9 ⊕ 020/7286 2929. ⊖ Maida Vale.
Yet another architectural gem – this time flamboyant Edwardian Art Nouveau – in an area replete with them. The interior is rich and satisfying, as are the draught beers and the Thai restaurant upstairs. It is, however, incredibly spilling-out-onto-the-street popular.

CAMDEN TOWN

Bar Vinyl

Map 2, H3. 6 Inverness St,
NW1 ⓣ 020/7681 7898,
ⓦ www.vinyl-addiction.co.uk
⊖ Camden Town.
Funky glass-bricked DJ bar
with a record shop downstairs
and a breakbeat and trip-hop
vibe.

Bartok

Map 2, H3. 78–79 Chalk Farm
Rd ⓣ 020/7916 0595.
⊖ Chalk Farm. Mon–Thurs
5pm–midnight, Fri 5pm–1am,
Sat noon–1am, Sun
noon–midnight.
Mean Fiddler-run bar where
punters can sink into the sofas
and sup beer or wine while
listening to classical music
instead of the usual muzak.

The Engineer

Map 2, H3. 65 Gloucester Ave,
NW1 ⓣ 020/7722 0950.
⊖ Chalk Farm.
A real pub, as well as a
gastropub, in the much-
sought-after residential area of
Primrose Hill, *The Engineer* is
a smart, grandiose place

which serves exceptional
Modern Brit/Med food; it's
pricey, though, and you're
best off booking if you intend
to nosh.

HAMPSTEAD AND HIGHGATE

The Flask

Map 2, G3. Flask Walk, NW3
ⓣ 020/7435 4580.
⊖ Hampstead.
Convivial Hampstead local,
hidden away along the
pedestrianized Flask Walk,
which retains much of its
original Victorian décor.

The Flask

Map 2, H2. 77 Highgate West
Hill, N6 ⓣ 020/8348 7346.
⊖ Highgate.
Ideally situated at the heart of
Highgate's village green, with
a rambling low-ceilinged
interior and a large, very
popular summer terrace. The
range of beers is good, but
the food is nothing special.

Freemason's Arms

Map 2, G3. 32 Downshire Hill,
NW3 ⓣ 020/7433 6811.

⊖ Hampstead.

Big, smart pub close to the Heath, popular on sunny days primarily for its large beer garden; also offers comfort pub food, a basement skittle alley, and an outdoor pell-mell pitch.

Holly Bush

Map 2, G3. 22 Holly Mount, NW3 ⓣ 020/7435 2892.
⊖ Hampstead. Mon–Fri 4.30–11pm, Sat 12.30–11pm, Sun 12.30–10.30pm.
A lovely old wood-panelled, gas-lit pub, tucked away in the steep backstreets of Hampstead village. You can sup the excellent range of real ales in a calm and cosy atmosphere during the week, but the place can get mobbed at the weekends.

DULWICH AND GREENWICH

Crown & Greyhound

Map 2, J7. 73 Dulwich Village, SE21 ⓣ 020/8299 4976. North Dulwich or West Dulwich train stations.
Grand, spacious Victorian pub with an ornate plasterwork ceiling, good food and beer, and a nice summer beer garden. Convenient for the Picture Gallery, but be prepared for the Sunday lunchtime crowds.

Cutty Sark

Map 2, L5. Ballast Quay, off Lassell St, SE10 ⓣ 020/8858 3146. Cutty Sark DLR or Maze Hill train station.
The nicest riverside pub in Greenwich, spacious, more of a local and much less touristy than the more famous *Trafalgar Tavern* (it's a couple of minutes walk further east, following the river). The views are great, as is the draught beer.

Trafalgar Tavern

See map on p.152, E2. 5 Park Row, SE10 ⓣ 020/8858 2437. Cutty Sark DLR or Maze Hill train station. Mon–Sat 11.30am–11pm, Sun noon–10.30pm.
A great riverside position and a mention in Dickens' *Our Mutual Friend* have made this Regency-style inn a firm

tourist favourite, which is fair enough really, as it's a convivial period piece, and serves good food (including whitebait).

CHISWICK TO RICHMOND

The Dove
Map 2, E5. 19 Upper Mall, W6 ⓣ 020/8748 5405.
⊖ Ravenscourt Park.
Old, old riverside pub with literary associations, the smallest bar in the UK (4ft by 7ft) and very popular Sunday roast dinners. Still by far the best of the Thameside inns within a short walk of Hammersmith, though you'll need to arrive early to get a seat on the tiny outdoor terrace.

White Cross Hotel
Map 2, C7. Water Lane, Richmond ⓣ 020/8940 6844.
⊖ Richmond.
With a longer pedigree and more character than its clinical chain rivals nearby, the *White Cross* is also much closer to the river (its front garden regularly gets flooded), and serves Young's beer.

White Swan
Map 2, C7. Riverside, Twickenham ⓣ 020/8892 2166. Twickenham train station.
Filling pub food, draught beer and a quiet riverside location – except on rugby match days – make this a good halt on any towpath ramble. The pub has a beer pontoon overlooking Eel Pie Island if you want to get even closer to the water.

CHISWICK TO RICHMOND

Live music
and clubs

ver the past five years London has established itself as the nightlife capital of not just Europe, but the world. Rio may be sunnier, Paris prettier and Madrid madder, but for sheer range and diversity there's little to beat London. The **live music** scene remains extremely diverse, encompassing all variations of rock, blues, roots and world music; and although London's jazz clubs aren't on a par with those in the big American cities, there's a highly individual scene of home-based artists, supplemented by top-name visiting players.

If you're looking for **dance music**, then welcome to Europe's party capital. After dark, London is thriving, with diverse scenes championing everything from hip-hop to house, techno to garage, samba to soca and drum'n'bass to R&B on virtually any night of the week. Venues once used exclusively by performing bands now pepper the week with club nights, and you often find dance sessions starting as soon as a band has stopped playing. Bear in mind that there's sometimes an overlap between "live music venues" and "clubs" in the listings below; we've indicated which places serve a double function.

The dance and club scene is, of course, pretty much in constant flux, with the hottest items constantly moving location, losing the plot or just cooling off. Weekly **listings magazines** like *Time Out* give up-to-date details of prices and access, plus previews and reviews.

For club-bars and pre-club drinking dens, see Chapter 18; for lesbian and gay clubs and discos, see Chapter 20.

LIVE MUSIC

London is hard to beat for its musical mix: whether you're into **jazz**, **indie**, **rock**, **R&B**, **blues** or **world music**, you'll find something worth hearing on almost any night of the week. **Entry prices** for gigs run from a couple of pounds for an unknown band thrashing it out in a pub to around £30 for the likes of U2, but you can reckon on around £10 for a good night out, not counting expenses at the bar. If you have a credit card, it's often cheaper to book tickets in advance online via sites like ⓦwww.ticketweb.co.uk, ⓦwww.tickets-online.co.uk or ⓦwww.gigsandtours.com. We've listed websites for all venues that have them.

ROCK AND BLUES

Astoria
Map 4, G5. 157 Charing Cross Rd, WC2 ☏020/7434 9592, ⓦwww.meanfiddler.com ⊖ Tottenham Court Road. One of London's best and most central medium-sized venues, this large, balconied, one-time theatre tends to host slightly alternative bands, with club nights on Friday and Saturday.

Borderline
Map 4, G5. Orange Yard, off

Manette St, W1 ℡ 020/7734 2095, ⓦ www.borderline.co.uk ⊖ Tottenham Court Road. Intimate basement joint with diverse musical policy. Good place to catch new bands, although big names sometimes turn up under a pseudonym.

Brixton Academy

Map 2, I6. 211 Stockwell Rd, SW9 ℡ 0870/771 2000, ⓦ www.ticketweb.co.uk ⊖ Brixton.
This refurbished Victorian hall, complete with Roman decorations, can hold 4000 but still manages to seem small and friendly, probably because most of the audience are standing, dancing or waving their beers about.

Forum

Map 2, G3. 9–17 Highgate Rd, NW5 ℡ 020/7344 0044, ⓦ www.meanfiddler.com ⊖ Kentish Town.
The Forum is north London's best medium-sized venue, and is still a frequent stop-off point for established jazz-funk and rock bands. Great views and good bars.

The Mean Fiddler

Map 2, F4. 24–28a Harlesden High St, NW10 ℡ 020/8961 5490, ⓦ www.meanfiddler.com ⊖ Willesden Junction.
An excellent – if inconveniently located – small venue with a main hall and smaller acoustic room. The bands veer from rock to world to folk.

The Orange

Map 2, F5. 3 North End Crescent, W14 ℡ 020/7751 1044 (answerphone outside office hours). ⊖ West Kensington.
Pub-like venue for serious-minded jazz-funkers. There are also varying club nights (call ahead).

Roadhouse

Map 4, H6. 35 The Piazza, WC2 ℡ 020/7240 6001, ⓦ www.roadhouse.co.uk ⊖ Covent Garden.
American food, 1950s US-style décor and a lineup of mainly blues and rock'n'roll bands performing to a mature, nostalgic crowd.

Shepherds Bush Empire

Map 2, E4. Shepherds Bush Green, W12 ⊤ 020/7771 2000, ⓦ www.shepherds-bush-empire.co.uk ⊖ Shepherds Bush.

The medium-sized venue and the one that both UK and US bands love to play at, this grand old west London theatre regularly draws the cream of the crop of non-stadium-rocking bands, from hip-hop acts through to singer-songwriters like Beth Orton. Upstairs balconies provide killer views, too.

Station Tavern

Map 2, F5. 41 Bramley Rd, W10 ⊤ 020/7727 4053. ⊖ Latimer Road.

Arguably London's best blues venue, with free – and occasionally great – blues six nights a week.

Subterania

Map 2, F5. 12 Acklam Rd, W10 ⊤ 020/8960 4590, ⓦ www.meanfiddler.com ⊖ Ladbroke Grove.

One of the original live music/club crossover venues, set in an arch under a bridge.

The crowd is as clued up as the music, which is often dance-oriented – look out for their great open-mic hip-hop nights.

12 Bar Club

Map 4, G5. 22–23 Denmark Place, WC2 ⊤ 020/7916 6989. ⊖ Tottenham Court Road.

A combination of live blues and contemporary country, seven nights a week.

Underworld

Map 2, H3. 174 Camden High St, NW1 ⊤ 020/7482 1932, ⓦ www.theunderworldcamden .co.uk ⊖ Camden Town.

Labyrinthine venue that's good for new bands, and has sporadic club nights.

JAZZ, WORLD MUSIC AND FOLK

Africa Centre

Map 4, H7. 38 King St, WC2 ⊤ 020/7836 1973, ⓦ www.africacentre.org.uk ⊖ Covent Garden.

The packed old hall was the venue that launched Soul II Soul; these days, it hosts

African bands and nights like Saturday's P-funk-heavy *Funkin Pussy*, but still draws a vibrantly enthusiastic crowd.

Bull's Head Barnes
Map 2, E5. 373 Lonsdale Rd, Barnes SW13 ⓣ 020/8876 5241. Bus #9 from ⊖ Hammersmith, or Barnes Bridge train station from Waterloo.

This riverside alehouse – with pub prices to boot – attracts Britain's finest jazz musicians, though it's now a little shabby round the edges.

Cecil Sharp House
Map 2, H3. 2 Regent's Park Rd, NW1 ⓣ 020/7485 2206. ⊖ Camden Town.

A centre for British folk music: singing, dancing and a folk-music shop.

Dover Street
Map 4, C9. 8–9 Dover St, W1 ⓣ 020/7629 9813. ⊖ Green Park.

London's largest jazz restaurant has music and dancing every night until 3am; the food is Modern British.

Jazz Café
Map 2, H3. 5 Parkway, NW1 ⓣ 020/7916 6060, ⓦ www.jazzcafe.co.uk ⊖ Camden Town.

Futuristic, white-walled venue with an adventurous booking policy exploring Latin, rap, funk, hip-hop and musical fusions. Die-hard trad-jazz fans won't be happy, despite the fact that there's a rather good restaurant upstairs with a few prime-view tables overlooking the stage (book ahead if you want one).

100 Club
Map 4, E5. 100 Oxford St, W1 ⓣ 020/7636 0933. ⊖ Tottenham Court Road.

After a brief spell as a stage for punk bands, the *100 Club* is once again an unpretentious and inexpensive jazz venue – in a very central location.

Pizza Express
Map 4, F5. 10 Dean St, W1 ⓣ 020/7439 8722. ⊖ Oxford Street.

Enjoy a good pizza, then listen to the resident band or highly skilled guest players in this long-running basement venue. There's also a late-night session on Saturdays, which starts at 9pm and finishes in the early hours.

Ronnie Scott's

Map 4, F6. 47 Frith St, W1 ⓣ 020/7439 0747, ⓦ www.ronniescotts.co.uk ⊖ Leicester Square.

The most famous jazz club in London: small, smoky and still going strong, even though the great man himself has passed away. The place for top-line names, who play two sets – one at around 10pm, the other after midnight. Book a table, or you'll have to stand.

606 Club

Map 2, F6. 90 Lots Rd, SW10 ⓣ 020/7352 5953. ⊖ Fulham Broadway.

A rare all-jazz venue, located just off the less trendy end of King's Road. You can book a table, and the licensing laws dictate that you must eat if you want to drink, but there's no cover charge.

Union Chapel

Map 2, I3. Compton Avenue, N1 ⓣ 020/7226 1686. ⊖ Highbury & Islington.

A wonderfully idiosyncratic chapel that hosts an array of world fusion nights. Wrap up warm for winter gigs.

CLUBS

Fifteen years after acid-house irreversibly shook up British clubs, London remains *the* place to come if you want to party after dark. The sheer diversity of dance music has enabled the city to maintain its status as **Europe's dance capital** – and it's still a port of call for DJs from around the globe. The so-called super-clubs may be on the way out, but, in their place, there's more variety than ever, in music and the venues available. The relaxation of late-night licensing has encouraged many venues to keep serving alcohol until 6am or even later, and the resurgence of alcohol in clubland (much to the relief

CLUBS

of the breweries) has been echoed by the meteoric rise of the club-bar (see chapter 18).

Nearly all of London's **dance clubs** open their doors between 10pm and midnight. Some are open six or seven nights a week, some keep irregular days, others just open at the weekend and very often a venue will host a different club on each night of the week. Many of the best nights take place during the week, especially Mondays, Wednesdays and Thursdays. For up-to-the-minute details of these, and all the nights listed below, pop into one of Soho's many record shops (see p.317) to pick up flyers, or check magazines like *Time Out* for details.

Admission charges vary wildly, with small midweek sessions starting at around £3 and large weekend events charging as much as £15; around £10 is the average for a Friday or Saturday night, but bear in mind that profit margins at the bar are often more outrageous than at live music venues.

CLUB VENUES

- - - - - - - - - - - - - - - - - - - -

Bagley's
Map 3, I1. King's Cross Goods Yard, off York Way, N1
ⓣ 020/7278 2777. ⊖ King's Cross.
Vast warehouse-style venue with a 2500-person capacity located in a post-apocalyptic industrial estate. The perfect place for enormous raves, with different music – normally including drum'n' bass, garage and old-school

house in each of the three rooms, and a chill-out bar replete with sofas.

Bar Rumba
Map 4, F7. 36 Shaftesbury Ave, W1 ⓣ 020/7287 2715, ⓦ www.barrumba.co.uk
⊖ Piccadilly Circus.
Fun, smallish West End venue with an adventurous mix of nights ranging from the future-jazz of *That's How It Is* on Mondays to top-notch house and R&B at weekends. Pop in during the early

CLUB VENUES

evening (when it's free) to sample some cocktails on the cheap during happy hour.

Café de Paris
Map 4, F7. 3 Coventry St, W1 ⓣ 020/7734 7700.
⊖ Leicester Square.
Elegantly restored ballroom that plays house, garage and disco to a smartly dressed crowd of wannabes – no jeans or trainers.

Camden Palace
Map 2, H3. 1 Camden High St, NW1 ⓣ 09062 100 200, ⓦ www.camdenpalace.com
⊖ Camden Town.
Home to popular Saturday garage nights with regular DJs such as Norris "Da Boss" Windross and Matt "Jam" Lamont – great lights, great sound, heaving crowds. Hard house dominates on Fridays at the long-running *Peach* club, hosted by DJ Graham Gold.

Cargo
Map 3, N2. Kingsland Viaduct, 83 Rivington St, EC2 ⓣ 020/7739 3446, ⓦ www.cargo-london.com
⊖ Old Street.

Still packing them in every weekend, *Cargo* complements live dance bands (it's the place where Röyksopp played their first shows) with a prescient music policy that covers deep house, drum'n'bass and jazzy grooves, as well as modern twists on Latin and African sounds. Worth getting there early in the summer, if only to lounge in the outdoor space at the back.

The Cross
Map 3, I1. King's Cross Freight Depot, Arches 27–31, off York Way, N1 ⓣ 020/7837 0828, ⓦ www.the-cross.co.uk
⊖ King's Cross.
Hidden underneath railway arches, the favourite flavours of this renowned club are house and garage. It's bigger than you imagine, but always crammed with Balearic clubby types, and there's a cool garden – perfect for those chill-out moments.

Cuba
Map 3, A6. 11–13 Kensington High St, W8 ⓣ 020/7938 4137.
⊖ Kensington High Street.
Grab a cocktail upstairs in the

CLUB VENUES

sociable bar before heading below for club nights that focus around Latin, salsa and Brazilian bossa nova.

Electric Ballroom

Map 2, H3. 184 Camden High St, NW1 ⚈ 020/7485 9006, ⊛ www.electricballroom.co.uk ⊖ Camden Town.

Attracts a truly mixed crowd of Camden regulars from punks to b-boys who come for the wide range of sounds: rock, hip-hop, jazz and house.

The End

Map 3, I3. 18 West Central St, WC1 ⚈ 020/7419 9199, ⊛ www.the-end.co.uk ⊖ Holborn.

Designed for clubbers by clubbers, *The End* is large and spacious, with chrome minimalist décor and a devastating sound system. Well-known for its focus on tech-house at weekends, and Monday's anything-goes bacchanalia, *Trash*.

Fabric

Map 3, K3. 77a Charterhouse St, EC1 ⚈ 020/7336 8898, ⊛ www.fabric-london.com

⊖ Farringdon.

If you're a serious dance music fan, then there really isn't a better weekend venue in London than *Fabric*, a cavernous, underground brewery-like space with three rooms, holding 2500 people. Fridays are *Fabric Live*, a mix of drum'n'bass and hip-hop that features lives acts, while Saturdays concentrate on the most cutting-edge house sounds around, played by the best DJs from around the globe. Get there early to avoid a night of queuing.

Fridge

Map 2, I6. Town Hall Parade, Brixton Hill, SW2 ⚈ 020/7326 5100, ⊛ www.fridge.co.uk ⊖ Brixton.

Weekends alternate between pumping mixed/gay nights, and trance favourites like the monthly *Escape from Samsara*, a Friday night with a psychedelic, trancey vibe, a hippy market and plenty of lightstick-waving action.

Gardening Club

Map 4, H6. 4 The Piazza, WC2 ⚈ 020/497 3154,

Ⓦ www.rockgarden.co.uk

⊖ Covent Garden.

A popular choice for house and garage, but be warned – you could well find yourself sharing the dancefloor with beer-boys and bemused tourists.

Gossips

Map 4, F5. 69 Dean St, W1
Ⓣ 020/7434 4480.

⊖ Tottenham Court Road.
Cave-like basement club that seems to have been around for aeons. Located deep in the heart of Soho, it's a popular stop for swing and hip-hop fans.

Herbal

Map 3, N2. 12–14 Kingsland Rd, E2 Ⓣ 020/7613 4462,
Ⓦ www.herbaluk.com

⊖ Old Street.
An intimate two-floored venue that's often home to big-name DJs for the entrance price of a packet of cigarettes. Check Thursdays or Sundays and you might just stumble across the likes of Groove Armada, DJ Harvey or Doc Martin in the cool New York-style loft or sweaty

ground-floor club.

HQs

Map 2, H3. West Yard, Camden Lock, NW1
Ⓣ 020/7485 6044.

⊖ Camden Town.
Smallish venue by the canal with a range of nights, though the emphasis is on hip-hop and jazz-fusion. Friendly vibe, good cocktails and free entry if you arrive early on weekdays.

ICA

Map 4, F10. The Mall, SW1
Ⓣ 020/7930 3647,
Ⓦ www.ica.org.uk

⊖ Piccadilly Circus.
The Institute of Contemporary Arts may not seem the perfect setting for a great club night, but weekends play host to some of the most cutting-edge audiovisual collaborations in town. If you're into Latin music, then the once-a-month, Friday-night *Batmacumba*, with DJ Cliffy, is a must. There's also a great bar and excellent modern European food.

Ministry of Sound

Map 3, L7. 103 Gaunt St, SE1
ⓣ 020/7378 6528,
ⓦ www.ministryofsound.co.uk
⊖ Elephant & Castle.

A vast, state-of-the-art enterprise based on New York's legendary *Paradise Garage*, with an exceptional sound system and the pick of visiting US and Italian DJs. Corporate clubbing and full of tourists, but it still draws the top talent, especially on Saturdays. Look out for their excellent, hedonistic Bank Holiday parties – turn up early to ensure you get in.

93 Feet East

Map 7, M1. 150 Brick Lane, E2
ⓣ 020/7247 3293,
ⓦ www.93feeteast.co.uk
⊖ Aldgate East.

One of East London's best mid-sized venues, this one-time brewery sports four varied rooms across two levels, as well as an excellent rooftop balcony and outdoor space that's well worth a visit in summer. Nights offer up the cream of the crop of the capital's cutting-edge club promoters. The party-hardy crowds dig everything from house to British hip-hop, as well as live acts.

Notting Hill Arts Club

Map 3, A5. 21 Notting Hill Gate, W11 ⓣ 020/7460 4459,
ⓦ www.nottinghillartsclub.com
⊖ Notting Hill Gate.

Basement club that's popular for everything from Latin-inspired funk, jazz and disco through to soul, house and garage, and famed for Ben Watt's Sunday-night deep-house session, *Lazy Dog*.

Office

Map 3, G4. 3–5 Rathbone Place, W1 ⓣ 020/7636 1598.
⊖ Tottenham Court Road.

Various music styles, often focusing on swing and hip-hop, but best known as home to a midweek session where you can play silly board games like Ker-Plunk. Booking a table in advance is advised.

Pacha London

Map 3, G7. Terminus Place, SW1 ⓣ 020/7834 4440,
ⓦ www.pachalondon.com
⊖ Victoria.

Don't expect the palm-tree-lined gardens and rooftop bars of the original (and best) *Pacha* in Ibiza. This soulless vast club hasn't really lived up to the hype since opening in 2001, and now draws a mix of Chelsea sloanes, suburban boys and clueless tourists to its Saturday-night house sessions. Even the dancers are lame.

Salsa!

Map 4, G5. 96 Charing Cross Rd, WC2 ⓣ020/7379 3277. ⊖ Leicester Square.
Funky and fun salsa-based club-cum-restaurant that's a popular choice for group birthday bookings; you can book a table to eat as you mambo.

Scala

Map 3, J1. 278 Pentonville Rd, N1 ⓣ020/7833 2022, ⓦwww.scala-london.co.uk ⊖ King's Cross.
Once a cinema (it was forced to shut down after illegally showing Kubrick's *Clockwork Orange*), the *Scala* is now one of London's best clubs, holding unusual and multifaceted nights that take

in film, live bands and music ranging from quirky hip-hop to drum'n'bass and deep house.

Subterania

Map 2, F5. 12 Acklam Rd, W10 ⓣ020/7960 4590, ⓦwww.meanfiddler.com ⊖ Ladbroke Grove.
Just off Portobello Road, *Subterania* is worth a visit for its diverse club nights at weekends. The superior hip-hop- and R&B-heavy *Rotation* is every Friday; also plays host to emerging hip-hop and R&B acts during club nights.

333

Map 3, N2. 333 Old St, EC1 ⓣ020/7630 5949. ⊖ Old Street.
One of London's best clubs for new dance music, in the heart of trendy-as-hell Hoxton. Three floors of drum'n'bass, twisted disco and breakbeat madness.

Turnmills

Map 3, K3. 63 Clerkenwell Rd, EC1 ⓣ020/7250 3409, ⓦwww.turnmills.com

CLUB VENUES

⊖ Farringdon.

The place to come if you want to sweat from dusk till dawn, with an alien-invasion-style bar and funky split-level dancefloor in the main room. Trance and house with top-name guest DJs rule Fridays, but it's rightly famed for the awesomely glorious gay extravaganza, *Trade*, which begins on Sunday morning at 4am.

Lesbian and gay London

L ondon's **lesbian and gay scene** is so huge, diverse
and well established that it's easy to forget just how
much – and how fast – it has grown over the last few
years. Pink power has given rise to the pink pound, gay liberation to gay lifestyle, and the ever-expanding Soho – now
firmly established as the homo heart of the city – is vibrant,
self-assured and unashamedly commercial. As a result of all
this high-profile activity, straight Londoners tend to be a
fairly homo-savvy bunch and, on the whole, happy to
embrace and even dip into the city's queer offerings.

Soho is the obvious place to start exploring London's gay
and lesbian scene, and **Old Compton Street** is, so to
speak, its main drag. Here, traditional gay pubs rub alongside café/bars selling expensive designer beers and lattes,
while hairdressers, letting agencies, sex boutiques and spiritual health centres offer a range of gay-run services. There
are clubs to cater for just about every musical, sartorial and
sexual taste and, while the bigger ones tend to cluster
around the West End, there are equally well-established
venues all over the city. Gay men still enjoy the best

permanent facilities London-wide, but today's **lesbian scene** is bigger and more eclectic than ever, and the cruisey girl bars which took up prize pitches on the boys' Soho turf a few years ago look like they're there to stay.

You can also find pockets of queer activity away from the centre in the city's funkier residential areas, most notably Brixton in South London, Islington (especially for dykes), Stoke Newington and Hackney. Bear in mind that although open anti-gay hostility is rare in London, it's probably wise not to hold hands or smooch too obviously in areas you don't know well.

The **outdoor event** of the year is **Mardi Gras** in July. A colourful, whistle-blowing march through the city streets followed by a huge, ticketed party in a central London park, Mardi Gras is the carnival child of Pride, which finally outgrew itself a few years ago. The newly branded event, now managed by a consortium of gay and lesbian entrepreneurs, is no longer free - tickets are roughly £15 - but the largest queer party of the year continues to draw people from all over the country. For up-to-date information, festival plans, tickets and transport information, call ☎020/7354 1100 or visit ⓦ www.londonmardigras.com.

London also boasts several queer-oriented annual arts events: in March and April, the National Film Theatre hosts the annual **Lesbian and Gay Film Festival**; the **Mardi Gras Arts Festival**, staged at venues throughout London, leads the run-up to Mardi Gras itself; and in mid-June there's the unmissably camp **Ms Lesbian UK & Ireland** hosted in a swish central London venue – check the gay press for details nearer the time.

Elsewhere, queer theatre and arts events take place all year round in the city's many fringe theatres, arts centres, galleries and clubs. If none of this is up your street, there are also a huge number of **gay groups and organizations** offering everything from ballroom dancing to spanking seminars.

For further details of lesbian and gay events, check out *Time Out* or the gay press – *The Pink Paper* (weekly, free), *Gay Times* (monthly, £2.95), and newish lesbian magazine *G3* (free) can be picked up from major newsagents, bookshops or cafés and bars in Soho. In addition, consumerist freesheets like *Boyz* and *qx* abound in clubs and bars and provide up-to-date club listings. Finally, check out the **websites** listed below.

WEBSITES

The following are the most useful **websites**, and the only ones to offer more than just an online version of printed publications.

ⓦ www.gaytoz.com

For a comprehensive online directory of gay, lesbian, bisexual and TV/TS-friendly organizations and businesses, you can't do better than GAY to Z. A print version is also available from Gay to Z Directories, 41 Cooks Rd, London SE17 3NG.

ⓦ www.gay.com

International and most commonly used website for gay men, with regular news stories, features and discount offers for hotels and selected club nights.

ⓦ www.rainbownetwork .com

Lifestyle e-zine for boys and girls, which, thanks to the vicissitudes of the dotcom market, is a shadow of its former self. Includes some news on the latest events, interviews with scene faces, listings and message boards.

ⓦ www.gingerbeer.co.uk

Well-designed and regularly updated website for London dykes, offering listings and reviews of bars, clubs and events. Gingerbeer also holds regular women-only club nights - check the site for details.

WEBSITES

255

Ⓦ **www.fruitcamp.com**

For a slice of London's lesbian and gay life online, fruitcamp provides useful info on flatshares, jobs, the scene and community events.

Ⓦ **www.gaydar.co.uk**

The gaydar revolution has transformed the lives of gay men who prefer to cut to the chase and order a date like they'd order a pizza. If it works for you, it's not a bad place to meet up-for-it guys of all persuasions.

Ⓦ **www.gaydargirls.com**

Online dating for queer girls nationwide. Tempting but often a little disappointing in the flesh – some of the ladies require careful vetting before you agree to meet up.

Ⓦ **www.crag.dircon.co.uk/news**

If it's free and up-to-date info on transsexual and transvestite news, events and venues you want, the online version of TS TV news, established in 1994, is a good place to start.

CAFÉS, BARS AND PUBS

There are loads of lesbian and gay **cafés, bars and pubs** in London, many of which have been around for years, while some pop up and disappear within months – such is the fickle nature of the scene. Our list is by no means exhaustive, as every corner of London has its own gay local. Many cafés and bars transform themselves into **drinking dens** at night and, as some open beyond licensing hours, they can be a cheap alternative to some clubs. Bear in mind that, although more and more lesbian bars admit gay men, "mixed," (as ever) tends to mean mostly men.

HELPLINES AND INFORMATION

All of the following services provide information, advice and counselling, but the **Lesbian & Gay Switchboard** is the one to turn to first: its volunteers have details on all the capital's resources and can point you in the direction of specific organizations and community or support groups.

Bisexual Helpline ☏ 0845/4501263. Tues & Wed 7.30–9.30pm, Sat 10.30am–12.30pm. Advice, support and information for bisexuals.

London Friend ☏ 020/7837 3337, ⓦ www.lf.org.uk; daily 7.30–10pm. Confidential information and support for lesbians and gay men. The women-only service (☏ 020/7837 2782; 7.30–10pm) is Sun to Thurs.

Lesbian, Gay, Bisexual & Transgender Liaison Team ☏ 020/7321 8788. Metropolitan Police helpline for anyone who is the victim of a hate crime. Supported by the LAGPA, the Lesbian & Gay Police Association.

London Lesbian & Gay Switchboard ☏ 020/7837 7324, ⓦ www.queery.org.uk. Huge database on everything you might ever want to know, plus legal advice, good counselling skills and good humour. Lines are 24hr; do keep trying if you can't get through.

National AIDS Helpline ☏ 0800/567 123, ⓦ www.lovelife .uk.com. Freephone 24hr service for anyone worried about HIV and AIDS-related issues and sexually transmitted infections.

Terrence Higgins Trust ☏ 0845/1221 20, ⓦ www.tht.org.uk; Mon–Fri 11am–8pm. Information and advice on all HIV and AIDS-related issues. Service also available in French and Spanish. For self-referrals to the counselling unit, call ☏ 020/7835 1495.

HELPLINES AND INFORMATION

MIXED CAFÉS, BARS AND RESTAURANTS

The Admiral Duncan
Map 4, F6. 54 Old Compton St, W1 ☎ 020/7437 5300.
⊖ Leicester Square.
Unpretentious, traditional-style gay bar in the heart of Soho, popular and busy with a post-work crowd, and now fully restored after the blast that ripped through it in 1999.

Ah Bar
Map 2, I6. 272 Brixton Hill, SW2 ☎ 020/8671 8992,
ⓦ www.ahbar.co.uk ⊖ Brixton.
Gay-friendly and gay-owned bar and restaurant with year-round heated terrace serving Mediterranean and modern English fusion menu. Breakfasts and brunch always popular.

Balans Café
Map 4, F6. 34 Old Compton St, W1 ☎ 020/7439 3309,
ⓦ www.balans.co.uk
⊖ Tottenham Court Road or Leicester Square.
This enduringly busy Soho institution is open until the early hours. Strong coffee and a range of cakes and snacks make it the obvious solution to mid- or post-party wooziness.

Bar Aquda
Map 4, H7. 13–14 Maiden Lane, WC2 ☎ 020/7557 9891.
⊖ Leicester Square or Covent Garden.
Bright, modern and fashionable café/bar with good food. Mixed, but mostly boys.

The Black Cap
Map 2, H3. 171 Camden High St, NW1 ☎ 020/7428 2721.
⊖ Camden Town.
Venerable north London institution offering cabaret of wildly varying quality almost every night. Laugh, sing and lip-synch along, and then dance to 1980s tunes until the early hours. The upstairs *Mrs Shufflewick's Bar* is quieter, and opens onto the Fong (after drag legend Regina) Terrace in the summer.

The Box
Map 4, G6. 32–34 Monmouth St, WC2 ☎ 020/7240 5828,

MIXED CAFÉS, BARS AND RESTAURANTS

ⓦ www.boxbar.co.uk
⊖ Covent Garden or Leicester Square.
Popular, bright café/bar serving good food for a mixed gay/straight crowd during the day, and becoming queerer as the night draws in.

The Edge

Map 4, F5. 11 Soho Square, W1 ☏ 020/7439 1313, ⓦ www.edge.uk.com
⊖ Tottenham Court Road.
Busy, style-conscious and pricey Soho café/bar spread over several floors, although this doesn't seem to stop everyone ending up on the pavement, especially in summer. Food daily, good art exhibitions and DJs most nights.

First Out

Map 4, G5. 52 St Giles High St, WC2 ☏ 020/7240 8042.
⊖ Tottenham Court Road.
The West End's original gay café/bar, and still permanently packed, serving good veggie food at reasonable prices. Upstairs is airy and non-smoking, downstairs dark and foggy.

Girl Friday is a busy pre-club Friday session for grrrls; gay men are welcome as guests.

Freedom

Map 4, F6. 60–66 Wardour St, W1 ☏ 020/7734 0071.
⊖ Leicester Square or Piccadilly.
Hip, busy, late-opening café/bar, popular with a mixed straight/gay Soho crowd. Great juices and healthy food in the daytime, cocktails and overpriced beer in the evening. The theatre space downstairs occasionally transforms itself into a funky basement club, and there are some intriguing art installations, too.

Oak Bar

Map 2, I3. 79 Green Lanes, N16 ☏ 020/7354 2791.
⊖ Manor House, or buses #73, #171A or #141 from ⊖ Angel.
Friendly, spacious local pub with a dancefloor and pool table, recently refurbished and with much-improved loos. Hosts a range of mixed and women-only special events and club nights, including the wildly popular women-only

MIXED CAFÉS, BARS AND RESTAURANTS

Liberté (see p.270) and the mixed (but mostly women) *Lower The Tone* (see p.268).

The Royal Oak

Map 2, J4. 73 Columbia Rd, E2 ⊤ 020/7739 8204. ⊖ Old Street or Shoreditch.

In the heart of the famous Columbia Road flower market (see p.100), this old, comfortable market pub caters for a mixed gay/straight crowd, and offers Sunday breakfasts or Tex-Mex meals at the upstairs restaurant.

The Royal Vauxhall Tavern

Map 3, I9. 372 Kennington Lane, SE11 (no phone). ⊖ Vauxhall.

A London institution with late opening hours, this huge, disreputable and divey drag and cabaret pub is home to legendary alternative club night, *Duckie* (Sat), with a staggeringly bonkers and queer range of appearances. Popular with alt/indie crowd.

Shadow Lounge

Map 4, G6. 5 Brewer St, W1 ⊤ 020/7287 7988,

ⓦ www.theshadowlounge.co.uk ⊖ Covent Garden or Leicester Square.

New glitzy gay lounge members' bar which attracts an A to Z of celebrity punters. More fag hag than leather lez, and the boys rule the school.

The Spiral Staircase

Map 2, N2. 138 Shoreditch High St, E1 ⊤ 020/7613 1351. ⊖ Old Street.

This notorious two-level dive attracts a mixed gay/straight, up-for-it crowd of drinkers. Comfy sofas upstairs, a singing, dancing basement area, and open until 4am at the weekends.

Teds Place

Map 2, F5. 305a North End Rd, W14 ⊤ 020/7385 9359. ⊖ West Kensington or West Brompton.

Friendly, late-opening local with a gay/lesbian/bi and TV/TS clientele, long-running lesbian *Blind Date* contest and assorted outbreaks of frivolity. Cheap drinks, too.

Village Soho

Map 4, E6. 81 Wardour St, W1
Ⓣ 020/7434 2124. ⊖ Leicester
Square or Piccadilly Circus.
Elegant three-floor café/bar
with a relaxed atmosphere
that attracts a young gay
crowd – more pretty boyz
than girlz.

The Yard

Map 4, F7. 57 Rupert St, W1
Ⓣ 020/7437 2652. ⊖ Piccadilly
Circus.
Attractive café/bar with
courtyard and loft areas.
Good food, weekly cabaret
and regular fortune tellers.

LESBIAN BARS AND PUBS

Blush

Map 2, J2. 8 Cazenove Rd,
Stoke Newington N16
Ⓣ 020/7923 9202. Stoke
Newington station.
This friendly local bar-club's
two floors of fun – quiz
nights, live music and a pool
bar – make it a popular
choice among lesbians north
of the city centre.

Candy Bar

Map 4, F2. Carlisle St, WC2
Ⓣ 020/7437 1977,
Ⓦ www.candybar.co.uk
⊖ Tottenham Court Road.
Now established at its
original venue, but still with
the same crucial, cruisey vibe
that has made its name as the
hottest girl bar in central
London.

The Glass Bar

Map 3, H2. West Lodge,
Euston Square Gardens, 190
Euston Rd, NW1 Ⓣ 020/7387
6184 or 7387 4153,
Ⓦ www.glassbar.ndo.co.uk
⊖ Euston. Mon–Fri from 5pm,
Sat from 6pm. No admission
after 11.30pm.
Difficult to find (and hard to
forget), this friendly and
intimate late-opening
women-only members' bar
(membership is automatic
once you're inside) is housed
in a listed building and
features a wrought-iron spiral
staircase, which gets
increasingly perilous as the
night wears on. Knock on the
door to get in.

LESBIAN BARS AND PUBS

Sewing Circle at *The Ritzy Café*

Map 2, I6. Ritzy Cinema, SW2
ⓣ 020/7733 2229. ⊖ Brixton.
Last Tues of month 7pm–late.
For alternative and artsy queer girls, this informal women-only culture club above Brixton's arts cinema has everything from films to DJs. Food also available.

Southopia

Map 3, L7. 146–148 Newington Butts, SE11
ⓣ 020/7735 5306, infoline
ⓣ 020/7735 5178,
ⓦ www.southopia.com
 ⊖ Kennington or Elephant & Castle. Mon–Sat 5–11pm, Sun noon–10.30pm.
One of the few women-only bars south of the river, run by Elaine from the northern *Glass Bar* (see p.261) so expect a friendly, grown-up atmosphere.

Vespa Lounge

Map 4, G4. Upstairs at *The Conservatory*, Centrepoint House, 15 St Giles High St, WC1 ⓣ 020/7836 8956,
ⓔ vespalounge@aol.com
 ⊖ Tottenham Court Road.

Daily 6–11pm.
This centrally located girls' bar gets super-busy at weekends. Pool table, video screen, cute bar staff and a predominantly young crowd. Gay men welcome as guests.

Y Bar

Map 2, I3. 142 Essex Rd, N1
ⓣ 020/7359 2661. ⊖ Angel.
Thurs 4pm–midnight.
Newish bar run by Yolanda (formerly of the legendary *Due South* bar) and now established as one of the cooler hangouts with the gorgeous girls.

GAY MEN'S CAFÉS, BARS AND PUBS

BarCode

Map 4, E7. 3–4 Archer St, W1
ⓣ 020/7734 3342. ⊖ Piccadilly Circus.
Busy, stylish cruise and dance bar on two floors.

Brief Encounter

Map 4, G7. 41–43 St Martin's Lane, WC2 ⓣ 020/7240 2221.
⊖ Leicester Square.
One of the oldest men's bars

GAY MEN'S CAFÉS, BARS AND PUBS

in London and still hard at it. A popular pre-*Heaven* or post-opera hangout (it's next door to the Coliseum): the front bar is bright, the back bar dark, and both are busy.

Brompton's

Map 3, A8. 294 Old Brompton Rd, SW5 ⓣ 020/7370 1344. ⊖ Earl's Court.

Long-established, leathery and immensely popular late-opening bar-cum-club that's packed at weekends, and features regular cabarets and PAs.

Central Station

Map 3, I1. 37 Wharfdale Rd, N1 ⓣ 020/7278 3294. ⊖ King's Cross.

Award-winning, late-opening community pub on three floors, offering cabaret, cruisey club nights in the *Underground* basement area, and the UK's only gay sports bar. Not strictly men-only, but mostly so.

The Champion

Map 3, A5. 1 Wellington Terrace, Bayswater Rd, W2 ⓣ 020/7243 9531. ⊖ Notting Hill Gate or Queensway.

Long-standing, unpretentious local, with basement bar – *Ruby's* – complete with pool table and a beer garden.

Chariots Café Bar

Map 3, N3. Chariots House, Fairchild St, EC2 ⓣ 020/7247 5222. ⊖ Liverpool Street or Old Street.

This large, stylish and friendly café/bar adjoins Chariots Sauna and offers regular late-licence extensions, cabaret and good-value food.

City of Quebec

Map 3, E4. 12 Old Quebec St, W1 ⓣ 020/7629 6159. ⊖ Marble Arch.

Long-established and busy gay venue with downstairs disco and a late licence six days a week. Especially popular with an older crowd.

The Coleherne

Map 3, A8. 261 Old Brompton Rd, SW5 ⓣ 020/7244 5951. ⊖ Earl's Court.

Famous and permanently packed former leather bar, now popular with a wide range of the gay community

GAY MEN'S CAFÉS, BARS AND PUBS

and still bristling with history.

Comptons of Soho

Map 4, F6. 53 Old Compton St, W1 ⓣ 020/7479 7961. ⊖ Leicester Square or Piccadilly Circus.
This large, traditional-style pub is a Soho institution, always busy with a youngish crowd, but still a relaxed place to cruise or just hang out.

79CXR

Map 4, G6. 79 Charing Cross Rd, WC2 ⓣ 020/7734 0769, ⓦ www.79cxr.co.uk
Busy, cruisey men's den on two floors, with industrial décor, late licence and a no-messing atmosphere.

TEA DANCES

Somewhere between a café and a club is the institution of the **tea dance**, a fun and friendly place to try out old-fashioned partner dancing. Traditionally, tea dancing happens on a Sunday, which means you're unlikely ever to get a serious tea dance habit – although be warned, as it has happened. It's best to arrive early, especially if you need a class; ring in advance for details.

Jackie's Jukebox

Map 2, L7. Rivoli Ballroom, 350 Brockley Rd, SE4 ⓣ 020/8692 5130. Crofton Park Station. First Sat of every month 7.30pm–midnight.
Glide your way round this fabulous original 1950s ballroom to a great mix of music from the 1930s to the present day with legendary DJ Jackie Appleton. Attracts a mixed gay/straight crowd.

Original Sunday Tea Dance at *BJs White Swan*

Map 2, K4. 556 Commercial Rd, E14 ⓣ 020/7780 9870. ⊖ Aldgate East or Limehouse DLR. Sun 5.30pm–midnight.
Hosted by popular local DJ Gary Malden, who plays ballroom, cheesy disco and everything in between. Tea and sandwiches served until 7pm.

Pink Jukebox, Warren Bar at the *Grafton Hotel*

Map 3, G3. 130 Tottenham Court Rd, W1 ⓣ 07774 443 627 ⊖ Tottenham Court Road. Second and fourth Sun of each month 6–11pm.

Jackie Appleton lesbian and gay Latin and ballroom dancing club, with friendly classes for beginners and intermediates.

Waltzing with Hilda at *Jackson's Lane Community Centre*

Map 2, H2. 269a Archway Rd, N6 ⓣ 079390 72958. ⊖ Highgate. Second and last Sat of the month 7.45pm–midnight.

Women-only Latin and ballroom dancing club – with a dash of country and western thrown in to keep you on your toes. Beer at pub prices and classes for beginners.

CLUBS

London's **clubs** tend to open up and shut down with surreal frequency, only to pop up again a few months later in another part of town, or in the same place under a different name. It's a good idea, therefore, to check the gay press, listings magazines and club websites for up-to-date times and prices before you plan your night out. Our listings are by club night where that's best known, or by venue where there's a variety of changing theme nights.

- -

For a guaranteed harassment-free drive home, call Freedom Cabs, 50 Rupert St, W1 ⓣ 020/7734 1313, or Liberty Cars, 330 Old St, EC1 ⓣ 020/7739 9080. Both offer a reasonably priced, London-wide 24-hour gay-run cab service.

- -

Entry charges start at around £4–5, but are more often between £8 and £14, rising to around £35 or even £50 for special events like New Year's Eve extravaganzas. Some places offer concessions for students and

CLUBS

those on benefits, and some extend **discounts** if you've managed to pick up the right flyer. Bear in mind also that clubs are usually significantly cheaper once you're out of the West End. Some clubs, especially the men's, stipulate **dress codes** – mainly leather, rubber, uniform and other fetish wear. We've specified such sartorial regulations, but it's best to check before setting out in your finery.

MIXED CLUBS

Bootylicious at *Crash*

Map 3, I9. 66 Goding St, SE11 (no phone), Ⓦ www.candybar .co.uk ⊖ Vauxhall. Every second Fri from around midnight.
London's only weekend club night devoted to urban dance music. Expect a full-on and sexy vibe at this hip-hop, R&B and ragga-tastic club night. For a hot'n'sweaty dance experience with a beautiful funky crowd, it doesn't get much better than this.

Ẃ̂ŵ̂ ŵ̂ Ŵ̂ŵ̂ŵ̂ at *The Dome*

Map 2, H3. 1 Dartmouth Park Hill, N19 Ⓦ www.clubkali.co.uk ⊖ Tufnell Park. Third Fri of the month.
Kali is a huge multi-ethnic extravaganza offering bhangra, Bollywood, Arabic, swing, Hindi and house flavours for a friendly, attitude-free crowd.

Club Travestie Extraordinaire at *Stepney's Nightclub*

Map 2, K4. 373 Commercial Rd, E1 (club entrance on Aylward St, off Jubilee St) ℡ 020/8788 4154. ⊖ Aldgate East or Shadwell DLR.
Long-running and popular Saturday-night club for TVs/TSs and their pals.

Crash

Map 3, I9. 66 Goding St, SE11 ℡ 020/7278 0995. ⊖ Vauxhall.
Four bars, two dancefloors, chill-out areas and hard bodies make this weekly Saturday club night busy, buzzy, sexy and mostly

boyzy.

DTPM at *Fabric*
Map 3, K3. 77a Charterhouse St, EC1 ⊤ 020/7251 8778, ⓦ www.dtpm-online.net ⊖ Farringdon.
This long-running Sunday-nighter can now be found in *Fabric*'s chic surroundings, with three dancefloors offering soul, jazz, funk, R&B, hip-hop, Latino house and progressive to hard house.

Duckie at the *Royal Vauxhall Tavern*
Map 3, I9. 372 Kennington Lane, SE11 ⊤ 020/7737 4043, ⓦ www.duckie.co.uk Sat weekly.
Duckie's modern, rock-based hurdy-gurdy provides a creative and cheerfully ridiculous antidote to the dreary forces of gay house domination. Cult DJs The Readers Wives are famed for playing *everything* from Kim Wilde to The Velvet Underground. Regular live art performances, occasional bouncy castles and theme nights.

Exilio Latino
Map 5, A4. UCL, Houghton St, WC2A ⊤ 07956 983230, ⓔ gexilio@aol.com ⊖ Holborn.
Every Saturday night, *Exilio* erupts in a lesbian and gay Latin frenzy, spinning salsa, cumbias and merengue, and also featuring live acts.

Fiction at *The Cross*
Map 3, I1 King's Cross Freight Depot, Arches 27–31, off York Way, N1 ⊤ 020/7837 0828, ⓦ www.the-cross.co.uk ⊖ King's Cross.
Brought to you by Blue Cube promotions of *Fabric* fame, *Fiction* is a huge, sweaty and mainly boyzy Friday night session that kicks off at 11pm.

G.A.Y. at *The Astoria*
Map 4, F4. 157 Charing Cross Rd, W1 ⊤ 020/7434 9592, ⓦ www.g-a-y.co.uk ⊖ Tottenham Court Road. Mon, Thurs and Sat.
Widely considered as the launch venue for new (and ailing) boy and girl bands, this huge, unpretentious and fun-loving dance night is where the young crowd gathers.

MIXED CLUBS

There are lots of cheap entry deals to be had at the *G.A.Y. Pink Pounder* trash bash (Mon) – just £1 for a night on the tiles.

The Ghetto

Map 4, F4. Falconberg Court, W1 ⓣ 020/7287 3726. ⊖ Tottenham Court Road. Late-night, cruisey club behind *The Astoria* (see above) with a range of nights catering to every taste (mainly male) from goth/indie to funk, including Wednesday's *Nag, Nag, Nag*, Friday's *The Cock*, and Saturday night's *Wig Out* – a very, very trashy disco.

Heaven

Map 4, H9. Under the Arches, Villiers St, WC2 ⓣ 020/7930 2020, ⓦ www.heaven-london .com ⊖ Charing Cross or Embankment.
Widely regarded as the UK's most popular gay club, this legendary, 2000-capacity venue continues to reign supreme. Big nights are Mondays (*Popcorn*), Wednesdays (*Fruit Machine*) and Saturdays (just *Heaven*),

all with big-name DJs, PAs and shows. More Muscle Mary than Diesel Doris.

Love Muscle at *The Fridge*

Map 2, I6. Town Hall Parade, Brixton Hill, SW2 ⓣ 020/7326 5100, ⓦ www.lovemusclexx .co.uk ⊖ Brixton.
A monthly Saturday night workout for oiled torsos, disco dykes and fag-hag friends, this sweaty, ten-year-old all-nighter offers everything from fluffy techno to hard house via Europop. Big stage shows, stunning lights, go-go dancers and a chill-out zone top off the party madness. Check the website for dates.

Lower The Tone at *Oak Bar*

Map 2, I3. 79 Green Lanes, N16 ⓣ 020/7354 2791.
⊖ Manor House, or buses #73, #171A or #141 from ⊖ Angel. Last Fri of the month.
This hugely popular monthly cult club night is the brainchild of painter Sadie Lee and rock-star pals Lea Andrews and Jonathan Kemp.

Billed as a club for people who don't like clubbing, *LTT* is a cocktail of sugar-coated hip-hop, classic 1970s pop, sleazy foreign disco and bizarre theme tunes.

Miss-Shapes at *The Ghetto*
Map 4, F4. Falconberg Court, W1 ⊤ 020/7287 3726, Ⓦ www.popstarz.co.uk
⊖ Tottenham Court Road.
Popular with indie girlz, this Thursday-nighter is the sister club to its neighbour, *Popstarz*, and plays trash and indie to entice a bevvied and up-for-it, grunge-cool crowd.

Popstarz at the *Scala*
Map 3, I1. 27 Pentonville Rd, N1 ⊤ 020/7738 2336, Ⓦ www.popstarz.co.uk
⊖ King's Cross.
A ground-breaking Friday-night indie club, now in its seventh year and its sixth venue, Popstarz has had to enforce a gay and lesbian majority door policy as its still-winning formula of alternative toons, 1970s and 1980s trash, cheap beer and no attitude attracts a growing

straight, studenty crowd.

Queer Nation at *Substation South*
Map 2, I6. 9 Brighton Terrace, SW9 ⊤ 020/7732 2095.
⊖ Brixton.
Long-running and popular New York-style house and garage Saturday-night club for funksters.

Trade at *Turnmills*
Map 3, K3. 63b Clerkenwell Rd, EC1 ⊤ 020/7250 3409, Ⓦ www.tradeuk.net
⊖ Farringdon.
This legendary Saturday all-nighter (business kicks off at 4am and carries on till Sunday lunchtime) is still going strong. Expect techno and hard house from some of the best DJs in the country, lots of lasers and special effects, and some very sweaty hard bodies – of all genders and flavours, but mostly boys.

WayOut Club at *Charlie's*
Map 7, K5. 9 Crosswall, off Minories, EC3 ⊤ 020/8363 0948, Ⓦ www.thewayout.com
⊖ Aldgate or Tower Hill.
Long-established Saturday

MIXED CLUBS

269

night for gays, straights, cross-dressers, drag queens, TVs, TSs and friends, which offers a warm welcome, changing rooms, video screen and regular cabaret.

LESBIAN CLUBS

Dolly Mixtures at *Candy Bar*

Map 4, F2. 4 Carlisle St, WC2
Ⓦ www.candybar.co.uk
Ⓔ Tottenham Court Road.
DJ Slamma plays house and soul while Crystal gets busy on the mic every Saturday. Friday nights see *Set It Off* with R&B classics and garage.

Liberté at *Oak Bar*

Map 2, I3. 79 Green Lanes, N16 Ⓣ 020/7354 2791.
Ⓔ Manor House, or buses #73, #171 or #141a from Angel tube. Last Sat of the month.
Great late-night watering hole offering women only the hugely popular *Liberté*, spinning soulful grooves, reggae and garage for girls who like to smile when they're swinging.

French Kiss at *Spirit*

Map 3, L3 2–5 Carthusian St, EC1 (no phone),
Ⓦ www.frenchkissclub.co.uk
Ⓔ Barbican. First Sat of the month.
This sexy new club playing progressive tribal and trance offers sophisticated clubbing for gay girls and their male guests.

Girl Friday at *First Out*

Map 4, G5. 52 St Giles High St, WC2 Ⓣ 020/7240 8042,
Ⓦ www.firstoutcafebar.com
Ⓔ Tottenham Court Road.
This long-standing Friday favourite is the place to meet girl pals at the end of a busy working week. Expect a packed basement for mingling and pre-club drinking.

Rumours at *Minories*

Map 7, K5. 64-73 Minories, EC3 Ⓣ 07961/158 375,
Ⓦ www.girl-rumours.co.uk
Ⓔ Tower Hill or Aldgate.
Biweekly Sat 8pm–2am.
There's room for 500 grrrls at this popular and cheap club night, which offers two bars, quiet lounges and two

dancefloors.

GAY MEN'S CLUBS
- - - - - - - - - - - - - - - - - - - -

Backstreet
Map 2, K4. Wentworth Mews, off Burdett Rd, E3 ⓣ 020/8980 8557 or 8980 7880 (outside club hours), ⓦ www .thebackstreet.com ⊖ Mile End.
Long-running, traditional leather and rubber club with a strict, *very* butch dress code.

Chariots Roman Baths
Map 2, J4. 201–207 Shoreditch High St, EC1 ⓣ 020/7247 5333, ⓦ www.gaysauna.co.uk ⊖ Liverpool Street.
London's largest and most fabulous gay sauna features everything you could wish for in the way of clearing out pores (and much else), and is open late all week and all night at weekends. Check the website for other city locations.

The Fort
Map 3, 7N. 131 Grange Rd, SE1 ⓣ 020/7237 7742.

⊖ Bermondsey or London Bridge.
There's no set dress code at this sleazy, sexy cruise bar, but check free press or phone for details about special themed nights like boots or underwear.

The Hoist
Map 3, I8. Railway Arch, 47c South Lambeth Rd, SW8 ⓣ 020/7735 9972. ⊖ Vauxhall.
Weekend men's cruise bar with a leather/rubber /industrial/uniform dress code. Hosts *SM Gays* every third Thursday.

Underground at *Central Station*
Map 3, I1. 37 Wharfdale Rd, N1 ⓣ 020/7278 3294. ⊖ King's Cross.
The basement of this friendly, three-tiered pub yields sleazy late-night cruising seven nights a week, and is also host to *Gummi*, Europe's only rubber-only club, every second Sunday of the month. Equally picturesque theme nights take place on other nights: call for details.

GAY MEN'S CLUBS

Classical music, opera and dance

With the South Bank, the Barbican and the Wigmore Hall offering year-round appearances by generally first-rank musicians, and numerous smaller venues providing a stage for less established or more specialized performers, the capital should satisfy most devotees of **classical music**. What's more, in the annual Promenade Concerts at the Royal Albert Hall London has one of Europe's greatest, most democratic music festivals – see p.274.

Despite its elitist image, **opera** in the capital continues to attract new audiences. With the Royal Opera House (ROH) seeming to have put its recent troubles behind it – though ticket prices are still far too high – it is now the turn of the English National Opera (ENO) to experience the trials and tribulations of a major overhaul to its theatre. The two major companies aside, there are also outfits, like the Almeida and Battersea Arts Centre, that are extending the boundaries of contemporary music theatre in lively and adventurous ways.

The more modest economics of **dance** means that you'll

often find a broad spectrum of ambitious work on offer, with some of the world's outstanding companies appearing on a regular basis at Sadler's Wells. Meanwhile, fans of classicism can revel in the **Royal Ballet** – a company with some of the most accomplished dancers in Europe.

CLASSICAL MUSIC

London is spoilt for choice when it comes to **orchestras**. On most days you'll be able to catch a concert by either the London Symphony Orchestra, the London Philharmonic, the Royal Philharmonic, the Philharmonia or the BBC Symphony Orchestra, or a smaller-scale performance from the English Chamber Orchestra or the Academy of St Martin-in-the-Fields. There are also more specialized ensembles, like the Orchestra of the Age of Enlightenment, who perform pre-twentieth-century repertoire on period instruments, and the London Sinfonietta, one of the world's finest contemporary music groups. Full houses are a rarity, so even at the biggest concert halls you should be able to pick up a ticket for around £12 (the usual range is about £6–30). During the week, there are also **free lunchtime concerts** by students or professionals in many of London's churches, particularly in the City; performances in the Royal College of Music and Royal Academy of Music are of an amazingly high standard, and the choice of work a lot riskier than the commercial venues can manage.

Barbican Centre

Map 7, D1. Silk St, EC2

ⓣ 020/7638 8891 or 7638 4141,

ⓦ www.barbican.org.uk

⊖ Barbican or Moorgate.

With the outstanding London Symphony Orchestra as its resident orchestra, and with top foreign orchestras and big-name soloists in regular attendance, the Barbican is one of the capital's best arenas for classical music. Programming is much more

273

THE PROMS

The Royal Albert Hall's **BBC Henry Wood Promenade Concerts** – known as the "Proms" – tend to be associated primarily with the raucous "Last Night", when the flag-waving audience sings its patriotic heart out. This jingoistic nonsense completely misrepresents the Proms, however, which from July to September feature at least one concert daily in an exhilarating melange of favourites and new or recondite works. You can book a seat as you would for any other concert, but for many the essence of the Proms is that all the stalls seats are removed to create hundreds of standing places costing around £4. The upper gallery is similarly packed with people sitting on the floor or standing, and tickets there are even cheaper. The acoustics aren't the world's best – OK for orchestral blockbusters, less so for small-scale works – but the performers are usually outstanding, the atmosphere is great, and the hall is so vast that the likelihood of being turned away if you turn up on the night is slim. A recent innovation is the **Proms Chamber Series**, a handful of lunchtime concerts (£6; booking in advance strongly advised) held in the lecture theatre of the nearby Victoria and Albert Museum.

The annual *Proms Guide*, available at most bookshops from May, gives information on every concert. You can also call the Albert Hall direct on ℡ 020/7589 8212, or visit the BBC Proms website at ⓦ www.bbc.co.uk/proms.

CLASSICAL MUSIC

adventurous than it was, and free music in the foyer is often very good. Unfortunately, it's a difficult place to find and to find your way around.

Royal Academy of Music

Map 3, F3. Marylebone Rd, NW1 ℡ 020/7873 7373, ⓦ www.ram.ac.uk ⊖ Regent's Park or Baker Street.
During term-time, you can catch at least one lunchtime

concert each week (Fri 1pm), and an early-evening recital, for which there's sometimes an entry charge.

Royal College of Music

Map 3, C7. Prince Consort Rd, SW7 ⓣ 020/7589 3643, ⓦ www.rcm.ac.uk ⊖ Kensington.

Free lunchtime (1pm) concerts are staged at London's top music college on Tuesdays, Wednesdays and Thursdays, and at nearby St Mary Abbots Church, Kensington High Street, on Fridays during term-time. There are also occasional evening concerts, for which there may be an entry charge.

St John's

Map 3, H7. Smith Square, SW1 ⓣ 020/7222 1061, ⓦ www.sjss.org.uk ⊖ Westminster.

This striking Baroque church, situated behind Westminster Abbey, was gutted in 1941 and later turned into a concert hall with a fine acoustic. Its varied musical menu includes orchestral and choral concerts, chamber

music and solo recitals. The restaurant in the crypt is good for before or after.

St Martin-in-the-Fields

Map 4, H8. Trafalgar Square, WC2 ⓣ 020/7839 8362, ⓦ www.stmartin-in-the-fields .org ⊖ Charing Cross or Leicester Square.

Free lunchtime recitals on Mondays, Tuesdays and Fridays, plus a few fee-charging candlelit concerts in the evenings, sometimes featuring the top-notch orchestra of the Academy of St Martin-in-the-Fields.

South Bank Centre

Map 6, B3. South Bank Centre, SE1 ⓣ 020/7960 4242, ⓦ www.sbc.org.uk ⊖ Waterloo.

The SBC has three concert venues, none of which is exclusively used for classical music. The Royal Festival Hall (RFH) is a gargantuan space, tailor-made for large-scale choral and orchestral works. It plays host to some big-name soloists as well, though only a few can fill it. The Queen Elizabeth Hall

CLASSICAL MUSIC

(QEH) is the prime location for chamber concerts, solo recitals and contemporary work, while the Purcell Room is the most intimate venue, excellent for chamber music and recitals by up-and-coming instrumentalists and singers. All concerts, other than the occasional performance in the foyer, are fee-paying.

The Warehouse
Map 6, D4. 13 Theed St, SE1
Ⓣ 020/7928 9251,
Ⓦ www.thewarehouselondon.com Ⓔ Waterloo.
A multipurpose commercial space that's one of the best and most exciting venues for contemporary music, with many concerts promoted by the Society for the Promotion of New Music (SPNM).

Wigmore Hall
Map 4, A4. 36 Wigmore St, W1
Ⓣ 020/7935 2141,
Ⓦ www.wigmore-hall.org.uk
Ⓔ Bond Street or Oxford Circus.
With its near-perfect acoustics, the small Wigmore Hall is a favourite with artists and audiences alike; concerts are best booked well in advance. An exceptional venue for chamber music, it is also well-known for its song recitals by some of the world's greatest singers. Stages very popular, fee-paying mid-morning concerts on a Sunday.

OPERA

Of the two main companies, the **Royal Opera House** is undergoing a new lease of life since its refurbishment and the appointment of a new music director. Meanwhile **English National Opera** has started renovating its theatre, the vast London Coliseum, while continuing to show what can be achieved with young, home-grown talent and lively, radical productions.

English National Opera

Map 4, H8. Coliseum, St Martin's Lane, WC2
ⓣ 020/7632 8300,
ⓦ www.eno.org ⊖ Leicester Square or Charing Cross.

English National Opera differs from its Royal Opera House counterpart in that all its operas are sung in English, productions tend to be more experimental, and the cost is far less. Ticket prices start from as little as £3, rising to just over £60; day seats are also available to personal callers after 10am on the day of the performance, with balcony seats going for just £3. Three hours before the performance, standbys (all tickets that are unsold) go on sale at £12.50 to students and £18 to senior citizens and the unemployed. Despite suffering the enforced resignation of its general director, and being in the throes of major restoration work, the company continues to produce challenging and often outstanding work.

Royal Opera House

Map 4, I6. Bow St, WC2
ⓣ 020/7304 4000,
ⓦ www.royaloperahouse.org
⊖ Covent Garden.

Since its recent refurbishment, the ROH has become more accessible – the Floral Hall foyer is open to the public during the day, there are regular free lunchtime recitals, and more modestly priced, small-scale productions in the new Linbury Theatre. As well as this, its dynamic new music director, Antonio Pappano, seems determined to rid the company of its conservatism. However, the ROH can still be snobbish and it remains ludicrously overpriced (over £120 for the very best seats). A small number of day seats (for £30 or under) are put on sale from 10am on the day of a performance – these are restricted to one per person, and you need to get there by 8am for popular shows. Four hours before performances, low-price standbys (subject to availability) can be bought for around £15 by students, senior citizen, etc. In

OPERA

summer, some performances are occasionally relayed live to a large screen in Covent Garden Piazza. All operas are performed in the original language, but are discreetly subtitled.

DANCE

For classical ballet lovers, the **Royal Ballet** possesses a number of truly world-class soloists; there's also the English National Ballet (ENB), a touring company who frequently perform in London including a regular Christmas slot at the Coliseum, and occasional visits to the Festival Hall (see p.275) and the Royal Albert Hall (see p.273). Those interested in more cutting-edge work can chose between the intimacy of **The Place** or the larger **Sadler's Wells**, both venues for the best contemporary work. London also has a good reputation for international dance festivals showcasing the work of a wide range of companies. The biggest of the annual events is the **Dance Umbrella** (℗ 020/8741 5881, ⓦ www.danceumbrella .co.uk), a six-week season (Sept–Nov) of often ground-breaking new work at various venues across town.

Barbican Centre
Map 7, D1. Silk St, EC2
℗ 020/7638 8891 or 7638 4141,
ⓦ www.barbican.org.uk
⊖ Barbican or Moorgate.
As part of its mixed programming, the Barbican regularly stages contemporary dance by top international companies. It is also used as a venue for Dance Umbrella events.

London Coliseum
Map 4, H8. St Martin's Lane, WC2 ℗ 020/7632 8300,
ⓦ www.eno.org ⊖ Leicester Square or Charing Cross.
The Coliseum (home to English National Opera) is used for dance between breaks in the opera season, most regularly by English National Ballet.

DANCE

CLASSICAL MUSIC, OPERA AND DANCE

The Place

Map 3, H2. 17 Duke's Rd, WC1 ⓣ 020/7387 0031, ⓦ www.theplace.org.uk ⊖ Euston.

The Place is the base of the Richard Alston Dance Company and home to the London Contemporary Dance School. Its small Robin Howard Dance Theatre presents the work of new choreographers and student performers, and plays host to some of the finest small-scale contemporary dance from across the globe.

Royal Ballet

Map 4 I6. Royal Opera House, Bow St, WC2 ⓣ 020/7304 4000, ⓦ www.royaloperahouse .org ⊖ Covent Garden.

The Royal Ballet is one of the most renowned classical companies in the world, whose outstanding principals include Darcey Bussell and Sylvie Guillem. The recent refurbishment added two small performing spaces, the Linbury Theatre and the Clore Studio, where more experimental work can be seen. Prices are almost half of those for the opera; you should be able to get decent seats for around £25 if you act quickly, though sell-outs are frequent (see Royal Opera House, p.277, for details of day tickets and standbys).

Sadler's Wells Theatre

Map 3, K2. Rosebery Ave, EC1 ⓣ 020/7863 8000, ⓦ www.sadlers-wells.com ⊖ Angel.

The newly rebuilt Sadler's Wells Theatre in Islington is home to Britain's best contemporary dance companies, including the Rambert, while many of the finest international companies are also regular visitors. The Lilian Baylis Theatre, tucked around the back, puts on smaller-scale shows, while the Peacock Theatre in the West End is where Sadler's Wells stages more populist dance, including flamenco and tango shows.

South Bank Centre

Map 6, B3. South Bank, SE1 ⓣ 020/7960 4242, ⓦ www.sbc.org.uk ⊖ Waterloo.

The South Bank Centre's

DANCE

three venues all stage dance performances, often as part of the Dance Umbrella Festival in the autumn. It is also the main venue for Asian dance in the capital, while the Festival Hall is occasionally home to English National Ballet.

Theatre, comedy and cinema

L ondon has enjoyed a reputation for quality **theatre** since the time of Shakespeare and, despite the continuing prevalence of blockbuster musicals and revenue-spinning star vehicles, the city still provides a platform for innovation. The **comedy** scene in London goes from strength to strength, so much so that the capital now boasts more comedy venues than any other city in the world. **Cinema** is rather less healthy, for London's repertory film theatres are a dying breed, edged out by the multi-screen complexes which show mainstream Hollywood fare some months behind America. There are a few excellent independent cinemas, though, including the National Film Theatre, which is the focus of the richly varied **London Film Festival** in November.

Current details of **what's on** in all these areas can be found in a number of publications, the most comprehensive being the weekly *Time Out*. Saturday's *Guardian* and Friday's *Evening Standard* are other good sources.

THEATRE

At first glance, it might seem as though London's **West End** theatres have become a province of the Andrew Lloyd Webber empire; however, few cities in the world can match the variety of the London scene. The State-funded **Royal Shakespeare Company** and the **National Theatre** often put on extremely original productions of mainstream masterpieces, while some of the most exciting work is performed in what have become known as the **Off West End** theatres, which consistently stage interesting and often challenging productions. Further still down the financial ladder are the **Fringe** theatres, more often than not pub venues, where ticket prices are low, and quality variable.

Unfortunately, most theatre-going doesn't come cheap. **Tickets** under £10 are restricted to the Fringe; the box-office average is closer to £15–25, with £30–40 the usual top whack. Tickets for the durable musicals and well-reviewed plays are like gold dust. Ticket agencies such as Ticketmaster (☎ 020/7344 4444, ⓦ www.ticketmaster.co.uk) or First Call (☎ 020/7497 9977, ⓦ www.firstcalltickets.com), can get seats for most West End shows, but add up to ten percent on the ticket price. The cheapest way to buy your ticket is to go to the theatre box office in person; if you book over the phone, you're likely to be charged a booking fee. Students, senior citizens and the unemployed can get **concessionary rates** on tickets for many shows, and many theatres offer reductions on standby tickets to these groups. Whatever you do, avoid the touts and the dodgy-looking ticket agencies that abound in the West End – there's no guarantee that the tickets are genuine.

The Society of London Theatre (ⓦ www.officiallondontheatre .co.uk) runs the **tkts ticket booth** in Leicester Square (Mon–Sat 10am–7pm, Sun noon–3pm), which sells on-the-day tickets for all the West End shows at discounts of up to fifty percent, though they tend to be in the top end of the price range, are limited to four per person, and carry a service charge of £2.50 per ticket.

What follows is a list of those West End theatres that offer a changing roster of good plays, along with the most consistent of the Off West End and Fringe venues. This by no means represents the full tally of London's stages, as there are scores of Fringe places that present work on an intermittent basis – *Time Out* provides the most comprehensive and detailed up-to-the-minute survey.

Almeida

Map 2, I3. Almeida St, N1
ⓣ 020/7359 4404,
ⓦ www.almeida.co.uk ⊖ Angel or Highbury & Islington.
A deservedly popular Off West End venue in Islington, which premieres excellent new plays and excitingly reworked classics, and has attracted some big Hollywood names. The Almeida has recently undergone a spectacular rebuilding programme.

Barbican Centre

Map 7, D1. Silk St, EC2
ⓣ 020/7638 8891,
ⓦ www.barbican.org.uk
⊖ Barbican or Moorgate.
The Barbican's two venues – the excellently designed Barbican Theatre and the much smaller Pit – put on a wide variety of theatrical spectacles from puppetry and musicals to new drama works, and, of course Shakespeare, courtesy of the Royal Shakespeare Company who perform here (and elsewhere in London) on and off from autumn to spring each year.

Battersea Arts Centre

Map 2, H6. 176 Lavender Hill, SW11 ⓣ 020/7223 2223,
ⓦ www.bac.org.uk Clapham Junction station, from Victoria or Waterloo.
The BAC is a triple-stage building, housed in an old town hall in south London, and has acquired a reputation

THEATRE

for excellent Fringe productions, from straight theatre to comedy and cabaret.

Bush

Map 2, F5. Shepherd's Bush Green, W12 ⓣ 020/7610 4224. ⊖ Goldhawk Road or Shepherd's Bush.

This minuscule above-pub theatre is London's most reliable venue for new writing after the Royal Court, and its productions have turned up some real crackers.

Donmar Warehouse

Map 4, H5. Thomas Neal's, Earlham St, WC2 ⓣ 020/7369 1732, ⓦ www .donmar-warehouse.com ⊖ Covent Garden.

A performance space that's noted for new plays and top-quality reappraisals of the classics. The theatre attracted media attention in recent years when its former artistic director, Sam Mendes, managed to entice several Hollywood stars to take to the stage.

Drill Hall

Map 4, F2. 16 Chenies St, WC1 ⓣ 020/7307 5060, ⓦ www.drillhall.co.uk ⊖ Goodge Street.

This studio-style venue off Tottenham Court Road specializes in gay, lesbian, feminist and politically correct new work. Monday evenings are women only; Thursdays are no-smoking.

Hampstead Theatre

Map 2, G3. Eton Avenue, NW3 ⓣ 020/7722 9301, ⓦ www.hampstead-theatre .co.uk ⊖ Swiss Cottage.

A spanking new zinc- and glass-fronted theatre in Swiss Cottage (not in Hampstead proper), whose productions often move on to the West End. Such is its prestige that the likes of John Malkovich have been seduced into performing here.

ICA

Map 4, F10. Nash House, The Mall, SW1 ⓣ 020/7930 3647, ⓦ www.ica.org.uk ⊖ Charing Cross.

The Institute of Contemporary Arts attracts

THEATRE

the most innovative practitioners in all areas of performance. It also attracts a fair quantity of modish junk, but the hits outweigh the misses.

King's Head

Map 2, I3. 115 Upper St, N1 ⓣ 020/7226 1916. ⊖ Angel or Highbury & Islington.

The oldest and probably most famous of London's thriving pub-theatres (with a useful late licence). Adventurous performances in a pint-sized room at lunchtimes and in the evenings.

National Theatre

Map 6, C2. South Bank Centre, South Bank, SE1 ⓣ 020/7452 3000, ⓦ www.nationaltheatre.org.uk ⊖ Waterloo.

The Royal National Theatre, as it's officially known, consists of three separate theatres: the 1100-seater Olivier, the proscenium-arched Lyttelton and the experimental Cottesloe. Standards set by the late Lawrence Olivier, founding artistic director, are maintained by the country's top actors and directors in a programme ranging from Greek tragedies to Broadway musicals. Some productions sell out months in advance, but 20–30 of the cheapest tickets go on sale on the morning of each performance – get there by 8am for the popular shows.

Open Air Theatre

Map 3, E2. Regent's Park, Inner Circle, NW1 ⓣ 020/7486 2431, ⓦ www.open-air-theatre .org.uk ⊖ Regent's Park or Baker Street.

If the weather's good, there's nothing quite like a dose of alfresco drama. This beautiful space in Regent's Park hosts a tourist-friendly summer programme of Shakespeare, musicals, plays and concerts.

Royal Court

Map 3, E8. Sloane Square, SW1 ⓣ 020/7565 5000, ⓦ www.royalcourttheatre.com ⊖ Sloane Square.

Newly refurbished, the Royal Court is one of the best places in London to catch radical new writing, either in

THEATRE

285

the proscenium-arch Theatre Downstairs, or the smaller-scale Theatre Upstairs studio space.

Shakespeare's Globe

Map 7, B7. New Globe Walk, SE1 ⓣ 020/7902 1400, Ⓦ www.shakespeares-globe.org ⊖ London Bridge, Blackfriars or Southwark.

This thatch-roofed replica Elizabethan theatre uses only natural light and the minimum of scenery, and currently puts on solid, fun Shakespearean shows from mid-May to mid-September, with "groundling" tickets (standing-room only) for around a fiver.

Tricycle

Map 2, F3. 269 Kilburn High Rd, NW6 ⓣ 020/7328 1000, Ⓦ www.tricycle.co.uk ⊖ Kilburn.

One of London's most dynamic Fringe venues, showcasing a mixed bag of new plays, with an emphasis on black and Irish issues, and international productions of the core repertoire.

Young Vic

Map 6, E5. 66 The Cut, SE1 ⓣ 020/7928 6363, Ⓦ www.youngvic.org ⊖ Waterloo.

A large, "in-the-round" space, perfect for Shakespeare, which is something of a speciality, as well as a studio for variable Fringe productions. Big names have appeared at the main stage over the years – Vanessa Redgrave's version of Ibsen's *Ghosts* is near-legendary.

COMEDY AND CABARET

London's **comedy scene** continues to live up to its media-coined status as the new rock'n'roll with the leading funnypersons catapulted to unlikely stardom on both stage and screen. The Comedy Store is the best-known and most central venue on the circuit, but just about every London suburb has a venue giving a platform to young hopefuls (full listings appear on Ⓦ www.chortle.co.uk, and in *Time Out*). Note that many venues operate only on Friday and Saturday nights, and that August is a lean month, as much of London's talent then heads north for the Edinburgh Festival. Tickets at smaller venues can be had for around £5, but in the more established places you're looking at £10 or more.

Backyard Comedy Club

Map 2, J4. 231 Cambridge Heath Rd, E2 Ⓣ 020/7739 3122, Ⓦ www.leehurst.com ⊖ Bethnal Green. Fri & Sat. Purpose-built club in Bethnal Green established by comedian Lee Hurst, who has successfully managed to attract a consistently strong lineup.

Banana Cabaret

Map 2, H7. The Bedford, 77 Bedford Hill, SW12 Ⓣ 020/8673 8904, Ⓦ www.bananacabaret .co.uk ⊖ Balham. Fri & Sat. This double-stage pub has become one of London's most welcoming comedy venues – well worth the trip out from the centre of town. It all kicks off at 9pm and is followed by a DJ.

Canal Café Theatre

Map 3, B3. The Bridge House, Delamere Terrace, W2 Ⓣ 020/7289 6054, Ⓦ www .chortle.co.uk/venues /canal.html ⊖ Warwick Avenue. Thurs–Sat. Perched on the water's edge in Little Venice, this venue is good for improvisation acts and is home to the "Newsrevue" team of topical gagsters.

Comedy Café

Map 3, N2. 66 Rivington St, EC2 Ⓣ 020/7739 5706, Ⓦ www.comedycafe.co.uk ⊖ Old Street. Wed–Sat. Long-established, purpose-built club in Shoreditch/Hoxton, often with impressive lineups, and free admission for the new-acts slot on Wednesday nights.

COMEDY AND CABARET

CHAPTER TWENTY-TWO

Comedy Store

Map 4, F8. Haymarket House, 1a Oxendon St, SW1 ⓣ 020/7344 0234, Ⓦ www.thecomedystore.co.uk ⊖ Piccadilly Circus.

Widely regarded as the birthplace of alternative comedy, though no longer in its original venue, the Comedy Store has catapulted many a stand-up onto primetime TV. Improvisation by in-house comics on Wednesdays and Sundays, in addition to a stand-up bill; Friday and Saturday are the busiest nights, with two shows, at 8pm and midnight – book ahead.

Jongleurs Camden Lock

Map 2, H3. Dingwalls Building, 36 Camden Lock Place, Chalk Farm Rd, NW1 ⓣ 020/7564 2500, Ⓦ www.jongleurs.com ⊖ Camden Town. Fri & Sat.

Jongleurs is the chain store of comedy, doling out high-quality stand-up and post-revelry disco dancing on Fridays. Also has branches at Bow and Battersea. Book well in advance.

Meccano Club

Map 3, K1. Dove Regent, 65 Graham St, N1 ⓣ 020/7813 4478, Ⓦ www.themeccanoclub .co.uk ⊖ Angel. Fri & Sat.

Popular, intimate, pub-based Islington venue that features consistently strong lineups.

CINEMA

There are an awful lot of **cinemas** in the West End, many of them now multiplexes, yet very few places committed to non-mainstream movies, and even fewer repertory cinemas programming serious films from the back catalogue. November's **London Film Festival** (Ⓦ www.lff.org.uk), which occupies half a dozen West End cinemas, is now a huge event, and so popular that most of the films sell out soon after publication of the festival's programme.

CINEMA

Tickets at the major screens in the West End cost £8 and upwards, although afternoon shows are usually discounted. The suburban screens run by the big companies (see *Time Out* for full listings) tend to be a couple of pounds cheaper, as do independent cinemas. Students, senior citizens and the unemployed can get **concessionary rates** for some shows at virtually all cinemas, usually all day Monday or at other off-peak times on weekdays.

Below is a selection of the cinemas that put on the most interesting programmes.

BFI London Imax Centre

Map 6, C4. South Bank, SE1
ⓣ 020/7902 1234,
ⓦ www.bfi.org.uk/imax
⊖ Waterloo.

The British Film Institute's remarkable glazed drum sits in the middle of the roundabout at the end of Waterloo Bridge. It's stunning, state-of-the-art stuff alright, showing 2D and 3D films on a massive screen, but like all IMAX cinemas it suffers from the paucity of good material that's been shot on the format.

Ciné Lumière

Map 8, C8. 17 Queensberry Place, SW7 ⓣ 020/7073 1350,
ⓦ www.institut-francais.org.uk
⊖ South Kensington.

Predominantly – but by no means exclusively – French films both old and new (sometimes with subtitles), put on by the Institut Français.

Electric

Map 2, F4. 191 Portobello Rd, W11 ⓣ 020/7299 8688,
ⓦ www.the-electric.co.uk
⊖ Notting Hill Gate or Ladbroke Grove.

One of the oldest cinemas in the country (opened 1910), the Electric has been restored to its former glory and now shows mostly mainstream films.

Empire

Map 4, F7. Leicester Square, WC2 ⓣ 0870/010 2030,
ⓦ www.uci-cinemas.co.uk
⊖ Leicester Square.

The huge, expensive, hi-tech

CINEMA

main auditorium here is London's second largest, and is the place where blockbusters tend to premiere and royalty occasionally turn up.

ICA Cinema

Map 4, E10. Nash House, The Mall, SW1 ☏ 020/7930 3647, ⓦ www.ica.org.uk ⊖ Piccadilly Circus or Charing Cross. Vintage and underground movies shown on one of two tiny screens in the avant-garde HQ of the Institute of Contemporary Arts.

National Film Theatre

Map 6, B2. South Bank, SE1 ☏ 020/7928 3232, ⓦ www.bfi .org.uk/nft ⊖ Waterloo. Known for its attentive audiences and an exhaustive, eclectic programme that includes directors' seasons and thematic series. Around six films daily are shown in the vast NFT1 and the smaller NFT2.

Odeon West End

Map 4, G7. 22–24 Leicester Square, WC2 ☏ 0870/5050 007, ⓦ www.odeon.co.uk

⊖ Leicester Square. London's largest cinema, and thus a favourite for celeb-packed premieres. There's just one screen here, so don't mistakenly enter the adjacent Odeon Mezzanine, which crushes five into a far smaller space.

Prince Charles

Map 4, G7. Leicester Place, WC2 ☏ 020/7494 3654, ⓦ www.princecharlescinema .com ⊖ Leicester Square or Piccadilly Circus. The bargain basement of London's cinemas (entry for most shows is just £3.50), with a programme of new movies, classics and cult favourites – the *Sing-Along-A-Sound-of-Music* is a regular.

Riverside Studios

Map 2, E5. Crisp Rd, W6 ☏ 020/8237 1111, ⓦ www.riversidestudios.co.uk ⊖ Hammersmith. This converted film studio in West London is worth checking out for its mini-festivals and innovative programming.

CINEMA

Galleries

T he vast **permanent collections** of the National
Gallery and the two Tates, the fascinating miscella-
nies of the Victoria and Albert Museum, and the
select holdings of such institutions as the Courtauld and the
Wallace Collection make London one of the world's great
repositories of Western art. However, the city is also a
dynamic creative centre, with artists such as Rachel
Whiteread, Sarah Lucas and Richard Wilson maintaining
the momentum established by the likes of Hockney, Caro,
Auerbach and Freud.

London's **commercial galleries** are scattered all over
the city, but there are two areas where the art world is particularly concentrated. Mayfair, the traditional epicentre of
the art market, continues to thrive around Bond Street, particularly in Cork Street, behind the Royal Academy; more
recently, however, galleries have sprung up all over the
Shoreditch/Hoxton area, just north of the City.

London fails to compete with Berlin, Paris and New
York in only one respect – it doesn't really have a designat-
ed **exhibition space** good enough to handle the blockbuster shows. Nevertheless, at any time of the year
London's public galleries will be offering at least one
absorbing exhibition, on anything from the art of the apoc-
alypse to Soviet supremacists.

Annual fixtures include the **Royal Academy's Summer Exhibition**, when hordes of amateur artists enter their efforts for sale, and November's controversial **Turner Prize**, devoted to new British work, which is preceded by a month-long display of work by the shortlisted artists at the Tate. More exciting than these, however, are the art-school **degree shows** in late May and June, when the current crop of student talent puts its work on display. For a rundown of the latest exhibitions, pick up a copy of the free listings handout *New Exhibitions of Contemporary Art* (Ⓦ www.newexhibitions.com), available at most galleries, or the weekly *Time Out*.

PERMANENT COLLECTIONS

Below is a list of London's principal permanent art collections, with a brief summary of their strengths and, where relevant, a cross-reference to the page of the guide where you'll find more detailed coverage.

British Museum
Map 4, G3. Great Russell St, WC1 Ⓣ 020/7323 8000, Ⓦ www.british-museum.ac.uk Ⓔ Russell Square or Tottenham Court Road. See p.56.
The BM owns a stupendous collection of drawings and prints, a small sample of which is always on show in room 90. It also stages excellent one-off exhibitions.

Dalí Universe
Map 6, A6. Riverside Building, County Hall, SE1 Ⓣ 020/7620 2420, Ⓦ www.daliuniverse.com Ⓔ Westminster. See p.112.
Permanent collection of works by Dalí, mostly little-known bronzes and illustrated books, plus one or two classics.

Dulwich Picture Gallery
Map 2, J7. College Rd, SE21 Ⓣ 020/8693 5254,

Ⓦ www.dulwichpicturegallery.org
.uk West Dulwich station from
Victoria. See p.150.
London's oldest public art
gallery houses a small but
high-quality selection of
work ranging from Poussin
and Gainsborough to
Rembrandt.

Estorick Collection

Map 2, I3. 39a Canonbury
Square, N1 Ⓣ 020/7704 9522,
Ⓦ www.estorickcollection.com
⊖ Highbury & Islington. £3.50.
Georgian mansion with a
small but interesting
collection of twentieth-
century Italian art, including
Modigliani, di Chirico and
the Futurists.

Guildhall Art Gallery

Map 7, D3. Gresham St, EC2
Ⓣ 020/7606 1632,
Ⓦ www.cityoflondon.gov.uk
⊖ Bank or St Paul's. See p.91.
Purpose-built gallery housing
the Corporation of London's
collection, which contains
one or two exceptional Pre-
Raphaelite works by the likes
of Rossetti and Holman
Hunt.

Iveagh Bequest

Map 2, G2. Kenwood House,
Hampstead Lane, NW3
Ⓣ 020/8348 1286. Bus #210
from ⊖ Archway, or walk from
Hampstead or ⊖ Archway. See
p.45.
Stately home overlooking
Hampstead Heath that's best
known for its pictures by
Rembrandt, Gainsborough,
Reynolds and Vermeer.

Leighton House

Map 2, F5. 12 Holland Park
Rd, W14 Ⓣ 020/7602 3316,
Ⓦ www.rbkc.gov.uk ⊖ High
Street Kensington. See p.133.
The house itself is a work of
art, but it also contains several
works by Lord Leighton
himself and his Pre-
Raphaelite chums.

National Gallery

Map 4, G8. Trafalgar Square,
WC2 Ⓣ 020/7306 0055,
Ⓦ www.nationalgallery.org.uk
⊖ Charing Cross or Leicester
Square. See p.19.
The country's premier
collection; it's difficult to think
of a major artist born between
1300 and 1850 whose work
isn't on show here.

PERMANENT COLLECTIONS

National Portrait Gallery

Map 4, G8. 2 St Martin's Place, WC2 ⓣ 020/7306 0055, ⓦ www.npg.org.uk ⊖ Leicester Square or Charing Cross. See p.21.

Interesting faces, but only a few works of art of a quality to match those on display in the neighbouring National Gallery.

Queen's Gallery

Map 4, C13. Buckingham Palace, Buckingham Palace Rd, SW1 ⓣ 020/7321 2233, ⓦ www.royal.gov.uk ⊖ St James's Park or Victoria. See p.25.

Changing exhibitions from the Royal Collection, which is three times larger than the National Gallery.

Somerset House

Map 5, A6. Strand, WC2 ⓣ 020/7845 4600, ⓦ www.somerset-house.org.uk ⊖ Covent Garden or Temple (Mon–Sat only). See p.69.
Several collections in one building: the Courtauld Institute boasts Impressionists and Post-Impressionists; the

Hermitage Rooms put on changing exhibitions from the Winter Palace in St Petersburg; the Gilbert Collection is a permanent display of decorative arts.

Tate Britain

Map 3, H8. Millbank, SW1 ⓣ 020/7887 8008, ⓦ www.tate.org.uk ⊖ Pimlico. See p.33.

The old Tate is now devoted to British art from the sixteenth century onwards (the British tag is fairly loosely applied), with several galleries permanently given over to Turner.

Tate Modern

Map 6, H2. Bankside, SE1 ⓣ 020/7887 8008, ⓦ www.tate.org.uk ⊖ Southwark. See p.116.
Housed in a spectacularly converted power station on the South Bank, the new Tate is the largest modern-art gallery in the world, and displays the city's finest international modern art collection.

PERMANENT COLLECTIONS

Victoria and Albert Museum

Map 8, E7. Cromwell Rd, SW7 ⓣ 020/7942 2000, ⓦ www.vam.ac.uk ⊖ South Kensington. See p.128.

The city's principal applied-arts museum, the V&A boasts a scattering of European painting and sculpture, a fine collection of English statuary, two remarkable rooms of casts, Raphael's famous tapestry cartoons, a photography gallery, plus works by Constable, Turner and Rodin.

Wallace Collection

Map 3, E4. Hertford House, Manchester Square, W1 ⓣ 020/7563 9500, ⓦ www.wallace-collection .org.uk ⊖ Bond Street. See p.43.

A country mansion just off Oxford Street, with a small, eclectic collection, including fine paintings by Rembrandt, Velázquez, Hals, Gainsborough and Delacroix.

William Morris Gallery

Map 2, K1. Forest Rd, E17 ⓣ 020/8527 3782, ⓦ www.lbwf.gov.uk/wmg ⊖ Walthamstow Central. Free.

Covers every aspect of Morris & Co's work, and there's a small gallery of Pre-Raphaelite work by Morris and his colleagues upstairs.

MAJOR GALLERIES AND EXHIBITION SPACES

Expect to pay around £5–10 for entry to one of the exhibitions at the Barbican or Hayward. Similar prices are charged for special shows at the National Gallery, the Tates and V&A (see above) and at the Royal Academy. Students, senior citizens and the unemployed are eligible for slight reductions. Hours vary, so it's always best to check the website or ring the gallery before setting off.

Barbican Art Gallery

Map 7, D1. Barbican Centre, Silk St, EC2 ⓣ 020/7638 8891, ⓦ www.barbican.org.uk

MAJOR GALLERIES AND EXHIBITION SPACES

⊖ Barbican or Moorgate.
The Barbican's two-floor gallery is badly designed, but its thematic exhibitions – ranging from African bush art to the latest photography – are often well worth the entrance fee.

Hayward Gallery

Map 6, B3. South Bank Centre, Belvedere Rd, SE1 Ⓣ 020/7960 5226, Ⓦ www.hayward-gallery.org.uk ⊖ Waterloo.
Part of the huge South Bank arts complex, the Hayward is one of London's most prestigious venues for major touring exhibitions, with the bias towards twentieth-century work. Closed for refurbishment until late 2003.

ICA Gallery

Map 4, F10. Nash House, The Mall, SW1 Ⓣ 020/7930 3647, Ⓦ www.ica.org.uk ⊖ Piccadilly Circus or Charing Cross.
The Institute of Contemporary Arts has two gallery spaces, in which it displays works that are invariably characterized as "challenging" or "provocative" – occasionally, they are. To visit, you must be a member of the ICA; a day's membership costs £1.50 (Mon–Fri) or £2.50 (Sat & Sun).

Royal Academy of Arts

Map 4, D8. Burlington House, Piccadilly, W1 Ⓣ 020/7300 8000, Ⓦ www.royalacademy .org.uk ⊖ Green Park or Piccadilly Circus. See p.40.
The Royal Academy is best known for its popular one-off exhibitions, though it dabbles in controversy every now and then. From early June to mid-August, the RA also stages its Summer Exhibition, when the public can submit work to be displayed (and sold) alongside the work of "Academicians". Tasteful landscapes, interiors and nudes tend to predominate, but there's the odd splash of experimentation. For the most popular shows here, you're best advised to pre-book a ticket.

Royal Institute of British Architects (RIBA)

Map 4, B2. 66 Portland Place, W1 ⊤ 020/7580 5533, ⓦ www.architecture.com ⊖ Oxford Circus. See p.44.

Regular architectural exhibitions by the leading lights, housed in a beautiful 1930s building, with an excellent café.

Serpentine Gallery

Map 8, D2. Kensington Gardens, Hyde Park, W2 ⊤ 020/7402 6075, ⓦ www.serpentinegallery.org ⊖ Lancaster Gate. Free.

This fine gallery displays dynamic work by new and established modern artists, as well as hosting interesting Sunday-afternoon lectures, and a performance-art festival in the summer.

Whitechapel Gallery

Map 7, M2. Whitechapel High St, E1 ⊤ 020/7522 7888, ⓦ www.whitechapel.org ⊖ Aldgate East.

The Whitechapel is a dedicated champion of contemporary art, housing major shows by living or not-long-dead artists. It's also the focal point of the Whitechapel Open, a biennial summer survey (the next one is in 2004) of the work of artists living in the vicinity; the show spreads into several local studios too.

COMMERCIAL GALLERIES

For gallery opening times, you're best off checking the website ⓦ www.newexhibitions.com, or the *Time Out* listings. Many galleries are closed throughout August, and rehangings or private viewings often interrupt the normal pattern of business. Some of these places can seem as intimidating as designer clothes shops, but all at least are free.

MAYFAIR AND MARYLEBONE

Annely Juda

Map 4, B5. 23 Dering St, W1 ⓣ 020/7629 7578, ⓦ www.annelyjudafineart.co.uk ⊖ Oxford Circus or Bond Street.

One of the city's best modernist galleries – specializes in early twentieth-century avant-garde works, but equally strong on contemporary painting and sculpture.

Entwistle

Map 4, C8. 6 Cork St, W1 ⓣ 020/7734 6440. ⊖ Green Park.

Box-like space often featuring small shows by major figures in the contemporary British and American art scenes.

Helly Nahmad

Map 4, C8. 2 Cork St, W1 ⓣ 020/7494 3200. ⊖ Green Park.

A gallery where you're guaranteed a glimpse of some very expensive works by very famous artists, from Monet to Picasso.

Lisson

Map 3, C3. 29 and 52–54 Bell St, NW1 ⓣ 020/7724 2739, ⓦ www.lisson.co.uk ⊖ Marylebone or Edgware Road.

An extremely important gallery, whose regularly exhibited sculptors – among them Anish Kapoor and Douglas Gordon – are hugely respected on the international circuit.

Marlborough Fine Art

Map 4, C8. 6 Albemarle St, W1 ⓣ 020/7629 5161, ⓦ www.marlboroughfineart.com ⊖ Green Park.

This is where you'll find the latest work of Britain's most celebrated artists, many in one-person shows. Essential viewing for anyone interested in modern British art.

Waddington Galleries

Map 4, C8. 11 & 12 Cork St, W1 ⓣ 020/7851 2200, ⓦ www.waddington-galleries .com ⊖ Green Park.

One of the chief Cork Street dealers, Waddington's concentrates on the established greats of the

COMMERCIAL GALLERIES

twentieth century, as well as showcasing newer international stars and younger upcoming artists.

HOXTON AND THE EAST END

- - - - - - - - - - - - - - - - - - - -

Flowers East

Map 2, J3. 199–205 Richmond Rd, E8 ⓣ 020/8985 3333, ⓦ www.flowerseast.com London Fields station, from Liverpool Street.

This outstanding East End gallery complex shows a huge variety of paintings, generally by young British artists. It has even opened its own Mayfair branch now, known as Flowers Central, at 21 Cork St, W1.

Victoria Miro

Map 3, L1. 16 Wharf Rd, N1 ⓣ 020/7336 8109, ⓦ www.victoria-miro.com ⊖ Angel or Old Street.

This large former factory on the Islington/Hoxton borders is one of the most impressive galleries in London. Victoria Miro herself has helped promote the likes of Chris Ofili and Tracey Moffatt.

Wapping Project

Map 2, J5. Wapping Hydraulic Power Station, Wapping Wall, E1 ⓣ 020/7680 2080. ⊖ Wapping.

Wonderful red-brick power station in Docklands that plays host to weird video installations and the like.

White Cube

Map 3, N2. 48 Hoxton Square, N1 ⓣ 020/7930 5373, ⓦ www.whitecube.com ⊖ Old Street.

Jay Jopling – who promotes the likes of Damien Hirst, Tracey Emin and various other Turner Prize artists – was one of the first major art dealers to move out to Hoxton, and he has since given up his Mayfair premises.

COMMERCIAL GALLERIES

PHOTOGRAPHY

The Barbican and the Hayward both host **photographic exhibitions** from time to time. The galleries listed below are places you can guarantee will always have photos on show – entry to all is free.

Hamilton's

Map 3, F5. 13 Carlos Place, W1 ⓣ 020/7499 9493, ⓦ www.hamiltonsgallery.com ⊖ Bond Street or Green Park. Classy Mayfair exhibition space for the most famous and fashionable contemporary photographers. Loads of pricey prints for sale as well.

Hulton Getty, Michael Hoppen & Shine

Map 3, D8. 3 Jubilee Place, SW3 ⓣ 020/7376 4525, ⓦ www.hultonarchive.com; ⓣ 020/7352 3669, ⓦ www.michaelhoppen-photo.com; ⓣ 020/7352 4499, ⓦ www.shinegallery.co.uk ⊖ Sloane Square or South Kensington. Three galleries in one building. Hulton Getty stages exhibitions from its massive photo archive on the ground floor, while upstairs Michael Hoppen shows off some of the finest photography of the last century and Shine concentrates on contemporary photography.

National Portrait Gallery

Map 4, G8. 2 St Martin's Place, WC2 ⓣ 020/7306 0055, ⓦ www.npg.org.uk ⊖ Leicester Square or Charing Cross. The NPG has lots of exceptional photos in its collection, with a fair sampling on permanent display; it also regularly holds special (fee-charging) exhibitions on internationally famous photo-portraitists.

Photographers' Gallery

Map 4, G7. 5 & 8 Great Newport St, WC2 ⓣ 020/7831 1772, ⓦ www.photonet.org.uk ⊖ Leicester Square. The capital's premier photography gallery shows work by new and established British and international photographers, often with a couple of exhibitions running concurrently. The prints are often for sale.

Victoria and Albert Museum

Map 8, E7. Cromwell Rd, SW7 ⓣ 020/7942 2000, ⓦ www.vam.ac.uk ⊖ South Kensington.

The V&A has a permanent gallery devoted to photography, though it's way too small to do justice to the museum's vast collection.

PHOTOGRAPHY

Shops and markets

Whether it's time or money you've got to burn, London is one big shopper's playground. And, although chains and superstores predominate along the high streets, you're still never too far from the kind of oddball, one-off establishment that makes shopping an adventure rather than a chore. From the *folie de grandeur* that is Harrods to the frantic street markets of the East End, there's nothing you can't find in some corner of the capital.

In the centre of town, **Oxford Street** is the city's most frantic chain-store mecca, and together with **Regent Street**, which crosses it halfway, offers pretty much every mainstream clothing label you could wish for. Just off Oxford Street, high-end designer outlets line **St Christopher's Place** and **South Molton Street**, and you'll find even pricier designers and jewellers along the very chic **Bond Street**.

Tottenham Court Road, which heads north from the east end of Oxford Street, is the place to go for electrical goods and, further along, furniture and design shops. **Charing Cross Road**, heading south, is the centre of London's book trade, both new and secondhand. At its north end, and particularly on **Denmark Street**, you can find music shops selling everything from instruments to sound equipment and sheet music. **Soho** offers an offbeat

OPENING HOURS

Opening hours for central London shops are generally Monday to Saturday 9.30am to 6pm, although some stay open later, especially on Thursdays. Many are now open on Sundays, although hours tend to be shorter, from around noon to 5pm. The cheapest time to shop is during one of the two annual sale seasons, centred on January and July, when prices can be slashed by up to fifty percent. Credit cards are almost universally accepted by shops. Always keep your receipts: whatever the shop may tell you, the law allows a full refund or replacement on purchases which turn out to be faulty.

mix of sex boutiques, specialist record shops and fabric stores, while the streets surrounding **Covent Garden** yield art and design shops, mainstream fashion stores and designer wear.

Just off Piccadilly, **St James's** is the natural habitat of the quintessential English gentleman, with **Jermyn Street** in particular harbouring shops dedicated to his grooming. **Knightsbridge**, further west, is home to Harrods and Harvey Nichols, and the big-name fashion stores of **Sloane Street** and **Brompton Road**.

DEPARTMENT STORES

Although all of London's **department stores** offer a huge range of high-quality goods under one roof, most specialize in fashion and food. Many of them are worth visiting if only to admire the scale, architecture and interior design, and most have cafés or restaurants.

DEPARTMENT STORES

303

Fortnum & Mason

Map 4, D9. 181 Piccadilly, W1
Ⓣ 020/7734 8040,
Ⓦ www.fortnumandmason.com
Ⓔ Green Park or Piccadilly Circus.

Beautiful and eccentric store featuring heavenly ceiling murals, gilded cherubs, chandeliers and fountains as a backdrop to its perfectly English offerings. Justly famed for its fabulous, gorgeously presented and pricey food, plus upmarket clothes, furniture and stationery.

Harrods

Map 3, D7. 87–135 Brompton Rd, Knightsbridge, SW1
Ⓣ 020/7730 1234,
Ⓦ www.harrods.com
Ⓔ Knightsbridge.

Put an afternoon aside to visit this enduring landmark of quirks and pretensions, most notable for its fantastic Art Nouveau tiled food hall, obscenely huge toy department, and supremely tasteless memorial to Diana and Dodi in the basement. Wear shorts and you may fail the rigorous dress code for entry. (See also p.133.)

Harvey Nichols

Map 3, E6. 109–125 Knightsbridge, SW1
Ⓣ 020/7235 5000,
Ⓦ www.harveynichols.com
Ⓔ Knightsbridge.

All the latest designer collections on the scarily fashionable first floor, where even the shop assistants look like catwalk models. The cosmetics department is equally essential, while the food hall offers famously frivolous and pricey luxuries.

John Lewis

Map 4, B5. 278–306 Oxford St, W1 Ⓣ 020/7629 7711,
Ⓦ www.johnlewis.com
Ⓔ Oxford Circus.

Famous for being "never knowingly undersold", this reliable institution can't be beaten for basics, from buttons to stockings to rugs, along with reasonably priced and well-made clothes, furniture, fabric and household goods. The staff are knowledgeable and friendly, too.

Liberty

Map 4, D6. 210–220 Regent St, W1 Ⓣ 020/7734 1234,

Ⓦ www.liberty-of-london.com
⊖ Oxford Circus.
This fabulous and rather regal emporium of luxury is most famous for its fabrics and accessories, but is also building an excellent reputation for both mainstream and new fashion. The perfume, cosmetics and household departments are good, too.

Marks & Spencer

Map 3, E4. 458 Oxford St, W1
Ⓣ 020/7935 7954,
Ⓦ www.marksandspencer.com
⊖ Marble Arch.
London's largest branch of this British institution offers a huge range of well-made own-brand clothes (the lingerie selection is fancier than in local branches), food, homeware and furnishings.

Selfridges

Map 3, F4. 400 Oxford St, W1
Ⓣ 020/7629 1234, Ⓦ www
.selfridges.com ⊖ Bond Street.
This huge, airy mecca of clothes, food and furnishings was London's first great department store, and remains one of its best, with a fashionable menswear department and a solid womenswear floor. The food hall is impressive, too.

CLOTHES AND ACCESSORIES

The listings below concentrate on the home-grown rather than the ubiquitous international names, but if you're after **designer wear** bear in mind that nearly all of the department stores listed on pp.303-5 stock lines from both major and up-and-coming designers. For designer-style fashion at lower prices, try the more upmarket high-street **chain stores** such as Jigsaw, French Connection and Whistles. Mango and Top Shop are a good bet for even cheaper versions of the same styles. For street, clubwear, secondhand and vintage gear, London's markets also have plenty to offer.

DESIGNER

Browns

Map 4, B6. 23–27 South
Molton St, W1 ⓣ 020/7514
0000, ⓦ www.brownsfashion
.com ⊖ Bond Street.
Huge range of designer wear
for men and women, with big
international names under the
same roof as the hip young
things. Browns' **Labels for
Less**, at 50 South Molton St,
W1 (ⓣ 020/7514 0052),
could save you precious
pennies.

Burberry

Map 4, C7. 21–23 New Bond
St, W1 ⓣ 020/7839 5222,
ⓦ www.burberry.com
⊖ Bond Street or Oxford
Circus.
The quintessential British
outdoors label has relaunched
itself as a fashion essential.
Get the traditional stock at a
huge discount from
Burberry's **Factory Shop**,
29–53 Chatham Place, E9
(ⓣ 020/8985 3344; Hackney
Central train).

Ghost

Map 4, A4 & Map 2, F5.
13–14 Hinde St, London W1
ⓣ 020/7486 0239 (⊖ Oxford
Circus) and 36 Ledbury Rd,
W11 ⓣ 020/7229 1057
(⊖ Notting Hill Gate)
ⓦ www.ghost.co.uk.
Romantic, floaty and hugely
popular modern Victoriana in
pastel shades.

Jean Paul Gaultier

Map 8, G9. Galerie Gaultier,
171–175 Draycott Ave, SW3
ⓣ 020/7584 4648,
ⓦ www.jpgaultier.fr ⊖ South
Kensington.
Outrageous, extravagant and
fun, JPG's designs continue to
raise a smile. Here you can
get the mid-price (which still
doesn't mean cheap) range,
too.

Jones

Map 4, H6. 13 & 15 Floral St,
WC2 ⓣ 020/7240 8312,
ⓦ www.jones-clothing.co.uk
⊖ Covent Garden.
Formal, casual and street
menswear from all the big
names and some of the smaller
ones. Sharp tailoring, jeans
and everything in between.

Joseph

Map 4, C7. 23 Old Bond St, W1 ⊤ 020/7629 3713 (and many other branches). ⊖ Bond Street.

Offering classic cuts in imaginative styles, Joseph is the last word in luxury fashion for men as well as women. The **Joseph Sale Shop** at 53 King's Rd, SW3 (⊤020/7730 7562; ⊖ Sloane Square), offers good discounts on womenswear.

Koh Samui

Map 4, G6. 65 Monmouth St, WC2 ⊤ 020/7240 4280. ⊖ Leicester Square or Covent Garden.

The leading promoter of young British designers, stocking a highly selective range of womenswear with an elegant, eclectic and urban feel.

Nicole Farhi

Map 4, C7. 158 New Bond St, W1 ⊤ 020/7499 8368 (and other branches). ⊖ Bond Street.

Classic designs and cuts for women, invariably in the shades of a chameleon resting on a sandy rock, but no less elegant and popular for that.

Paul Smith

Map 4, H6 & Map 4, B6. Westbourne House, 122 Kensington Park Rd, W11 ⊤ 020/7727 3553 (⊖ Notting Hill Gate) and 40–44 Floral St, WC2 ⊤ 020/7379 7133 (⊖ Covent Garden), Ⓦ www .paulsmith.co.uk

The Covent Garden store is more accessible, but the Notting Hill shop-in-a-house is worth a visit, selling Smith's whole range of well-tailored, very English clothes for men, women and children. The **Smith Sale Shop**, at 23 Avery Row, W1 (⊤020/7493 1287; ⊖ Bond Street), offers huge discounts.

Vexed Generation

Map 4, E6. 3 Berwick St, W1 ⊤ 020/7287 6224, Ⓦ www .thing-is.com ⊖ Piccadilly Circus.

Created in all kinds of new fabrics and coatings, the clothes here are so cool it hurts.

CLOTHES AND ACCESSORIES

Vivienne Westwood
Map 4, A6. 6 Davies St, W1
☎ 020/7629 3757 (and other
branches). ⊖ Bond Street.
Somewhat eccentric but
revered by the international
fashion pack, this
quintessentially English
maverick is still going strong.

MID-RANGE AND HIGH-STREET

Agnès B
Map 4, H6. 35–36 Floral St,
WC2 ☎ 020/7379 1992 (and
other branches). ⊖ Covent
Garden.
Sitting with one foot in the
designer camp, this French
fashion house brings
understated Parisian chic to
the high street. Classic
clothing, a few more
adventurous designs, plus
hats, bags and other
accessories.

French Connection
Map 3, F4. 396 Oxford St, W1
☎ 020/7629 7766 (and many
other branches), Ⓦ www
.frenchconnection.com
⊖ Bond Street.

A tongue-in-cheek
advertising campaign has seen
French Connection relaunch
itself for a younger, funkier
market. Top-quality fabrics
and cuts don't come cheap,
but for your money you get
catwalk styling at a fraction of
the cost of the real thing.

Gap
Map 4, A5. 376–384 Oxford
St, W1 ☎ 020/7408 4500,
Ⓦ www.gap.com ⊖ Bond
Street.
The flagship branch of this
ubiquitous and enduringly
popular casual-clothing store.
Reasonably priced quality
basics; catering for all the
family.

H&M
Map 4, C5. 261–271 Regent
St, W1 ☎ 020/7493 4004 (and
other branches), Ⓦ www.hm
.com ⊖ Piccadilly Circus or
Oxford Circus.
Fashion basics for men and
women for very little outlay,
though quality can be a little
erratic.

Jigsaw
Map 4, C7. 126–127 Bond St,

W1 ⊕ 020/7491 4484 (and many other branches), ⓦ www.jigsaw-online.com ⊖ Bond Street.
Very feminine, very fashionable casuals and formal wear at mid-range prices; think floaty summer dresses and luxury knitwear.

Mango
Map 4, H6. 8–12 Neal St, WC2 ⊕ 020/7240 6099 (and other branches), ⓦ www.mango.es ⊖ Covent Garden.
Up-to-the-minute, well-put-together designs sold in stylish surroundings at rock-bottom prices. Mango is stealing the march on the Top Shop and H&M end of the market.

Next
Map 4, H6. 15–17 Long Acre, WC2 ⊕ 020/7420 8280 (and many other branches), ⓦ www.next.co.uk. ⊖ Covent Garden or Leicester Square.
Safe, reliable casual, office and evening wear at very reasonable prices; there's a nod towards the latest fashion trends rather than a stampede to keep up with them, but so long as you don't expect anything cutting edge you should find some bargains.

Press & Bastyan
Map 4, B6. 22 South Molton St, W1 ⊕ 020/7491 0597 (and other branches). ⊖ Bond Street.
Understatedly feminine and fashionable pieces, from office wear to evening wear, at the top end of this price band.

Top Shop
Map 4, C5. 214 Oxford St, W1 ⊕ 020/7636 7700 (and many other branches), ⓦ www.tops.co.uk ⊖ Oxford Circus.
Proving a big hit with the celebs as well as mere mortals, Top Shop's remodelled flagship store is *the* place to go for this season's must-have item at a snip of the designer prices. One floor is entirely given over to accessories, another to Top Shop's own-brand stuff and a third to independent labels.

CLOTHES AND ACCESSORIES

STREET AND CLUBWEAR

- - - - - - - - - - - - - - - - - - - -

AdHoc/Boy

Map 4, G6. 10–11 Moor St, W1 ⓣ 020/7287 0911, ⓦ www .adhoclondon.com
⊖ Leicester Square.
Party gear for exhibitionists: plenty of PVC, Lycra, feathers and spangles, with fairy wings and magic wands to match your outfit, and a body-piercing studio downstairs.

Burro

Map 4, H6. 29a Floral St, WC2 ⓣ 020/7240 5120. ⊖ Covent Garden.
Funky but with an air of studied nonchalance, this is for boys who want to look cool without looking like they want to look cool.

Cyberdog

Map 4, G6. 9 Earlham St, WC2 ⓣ 020/7836 7855, ⓦ www.cyberdog.co.uk
⊖ Covent Garden.
Club ambience for club gear, with a UV light showing off the goods to good effect:

funky T-shirts, combat ski pants, and glowing accessories to show you the way home.

Diesel

Map 4, H6. 43 Earlham St, WC2 ⓣ 020/7497 5543, ⓦ www.diesel.com ⊖ Covent Garden.
Still cool despite the hype, this industrial-looking store for label-conscious men and women continues to offer that retro-denim look in a dazzling variety of colours and styles.

Duffer of St George

Map 4, H5. 29 Shorts Gardens, WC2 ⓣ 020/7379 4660, ⓦ www.dufferofstgeorge .com ⊖ Covent Garden.
Covetable own-label boys' casuals and streetwear, plus a range of other hip labels in the land of jeans, shoes, jackets and so on.

Home

Map 4, D7. 39 Beak St, W1 ⓣ 020/7287 3708. ⊖ Covent Garden.
The cheeky monkey featured on some of the capital's cooler streetwear accessories

originated here. Jeans, shirts, trainers, shoes, bags, wallets and hats all serve to produce a one-stop, Paul Frank-style combo.

Mambo

Map 4, H6. 2–3 Thomas Neal Centre, 37 Earlham St, WC2 Ⓣ 020/7379 6066, Ⓦ www.mambo.com.au ⊖ Covent Garden.

Surf, skate and graffiti gear, including a range of books, mugs and hats.

Shop

Map 4, E7. 4 Brewer St, W1 Ⓣ 020/7437 1259. ⊖ Piccadilly Circus.

Lots of cabinets stuffed with fashion accessories, some cushions and bedding, plus blaxploitation mugs and plates, and clothes – fleeces, jeans, T-shirts, slip dresses and more.

VINTAGE, RETRO AND SECONDHAND

The Antiques Clothing Shop

Map 2, F4. 282 Portobello Rd, W10 Ⓣ 020/8946 4830. ⊖ Ladbroke Grove.

Lots of treasures in this store, with affordable Victoriana and vintage menswear a speciality.

The Emporium

See map on p.152. A2. 330–332 Creek Rd, SE10 Ⓣ 020/8305 1670. ⊖ Greenwich or train.

Elegant retro store specializing in 1940s to 1960s clothes for men and women, and featuring kitsch displays in its beautiful glass-fronted cases. Well-kept bargains start at a tenner.

Laurence Corner

Map 2, H4. 62–64 Hampstead Road, NW1 Ⓣ 020/7813 1010. ⊖ Warren Street.

London's oldest and most eccentric army-surplus shop, with lots of bargains and an extensive theatrical and fancy-dress hire section.

Modern Age Vintage Clothing

Map 2, H3. 65 Chalk Farm Rd, NW1 Ⓣ 020/7482 2787. ⊖ Chalk Farm.

CLOTHES AND ACCESSORIES

Splendid clobber (mostly menswear) for lovers of 1940s and 1950s American-style gear. The best bargains are on the rails outside: inside, the very lovely cashmere and leather coats are a bit pricier.

162 Holloway Road
Map 2, I3. 162 Holloway Rd, N7 ⓣ 020/7700 2354.
⊖ Holloway Road.
Cheap, enormous and unmissable if your idea of heaven is American-style jeans, shirts, frocks, army surplus, sportswear or shoes for less than a fiver.

SHOES

Birkenstock
Map 4, H5. 37 Neal St, WC2
ⓣ 020/7240 2783,
ⓦ www.Birkenstock.co.uk
⊖ Covent Garden.
Comfortable, classic sandals and shoes in leather, suede and nubuck, with vegetarian options too.

Buffalo Boots
Map 4, H5. 47–49 Neal St,

WC2 ⓣ 020/7379 1051,
ⓦ www.buffalo-boots.com
⊖ Covent Garden.
Everything from the practical to the clubby via spike-heeled boots and enormous platform shoes.

Natural Shoe Store
Map 4, H5. 21 Neal St, WC2
ⓣ 020/7836 5254 (and other branches) ⊖ Covent Garden.
Well-made, stylish, comfortable and sometimes strange shoes. Good value, although not cheap.

L.K. Bennett
Map 4, H6. 130 Long Acre, WC2 ⓣ 020/7379 1710 (and other branches),
ⓦ www.lkbennett.com
⊖ Covent Garden.
Girlie shoes galore: glamorous kitten heels, sharp boots and strappy sandals. Well made, very stylish and with a price tag to match.

Office
Map 4, H5. 57 Neal St, WC2
ⓣ 020/7379 1896 (and many other branches),
ⓦ www.officelondon.co.uk
⊖ Covent Garden.

Good, broad range of basics, including many own-label creations, at reasonable prices, plus some more frivolous fashion moments, too.

Pied à Terre
Map 3, E7. 3 Sloane St, SW1 ⓣ 020/7235 0564 (and many other branches), ⓦ www.theshoestudio.com ⊖ Knightsbridge.
Elegant but pricey women's footwear, with an interesting combination of classic and modern styles.

Shellys
Map 4, C5. 266–270 Regent St, W1 ⓣ 020/7287 0939 (and many other branches), ⓦ www.shellys.co.uk ⊖ Oxford Circus.
Offering pretty much everything from the sensible to the silly and with a good deal in between, this always madly busy store has a huge range, over several floors and at every price, for both men and women.

BOOKS

As well as the big-name **chain bookstores**, most of which have branches throughout the city, London is blessed with a wealth of **local, independent and specialist bookshops**. Charing Cross Road has the highest concentration of the latter and, though these may not have as extensive a stock as the chains, they will almost certainly be more interesting to browse around, and you may well find some hidden jewels on their shelves.

Secondhand books are also sold at the Riverside Walk stalls, under Waterloo Bridge on the South Bank, SE1 (Sat & Sun 10am–5pm, and occasionally midweek); ⊖ Waterloo or train.

Any Amount of Books

Map 4, G7. 62 Charing Cross Rd, WC2 ☏ 020/7240 8140, Ⓦ www.anyamountofbooks .com ⊖ Leicester Square. Sprawling secondhand bookshop stocking everything from obscure 50p bargains to rare and expensive first editions. Especially strong on fiction, the arts and literary biography.

Arthur Probsthain Oriental & African Bookseller

Map 4, G3. 41 Great Russell St, WC1 ☏ 020/7636 1096. ⊖ Tottenham Court Road. Connected to the School of Oriental and African Studies, this impressive academic store covers all relevant aspects of art, history, science and culture.

Atlantis Bookshop

Map 4, H4. 49a Museum St, WC1 ☏ 020/7405 2120, Ⓦ www.atlantisbookshop .demon.co.uk ⊖ Tottenham Court Road. Splendid occult-oriented place with the perfect ambience for browsing

through books and magazines covering spirituality, psychic phenomena, witchcraft and so on.

Blackwell's

Map 4, G5. 100 Charing Cross Rd, WC2 ☏ 020/7292 5100 (and other branches), Ⓦ www.bookshop.blackwell. co.uk ⊖ Tottenham Court Road or Leicester Square. The London flagship of Oxford's best academic bookshop has a wider range than you might expect; academic stock is unsurprisingly excellent, but so is the range of computing, travel and fiction titles.

Bookmarks

Map 4, G4. 1 Bloomsbury St, WC1 ☏ 020/7637 1848, Ⓦ www.bookmarks.uk.com; ⊖ Tottenham Court Road. Leftist and radical fare in the heart of Bloomsbury, with a wide range of political biography, history, theory and assorted political ephemera. There's even a children's section.

Books for Cooks

Map 2, F5. 4 Blenheim Crescent, W11 ⓣ 020/7221 1992, ⓦ www.booksforcooks .com. ⊖ Ladbroke Grove. Anything and everything to do with food can be found on the shelves of this wonderful new and secondhand bookshop, which also has a tiny café (see p.205) offering cookery demonstrations, coffee for browsers, and lunch.

Books Etc

Map 5, B1. 264 High Holborn, WC1 ⓣ 020/7404 0261 (and other branches), ⓦ www .booksetc.co.uk ⊖ Holborn. Large, laid-back and user-friendly, with an on-site coffee shop and a wide and well-stocked range of mainstream and specialist titles, and especially good on contemporary fiction. This branch is closed on Saturdays.

Borders Books & Music

Map 4, D5. 203 Oxford St, W1 ⓣ 020/7292 1600 (and other branches), ⓦ www.borders .com ⊖ Oxford Circus or Tottenham Court Road. Enormous London flagship of the American import, boasting four floors of books alongside a huge range of CDs and magazines. Good range of titles, with staff recommendations and reviews, and a solid children's section.

Daunt Books

Map 3, E3. 83–84 Marylebone High St, W1 ⓣ 020/7224 2295 (and other branches). ⊖ Bond Street or Baker Street. Wide and varied range of travel literature as well as the usual guidebooks, presented by expert staff in the beautiful, galleried interior of this famous shop.

Forbidden Planet

Map 4, G4. 71–75 New Oxford St, WC1 ⓣ 020/7836 4179. ⊖ Tottenham Court Road. Two permanently packed floors of all things science-fiction and fantasy-related, ranging from books and comics to games and ephemera.

BOOKS

Foyles

Map 4, G5. 113–119 Charing Cross Rd, WC2 ⓣ 020/7437 5660, ⓦ www.foyles.co.uk
⊖ Tottenham Court Road.
Long-established, huge and famous London bookshop with a big feminist section and Ray's Jazz Shop and café on the first floor.

Gay's the Word

Map 3, H3. 66 Marchmont St, WC1 ⓣ 020/7278 7654, ⓦ www .gaystheword.co.uk ⊖ Russell Square.
Extensive collection of lesbian and gay classics, pulps, contemporary fiction and non-fiction, plus cards, calendars, magazines and more. Known for the weekly lesbian discussion groups and readings held in the back of the shop.

Gosh!

Map 4, G3. 39 Great Russell St, WC1 ⓣ 020/7636 1011.
⊖ Tottenham Court Road.
All kinds of comics for all kinds of readers, whether you're the casually curious or the serious collector. Check out the Cartoon Gallery in the basement.

Offstage Theatre & Cinema Bookshop

Map 2, H3. 37 Chalk Farm Rd, NW1 ⓣ 020/7485 4996.
⊖ Camden Town or Chalk Farm.
Excellent, well-stocked shop covering all aspects of stage and screen craft, plus theory, criticism, scripts and biographies.

Politico's

Map 3, G7. 8 Artillery Row, SW1 ⓣ 020/7828 0010, ⓦ www.politicos.co.uk.
⊖ St James's Park.
Mainstream political fare, new and secondhand, with plenty of big biographies. A cosy café, board games and irreverent window displays give it a more frivolous edge.

Souls of Black Folks

Map 2, I6. 407 Coldharbour Lane, SW9 ⓣ 020/7738 4141.
⊖ Brixton or Brixton station.
Dedicated black bookshop specializing in African, Caribbean and African-American literature, with regular readings, a buzzing café and late opening hours.

BOOKS

Stanford's Map and Travel Bookshop

Map 4, H6. 12–14 Long Acre, WC2 ☎ 020/7836 1321, ⓦ www.stanfords.co.uk ⊖ Leicester Square or Charing Cross.

The world's largest specialist travel bookshop, this features pretty much any map of anywhere, plus a huge range of travel books and guides.

Unsworths Booksellers

Map 4, G4. 12 Bloomsbury St, WC1 ☎ 020/7436 9836. ⊖ Tottenham Court Road.

Good for bargains, including recent and just-out-of-print novels and academic titles. Specializes in the humanities, and features an interesting antiquarian selection.

Waterstone's

Map 4, E8. 203–206 Piccadilly, W1 ☎ 020/7851 2400 (and other branches), ⓦ www.waterstones.co.uk ⊖ Piccadilly Circus or Green Park.

This flagship bookshop – Europe's largest – occupies the former Simpson's department store building and boasts a café, bar, gallery and events rooms, as well as five floors of books.

Zwemmer Arts & Architecture

Map 4, G6. 24 Litchfield St, WC2 ☎ 020/7240 4158, ⓦ www.zwemmer.com ⊖ Leicester Square.

Specialist art bookshop with a fantastic and expert selection. **Zwemmer Media Arts**, nearby (80 Charing Cross Rd, WC2 ☎ 020/7240 4157; ⊖ Leicester Square), specializes in film, design and photography.

MUSIC

There are hundreds of mainstream, independent and specialist **music shops** in London, catering equally well for the CD bulk-buyer and the obsessive rare-vinyl collector. This is a selection of the best and best known. Bear in mind

MUSIC

that London's markets, especially Camden, are also good sources of vinyl (see "Markets", p.320).

MEGASTORES

- - - - - - - - - - - - - - - - - - -

HMV

Map 4, D4. 150 Oxford St, W1 ⓣ 020/7631 3423, ⓦ www.hmv .co.uk ⊖ Oxford Circus.
All the latest releases, as you'd expect, but also an impressive backlist, a reassuring amount of vinyl, and a good classical section downstairs. Dance music is also a strength.

Tower Records

Map 4, E8. 1 Piccadilly Circus, W1 ⓣ 020/7439 2500, ⓦ www.towerrecords.co.uk ⊖ Piccadilly Circus.
Fantastic range, although it's not always easy to find what you're looking for, and genre classifications sometimes seem a little random. The jazz, folk and world music department upstairs is especially impressive.

Virgin Megastore

Map 4, F4. 14–16 Oxford St, W1 ⓣ 020/7631 1234, ⓦ www.virgin.com

⊖ Tottenham Court Road.
The mainstream floor here is better stocked than the specialist sections: the bias is rock-heavy, but there's a little of everything else, and plenty of books, magazines, T-shirts and assorted music ephemera.

INDEPENDENT STORES

- - - - - - - - - - - - - - - - - - -

Caruso & Company

Map 4, E3. 10 Charlotte Place, W1 ⓣ 020/7636 6622. ⊖ Goodge Street.
Comfortable, well-stocked shop specializing in opera, but also stocking world music, French cabaret and the like.

Daddy Kool

Map 4, E6. 12 Berwick St, W1 ⓣ 020/7437 3535, ⓦ www.daddykoolrecords.com ⊖ Oxford Circus or Tottenham Court Road.
Lots of collectable reggae vinyl, most of it classic roots

MUSIC

and Studio One, as well as the latest ragga and drum'n'bass.

Eukatech
Map 4, H5. 49 Endell St, WC2
ⓣ 020/7240 8060,
ⓦ www.ucmguk.com
⊖ Covent Garden.
House, techno and trance on two floors, both vinyl and CD.

Gramex
Map 6, C7. 25 Lower Marsh, SE1 ⓣ 020/7401 3830.
⊖ Waterloo or Waterloo station.
A splendid find for classical music lovers, this new and secondhand record store features both CDs and vinyl, and offers comfy leather armchairs to sample or discuss your finds at leisure.

Honest Jon's
Map 2, F5. 276 & 278 Portobello Rd, W10 ⓣ 020/8969 9822, ⓦ www.honestjohns .co.uk ⊖ Ladbroke Grove.
Jazz, soul, funk, R&B, rare groove, dance and plenty more make this place a browser's delight, with

current releases, secondhand finds and reissues on vinyl and CD.

MDC Classic Music
Map 4, H8. 437 Strand, WC2
ⓣ 020/7240 2157 (and many other branches),
ⓦ www.mdcmusic.com
⊖ Charing Cross or Embankment.
Big and brassy, this central chain store has an impressive range of stock, but specializes in special offers and cut-price CDs.

Mr Bongo
Map 4, D3. 44 Poland St, WC1
ⓣ 020/7287 1887, ⓦ www .mrbongo.com ⊖ Oxford Circus.
Good on 12-inch singles, and equally reliable for hip-hop, jazz, funk, Latin American and Brazilian sounds.

Sister Ray
Map 4, E6. 94 Berwick St, W1
ⓣ 020/7287 8385, ⓦ www .sisterray.co.uk
⊖ Oxford Circus or Piccadilly Circus.
Up-to-the minute indie sounds, with lots of

MUSIC

electronica and some forays into the current dance scene, most on vinyl as well as CD.

Stern's African Record Centre
Map 3, G2. 293 Euston Rd, NW1 ⓣ 020/7387 5550, ⓦ www.sternsmusic.com
⊖ Euston Square.
World-famous for its global specialisms, this knowledgeable store has an unrivalled stock of African

music and excellent selections from pretty much everywhere else in the world.

Steve's Sounds
Map 4, G7. 20–20a Newport Court, WC2 ⓣ 020/7473 4638.
⊖ Leicester Square.
Quick-moving stock of CDs and vinyl, from rock and pop to dance, jazz, world and classical music. Irresistible prices.

MARKETS

London's **markets** are more than just a cheap alternative to high-street shopping: many of them are significant remnants of communities endangered by the heedless expansion of the city. You haven't really got to grips with London unless you've rummaged through the junk at Brick Lane on a Sunday morning, or haggled over a leather jacket at Camden. Do keep an eye out for **pickpockets**: the weekend markets provide them with easy pickings.

The East End markets of Brick Lane, Columbia Road, Petticoat Lane and Spitalfields are reviewed on p.100.

Bermondsey (New Caledonian) Market
Map 3, N6. Bermondsey

Square, SE1. ⊖ Borough or London Bridge. Fri 5am–2pm.
Huge, unglamorous but

highly regarded antique market offering everything from obscure nautical instruments to attractive but pricey furniture. The real collectors arrive at dawn to pick up the bargains, and you need to get here by midday at the latest to ensure you don't go home empty-handed.

Camden Market

Map 2, H3. Camden High St to Chalk Farm Rd, NW1.

⊖ Camden Town. Mainly Thurs–Sun 9.30am–5.30pm.

Camden Market (Camden High Street, on the junction of Buck Street; Thurs–Sun 9am–5.30pm) offers a good mix of new, secondhand, retro and young designer clothes, as well as records and ephemera, while the Electric Market (Camden High Street, just before the junction of Dewsbury Terrace; Sun 9am–5.30pm) and Camden Canal Market (just over Camden Lock bridge; Sat & Sun 10am–6pm) offer cheap fashion, hippy wear, smoking paraphernalia and souvenir knick-knacks. Camden Lock (Camden Lock Place, off Chalk Farm Road; indoor stalls Tues–Sun 10am–6pm; outdoor stalls Sat & Sun 10am–6pm) offers mainly arts, crafts and clothes stalls, with the shops adding a few hip designers, antique dealers and booksellers to the mix. The Stables Yard (leading off from Camden Lock or from Chalk Farm Road; Sat & Sun 8am–6pm) is a sprawling adventure of clubwear, more young designers, furniture, retro design, trinkets and antiques.

Covent Garden Market

Map 4, I7. Apple Market, The Piazza, and Jubilee Market, off Southampton St, WC2.

⊖ Covent Garden. Daily 9am–5pm.

The Apple Market offers handmade, rather twee craft stalls most days, while Jubilee Market offers endless cheap T-shirts, jewellery, souvenirs and so on. On Mondays, Jubilee is taken over by an antiques market, which has some more enjoyable stalls (closes 3pm). Whichever day you visit, there are street performers to

MARKETS

distract you in the Piazza, and it's an amiable area in which to wander about.

Greenwich Market

See map on p.152, B2.
Greenwich High Rd, Stockwell St and College Approach, SE10. ⊖ North Greenwich or train, or Cutty Sark DLR. Mainly Thurs–Sun 9.30am–5pm.

The covered Crafts Market on College Approach sells mostly twentieth-century antiques on a Thursday (7.30am–5pm) and handmade goods, clothes and gifts from Friday to Sunday (9.30am–5.30pm), while the Central Market, off Stockwell Street (indoor Fri & Sat 10am–5pm, Sun 10am–6pm; outdoor Sat 7am–6pm, Sun 7am–5pm), hosts funky secondhand clothes, bric-a-brac and furniture. The surrounding streets, and the shops inside the covered market, offer obscure maritime devices, new and old, plus lots of secondhand books and retro clothes.

Portobello Road Market

Map 2, F5. Portobello Rd, W10, and Golborne Rd, W10/W11, ⓦ www .portobelloroad.co.uk (antiques) ⊖ Ladbroke Grove or Notting Hill Gate. Antique market Sat 4am–6pm; general market Mon–Wed 8am–6pm, Thurs 9am–1pm, Fri & Sat 7am–7pm; organic market Thurs 11am–6pm; Golborne Road market Mon–Sat 9am–5pm.

Start at the Notting Hill end and make your way through the antiques and bric-a-brac down to the fruit and veg stalls, and then under the Westway to the seriously hip new and secondhand clothes stalls and shops around which local style vultures circle and swoop. The Golborne Road market is cheaper and less crowded, with some very attractive antiques and retro furniture.

MISCELLANEOUS

The listings below are a small selection of shops which don't really fit into any particular category, or which are just interesting to visit.

Anything Left-Handed
Map 4, E7. 57 Brewer St, W1 ⓣ 020/7437 3910, ⓦ www.anythingleft-handed .co.uk ⊖ Piccadilly Circus. *The* place to go for left-handed tools, implements and gifts.

Davenport's Magic Shop
Map 4, H9. 7 Charing Cross Tube Arcade, Strand, WC2 ⓣ 020/7836 0408. ⊖ Charing Cross or Embankment. The world's oldest family-run magic business, stocking marvellous tricks for both amateurs and professionals.

Flying Duck Enterprises
See map on p.152, A2. 320–322 Creek Rd, SE10 ⓣ 020/8858 1964. ⊖ North Greenwich or train, or Cutty Sark DLR. Kitsch aplenty, whether you're after tacky 1970s board games, Elvis soap or a 1950s polka-dotted dinner service.

G. Smith & Sons
Map 4, G6. 74 Charing Cross Rd, WC2 ⓣ 020/7836 7422. ⊖ Leicester Square. Exactly what an old English tobacconist's ought to look and smell like. Every variety of tobacco, including some of the shop's own creations, plus a huge range of snuff and a walk-in humidor featuring some very classy cigars.

Gadget Shop
Map 4, H6. Unit 9, North Piazza, Covent Garden Piazza, WC2 ⓣ 0800/783 8343, ⓦ www.gadgetshop.com ⊖ Covent Garden. Great for weird and wacky gifts, from Leatherman toolkits and Homer Simpson bottle openers, to inflatable chairs and lava lamps.

Radio Days
Map 6, C7. 87 Lower Marsh, SE1 ⓣ 020/7928 0800. ⊖ Waterloo or train.

MISCELLANEOUS

A fantastic collection of memorabilia and accessories from the 1930s to the 1970s, including shoes, shot glasses, cosmetics and vintage magazines, plus a huge stock of well-kept ladies' and menswear from the same period.

Sport

A s a quick glance at the national press will tell you, **sport** in Britain is a serious matter, with each international defeat being taken as an index of the country's slide down the scale of world powers. Many of the crucial domestic and international fixtures of the **football**, **rugby** and **cricket** seasons take place in the capital, and London also hosts one of the world's greatest tennis tournaments, the **Wimbledon** championships.

For **up-to-the-minute details** of sporting events in London, check the *Evening Standard* or *Time Out*, or ring the London Sportsline on ☎020/7222 8000.

FOOTBALL

English **football** (or soccer) is passionate and, if you have the slightest interest in the game, then catching a league or FA Cup fixture is a must. The season runs from mid-August to early May, when the **FA Cup Final** rounds things off. There are four league divisions: one, two, three and, at the top of the pyramid, the twenty-club **Premier League**. There are London clubs in every division, with around five or six in the Premiership at any one time.

Most Premiership fixtures kick off at 3pm on Saturday – the highlights of the day's best games are shown on ITV on

Saturday nights. However, there are usually one or two games each Sunday (kick-off between 2pm and 4pm) and Monday (kick-off around 8pm), broadcast live on Sky TV.

London's top club at the moment is **Arsenal** (☎020 /7704 4000, ⓦwww.arsenal.co.uk; ⊖ Arsenal), who won the double (Premier League and FA Cup) in the 1997–98 and 2001–2002 seasons. There's an intense rivalry between Arsenal and north London neighbours, Tottenham Hotspur (☎0870/011 2222, ⓦwww.spurs.co.uk; White Hart Lane station from Liverpool Street), though **Chelsea** (☎020/7915 2951, ⓦwww.chelseafc.co.uk; ⊖ Fulham Broadway), based in west London, are usually closer to Arsenal in the league.

Tickets for most Premiership games start at £20–25 and are very difficult to get hold of: you need to book in advance, or try and see one of the European or knockout cup fixtures.

CRICKET

In the days of the Empire, the English took **cricket** to the colonies as a means of instilling the gentlemanly values of fair play while administering a sound thrashing to the natives. These days, the former colonies – such as Australia, the West Indies and India – all beat England on a regular basis, and to see the game at its best you should try to get into one of the **Test matches** between England and the summer's touring team. These international fixtures are played in the middle of the cricket season, which runs from April to September.

Two of the matches are played in London: one at **Lord's** (☎020/7432 1000, ⓦwww.lords.org), the home of English cricket, in St John's Wood (⊖ St John's Wood), the other at **The Oval** (☎020/7582 6660, ⓦwww.surreycricket.com), in Kennington (⊖ Oval). In tandem with the full-blown five-day Tests, there's also a series of **one-day internationals**, two of which are usually held in London.

Getting to see England play one of the big teams can be difficult unless you book months in advance. If you can't wangle your way into a Test, you could watch it live on television, or settle down to an inter-county match, either in the **county championship** (these are four-day games) or in one of the fast-and-furious one-day competitions. Two county teams are based in London – **Middlesex**, who play at Lord's, and **Surrey**, who play at The Oval.

RUGBY

Rugby gets its name from Rugby public school, where the game mutated from football (soccer) in the nineteenth century. A rugby match may at times look like a bunch of weightlifters grappling each other in the mud – as they say, rugby is a hooligan's game played by gentlemen, while football is a gentleman's game played by hooligans – but it is in reality a highly tactical and athletic game. England's rugby team tends to represent the country with rather more success than the cricket squad.

There are two types of rugby played in Britain. Thirteen-a-side **Rugby League** is a professional game played almost exclusively in the north of England. The Super League features the big-name northern clubs and one London club, the **London Broncos** (☏ 0871/222 1132, ⓦ www .londonbroncos.co.uk), who share a ground with Brentford football club in west London (Brentford train station from Waterloo). The season runs from March to September, and games traditionally take place on Sundays at 3pm, but there are also matches on Friday and Saturday nights.

In London, however, virtually all rugby clubs play fifteen-a-side **Rugby Union**, which has upper-class associations (though the game is also very strong in working-class

RUGBY

Wales) and only became a professional sport in 1995. The only Premiership team that actually plays its games in London is **Harlequins** (ⓣ020/8410 6000, ⓦwww.quins.co.uk), who play at the Stoop Memorial Ground in Twickenham in southwest London (Twickenham train station from Waterloo). The season runs from September until May, finishing off with the knock-out cup final. The cup final and international matches are played at **Twickenham Stadium**, Whitton Road (ⓣ020/8831 6666, ⓦwww.rfu.com). Unless you are affiliated to one of the 2000 clubs of the Rugby Union, or willing to pay well over the odds at a ticket agency, it is tough to get a ticket for one of these big Twickenham games. A better bet is to go and see a Harlequins league game, where there's bound to be an international player or two on display – you can usually get in for around £10–15.

TENNIS

Tennis in England is synonymous with **Wimbledon** (ⓣ020/8946 2244, ⓦwww.wimbledon.com), the only Grand Slam tournament in the world to be played on grass, and for many players the ultimate goal of their careers. The Wimbledon championships last a fortnight, and are always held during the last week of June and the first week of July. Most of the **tickets**, especially seats for the main show courts (Centre and No. 1), are allocated in advance to the Wimbledon tennis club's members, other clubs and corporate "sponsors" – as well as by public ballot – and once these have taken their slice there's not a lot left for the general public.

On tournament days, **queues** start to form around dawn – if you arrive by around 7am, you have a reasonable chance of securing one of the limited number of Centre and No. 1 court tickets held back for sale on the day. If you're there by around 9am, you should get admission to the outside courts (where you'll catch some top players in the first week of the tournament). Either way, you then have a long wait until play commences at noon – and if it rains you don't get your money back.

If you want to see big-name players in London, an easier opportunity is the Stella Artois men's championship at **Queen's Club** (☎020/7385 3421, ⓦwww.queensclub.co.uk) in Hammersmith, which finishes a week before Wimbledon. Many of the male tennis stars use this tournament to acclimatize themselves to British grass-court conditions. As with Wimbledon, you have to apply for tickets in advance, although there is a limited number of returns on sale at 10am each day. For the unlucky, there's the consolation of TV coverage, which is pretty all-consuming for Wimbledon.

If you want to play tennis, there are **public courts** in most of London's parks, including Hyde Park (☎020/7262 3474) and Regent's Park (☎020/7486 4216); again, you'll need to book in advance.

HORSE RACING

There are five **horse racecourses** within easy reach of London: **Kempton Park** (☎01932/782292, ⓦwww.kempton.co.uk), near Sunbury-on-Thames; **Sandown Park** (☎01372/463072, ⓦwww.sandown.co.uk), near Esher in Surrey; and **Windsor** (☎01753/498400, ⓦwww.windsor-racecourse.co.uk), all of which hold top-quality races on the flat (April–Sept) and over jumps (Aug–March). There's also **Ascot** (☎01344/622211, ⓦwww.ascot.co.uk), in Berkshire, and **Epsom** (☎01372/726311, ⓦwww.epsomderby.co.uk) in Surrey, which are the real glamour courses, hosting major races of the flat-racing season every June.

Thousands of Londoners have a day out at Epsom on Derby Day, which takes place on the first or second Saturday in June. **The Derby**, a mile-and-a-half race for three-year-old thoroughbreds, is the most prestigious of the five classics of the April to September English flat season, and is preceded by another classic, **the Oaks**, which is for fillies only. The three-day Derby meeting is as much a social ritual as a sporting event, but for sheer snobbery nothing can match the **Royal Ascot** week in mid-June, when the Queen and selected members of the royal family are in attendance, along with half the nation's blue bloods. The best seats are the preserve of the gentry, who get dressed up to the nines for the day; but, as is the case at most racecourses, the rabble are allowed into the public enclosure for around a fiver.

GREYHOUND RACING

A night out at the **dogs** is still a popular pursuit in London. It's an inexpensive, cheerful and comfortable spectacle: a grandstand seat costs less than £5 and all the London stadiums have one or more restaurants, some surprisingly good. Indeed, the sport has become so popular that you'd be best advised to book in advance if you want to watch the races from a restaurant table, particularly around Christmas. Meetings usually start around 7.30pm and finish at 10.30pm, and usually include around a dozen races. The two easiest stadiums to get to are in South London: **Catford** (℡020/8690 8000, ⊛www.thedogs.co.uk; Catford Bridge train station from Charing Cross or Catford train station from Victoria) and **Wimbledon** (℡0870/840 8905, ⊛www.wimbledondogs.co.uk; ⊖ Wimbledon Park or Haydons Road train station from Blackfriars).

ICE SKATING

From October to March, there's the Broadgate **outdoor ice rink** (see below), supplemented in the Christmas and New

Year period with outdoor rinks at Somerset House (ⓦwww.somerset-house.org.uk) and Marble Arch (ⓦwww.marblearchicerink.com). Otherwise, London has just one centrally located **indoor ice rink**. Session times tend to vary quite a lot, but generally last for around two to three hours.

Broadgate Ice Rink

Map 7, H1. Broadgate Circus, Eldon St, EC2 ☎020/7505 4068, ⓦwww.broadgateestates.co.uk/ice/frameset.htm ⊖ Liverpool Street.

A little circle of ice open from Oct–March. It's fun (in fine weather), but can get crowded during the weekend. Mon–Wed evenings are for "broomball" matches

(ⓦwww.vicinitee.com). Admission £7.

Leisurebox

Map 3, A5. 17 Queensway, W2 ☎020/7229 0172. ⊖ Queensway or Bayswater. The whole family can skate at this rink, which has ice-discos on Fri and Sat evenings. Admission £6.

SWIMMING, GYMS AND FITNESS CENTRES

Below is a selection of the best-equipped, most central of London's multipurpose **fitness centres**. We haven't given the addresses of the city's many council-run swimming pools, virtually all of which now have fitness classes and gyms. Wherever you go, however, a swim will usually cost you around £3.

If you fancy an alfresco dip, then the Serpentine Lido in Hyde Park (see p.126) or the **open-air pools** on Hampstead Heath are your best bet.

Ironmonger Row Baths

Map 3, M2. Ironmonger Row, EC1 ☎020/7253 4011. ⊖ Old Street. Men: Tues & Thurs

9am–9.30pm, Sat 9am–6.30pm. Women: Mon 9am–2.30pm, Wed & Fri 9am–9.30pm, Sun 10am–6.30pm. Mixed: Mon

ICE SKATING • SWIMMING, GYMS AND FITNESS CENTRES

2.30–9.30pm.

An old-fashioned kind of place that attracts all classes, with a steam room, sauna, small plunge pool, masseurs, a lounge area with beds, and a large pool. Admission for a 3hr session is a bargain at around £6 (Mon–Fri) or £10 (weekends).

Oasis Sports Centre

Map 4, H5. 32 Endell St, WC2 ⓣ 020/7831 1804. ⊖ Covent Garden. Pools: Mon–Fri 6.30am–9pm, Sat & Sun 9.30am–6pm.

The Oasis has two pools, one of which is the only heated outdoor pool in central London. Other facilities include a gym, a health suite with sauna and sunbed, massage, and badminton and squash courts.

Porchester Spa

Map 3, A4. 225 Queensway, W2 ⓣ 020/7792 3980. ⊖ Bayswater or Queensway. Men: Mon, Wed & Sat 10am–10pm. Women: Tues,

Thurs & Fri 10am–10pm, Sun 10am–4pm. Mixed: Sun 4–10pm.

Built in 1926, the Porchester is one of only two Turkish baths in central London, and is well worth a visit for the Art Deco tiling alone. Admission is around £20 and entitles you to use the saunas, steam rooms, plunge pool, Jacuzzi and swimming pool.

The Sanctuary

Map 4, H6. 12 Floral St, WC2 ⓣ 0870/770 3350, ⓦ www.thesanctuary.co.uk ⊖ Covent Garden. Mon, Tues, Sat & Sun 9.30am–6pm, Wed–Fri 9.30am–10pm.

For a serious day of self-indulgence, this women-only club in Covent Garden is a real treat: the interior is filled with lush tropical plants and you can swim naked in the pool. It's a serious investment, at £40–75 for day membership, but your money gets you unlimited use of the pool, Jacuzzi, sauna and steam room, plus one sunbed session.

Festivals and events

T his chapter is simply a rundown of the principal **festivals and annual events** in the capital, ranging from the upper-caste rituals of Royal Ascot to the sassy street party of the Notting Hill Carnival, plus a few oddities like Oak Apple Day and Horseman's Sunday. Our listings cover a pretty wide spread of interests, but they are by no means exhaustive; London has an almost endless roll-call of ceremonials and special shows, and for daily information, as always, it's well worth checking the weekly *Time Out* or the weekday *Evening Standard*.

JANUARY 1

London Parade

To kick off the new year, a procession of floats, marching bands, clowns, American cheerleaders and classic cars wends its way from Parliament Square at noon, through the centre of London, to Berkeley Square, collecting money for charity from around one million spectators en route. Admission charge for grandstand seats in Piccadilly, otherwise free. Information

Ⓣ020/8566 8586,
Ⓦwww.londonparade.co.uk.

LATE JANUARY

London International Mime Festival

Annual mime festival which takes place in the last two weeks of January on the South Bank, and in other funky venues throughout London. It pulls in some very big names in mime, animation and puppetry. Information Ⓣ020/7637 5661, Ⓦwww.mimefest.co.uk

LATE JANUARY/ EARLY FEBRUARY

Chinese New Year Celebrations

The streets of Soho's Chinatown explode in a riot of dancing dragons and firecrackers on the night of this vibrant annual celebration, and the streets and restaurants are packed to capacity. Information Ⓦwww .chinatown-on-line.org.uk

MARCH

Head of the River Race

Less well-known than the Oxford and Cambridge Boat Race, but much more fun; there are over 400 crews setting off at ten-second intervals and chasing each other from Mortlake to Putney. Information Ⓦwww.horr.co.uk

LATE MARCH/ EARLY APRIL

Oxford and Cambridge Boat Race

Since 1845, the rowing teams of Oxford and Cambridge universities have battled it out on a four-mile, upstream course on the Thames from Putney to Mortlake. It's as much a social as sporting event, and the pubs at prime vantage points pack out early. Alternatively, you can catch it on TV. For details, Ⓦwww.theboatrace.org.uk

THIRD SUNDAY IN APRIL

London Marathon

The world's most popular city marathon, with over 40,000 runners sweating the 26.2 miles from Greenwich Park to Westminster Bridge. Only a handful of world-class athletes enter each year; most of the competitors are club runners or obsessive flab-fighters. There's always someone dressed up as a gorilla, and you can generally spot a fundraising celebrity or two. Information ☎020/7620 4117, ⓦwww .london-marathon.co.uk

MAY BANK HOLIDAY WEEKEND

IWA Canal Cavalcade

Lively celebration of the city's inland waterways held at Little Venice (near ⊖ Warwick Avenue), with scores of decorated narrowboats, Morris dancers and lots of children's activities. Information ⓦwww.waterways.org.uk

SUNDAY NEAREST TO MAY 9

May Fayre and Puppet Festival

The garden of St Paul's church in Covent Garden is taken over by puppet booths to commemorate the first recorded sighting of a Punch and Judy show, by diarist Samuel Pepys in 1662. Information ☎020/7375 0441.

THIRD OR FOURTH WEEK IN MAY

Chelsea Flower Show

Run by the Royal Horticultural Society, the world's finest horticultural event transforms the normally tranquil grounds of the Royal Hospital in Chelsea for four days, with a daily inundation of up to 50,000 gardening gurus and amateurs. It's a solidly bourgeois event, with the public admitted only for the closing stages (the last two days), and charging an exorbitant fee for the

THIRD SUNDAY IN APRIL TO MAY

335

privilege. Tickets must be bought in advance: ℡0870/906 3781, Ⓦwww.rhs.org.uk

MAY 29

Oak Apple Day

The Chelsea Pensioners of the Royal Hospital honour their founder, Charles II, by wearing their posh uniforms and decorating his statue with oak leaves, in memory of the oak tree in which the king hid after the Battle of Worcester in 1651. Information ℡020/7730 5282.

LATE MAY/EARLY JUNE

Beating the Retreat

This annual display takes place on Horse Guards' Parade over three evenings, and marks the old military custom of drumming the troops back to base at dusk. Soldiers on foot and horseback provide a colourful, very British

ceremony, which precedes a floodlit performance by the Massed Bands of the Queen's Household Cavalry. Information ℡020/7739 5323.

FIRST OR SECOND SATURDAY IN JUNE

Derby Day

Run at the Epsom racecourse in Surrey, the Derby is the country's premier flat race: the beast that gets its snout over the line first is instantly worth millions. Admission prices reflect proximity to the horses and to the watching nobility. The race is always shown live on TV. Information ℡01372/726311, Ⓦwww.epsomderby.co.uk

EARLY JUNE TO MID-AUGUST

Royal Academy Summer Exhibition

Thousands of prints, paintings, sculptures and sketches, most by amateurs

MAY 29 TO MID-AUGUST

and nearly all of them for sale, are displayed at one of the city's finest galleries. See p.40. Information ⓣ020/7300 8000, ⓦwww .royalacademy.org.uk

JUNE

Fleadh

Pronounced "flaa", this is a raucous (by no means exclusively) Irish music festival in Finsbury Park, north London. Van Morrison has pitched up here on more than a few occasions, but then so too have Bob Dylan and the briefly re-formed Sex Pistols. Information ⓣ020/8951 5490, ⓦwww.meanfiddler .com

Spitalfields Festival

Classical music recitals in Hawksmoor's Christ Church, the parish church of Spitalfields, and other events in and around the old Spitalfields Market for a fortnight or so in June. In 2003, the festival will take place in Shoreditch church,

while Christ Church is being restored. Information ⓣ020/7377 1362, ⓦwww .spitalfieldsfestival.org.uk

SECOND SATURDAY IN JUNE

Trooping of the Colour

This celebration of the Queen's official birthday (her real one is on April 21) features massed bands, gun salutes, fly-pasts and crowds of tourists and patriotic Britons paying homage. Tickets for the ceremony itself (limited to two per person, allocated by ballot) must be applied for before the end of February; send an SAE to the Brigade Major, HQ Household Division, Horse Guards, Whitehall, London SW1A 2AX, ⓣ020/7414 2479. Otherwise, the royal procession along the Mall lets you glimpse the nobility for free, and there are rehearsals (minus Her Majesty) on the two preceding Saturdays.

JUNE

●

MID-JUNE

Royal Ascot

A highlight of the society year, held at the Ascot racecourse in Berkshire, this high-profile meeting has the Queen and sundry royals completing a crowd-pleasing lap of the track in open carriages prior to the opening races. The event is otherwise famed for its fashion statements, especially on Ladies' Day, and there's TV coverage of both the races and the more extravagant headgear of the female racegoers. Information ☎01344/622211, ⓦwww.ascot.co.uk

LAST WEEK OF JUNE AND FIRST WEEK OF JULY

Wimbledon Lawn Tennis Championships

This Grand Slam tournament attracts the cream of the world's professionals and is one of the highlights of the sporting and social calendar. For information on how to get hold of tickets, see p.328. Information ☎020/8946 2244, ⓦwww.wimbledon .org

LATE JUNE TO MID-JULY

City of London Festival

For nearly a month, churches (including St Paul's Cathedral), livery halls and corporate buildings around the City play host to classical and jazz musicians, theatre companies and other guest performers. Information ☎020/7377 0540, ⓦwww.colf.org

EARLY JULY

Mardi Gras

A colourful, whistle-blowing lesbian and gay march through the city streets followed by a huge, ticketed party in a London park. See p.254. Information from ⓦwww.londonmardigras.com

MID-JULY

Greenwich & Docklands Festival

Ten-day festival of fireworks, music, dance, theatre, art and spectacles at venues on both sides of the river, plus a village fayre in nearby Blackheath. Information ☎ 020/858 7755, Ⓦ www.festival.org

MID-JULY TO MID-SEPTEMBER

BBC Henry Wood Promenade Concerts

Commonly known as the Proms, this series of nightly classical concerts at the Royal Albert Hall is a well-loved British institution. See p.274. Information ☎ 020/7589 8212, Ⓦ www.bbc.co.uk/proms

MID-JULY

Doggett's Coat and Badge Race

The world's oldest rowing race, from London Bridge to Chelsea, established by Thomas Doggett, an eighteenth-century Irish comedian, to commemorate George I's accession to the throne. The winner receives a Hanoverian costume and silver badge. Information ☎ 020/7626 3531, Ⓦ www.watermenshall.org /doggett_race.htm

THIRD WEEK OF JULY

Swan-Upping

Five-day scramble up the Thames, from Sunbury to Pangbourne, during which liveried rowers search for swans, marking them (on the bill) as belonging to either the Queen, the Dyers' or the Vintners' City liveries. At Windsor, all the oarsmen stand to attention in their boats and salute the Queen. Details of the daily whereabouts of the Swan Marker and his crew can be found on ☎ 01628/523030, Ⓦ www.royal.gov.uk

JULY

LAST BANK HOLIDAY WEEKEND IN AUGUST

- - - - - - - - - - - - - - - - - -

Notting Hill Carnival

The three-day free festival in Notting Hill Gate is the longest-running, best-known and biggest street party in Europe. Dating back forty years, Carnival is a tumult of imaginatively decorated floats, eye-catching costumes, thumping sound systems, live bands, irresistible food and huge crowds.

SATURDAY IN EARLY SEPTEMBER

- - - - - - - - - - - - - - - - - -

Great River Race

Hundreds of boats are rowed or paddled from Ham House, Richmond, down to Island Gardens on the Isle of Dogs. Starts are staggered and there's any number of weird and wonderful vessels taking part. Information ⓦwww .greatriverrace.co.uk

THIRD SUNDAY IN SEPTEMBER

- - - - - - - - - - - - - - - - - -

Horseman's Sunday

In an eccentric 11.30am ceremony at the Hyde Park church of St John & St Michael, a vicar on horseback blesses a hundred or so horses; the newly consecrated beasts then parade around the neighbourhood before galloping off through the park, and later taking part in showjumping. Information ⓣ020/7262 1732.

THIRD WEEKEND IN SEPTEMBER

- - - - - - - - - - - - - - - - - -

Open House

A once-a-year opportunity to peek inside over 400 buildings around London, many of which don't normally open their doors to the public. You'll need to book in advance for some of the more popular places. Information ⓦwww .londonopenhouse.org

AUGUST TO SEPTEMBER

LATE SEPTEMBER/EARLY OCTOBER

- - - - - - - - - - - - - - - - - - - -

Soho Jazz Festival

Headed by *Ronnie Scott's*, this is a week-long celebration of one of Soho's most famous attributes – its jazz culture – including free concerts in Soho Square. Information ⓦ www.sohojazzfestival.co.uk

FIRST SUNDAY IN OCTOBER

- - - - - - - - - - - - - - - - - - - -

Costermongers' Pearly Harvest Festival Service

Cockney fruit and vegetable festival at St Martin-in-the-Fields Church. Of most interest to the onlooker are the Pearly Kings and Queens who gather at around 3pm in their traditional pearl-button-studded outfits. Information ⓣ 020/7930 0089, ⓦ www.pearlies.co.uk

LATE OCTOBER/EARLY NOVEMBER

- - - - - - - - - - - - - - - - - - - -

State Opening of Parliament

The Queen arrives by coach at the Houses of Parliament at 11am accompanied by the Household Cavalry and gun salutes. The ceremony itself takes place inside the House of Lords and is televised; it also takes place whenever a new government is sworn in. Information ⓣ 020/7219 4272, ⓦ www.parliament.uk

NOVEMBER

- - - - - - - - - - - - - - - - - - - -

London Film Festival

A three-week cinematic season with scores of new international films screened at the National Film Theatre and some West End venues. Information ⓣ 020/7928 3232, ⓦ www.bfi.org.uk or (nearer the time) ⓦ www.rlff.org.uk

LATE SEPTEMBER TO NOVEMBER

EARLY NOVEMBER

London Jazz Festival
Big ten-day international jazz-fest held in all London's jazz venues, large and small, in association with BBC Radio 3. Information ☏ 020/7405 9900, ⓦ www.bbc.co.uk/radio3

FIRST SUNDAY IN NOVEMBER

London to Brighton Veteran Car Run
In 1896 Parliament abolished the Act that required all cars to crawl along at 2mph behind someone waving a red flag. Such was the euphoria in the motoring community that a rally was promptly set up to mark the occasion, and a century later it's still going strong. Classic cars built before 1905 set off from Hyde Park at 7.30am and travel the 58 miles to Brighton along the A23 at the heady maximum speed of 20mph. Information ⓦ www .vccofgb.co.uk/lontobri

NOVEMBER 5

Bonfire Night
In memory of Guy Fawkes – executed for his role in the 1605 Gunpowder Plot to blow up King James I and the Houses of Parliament – effigies of the hapless Mr Fawkes are burned on bonfires all over Britain. There are also council-run fires and firework displays right across the capital – Alexandra Palace provides a good vantage point from which to take in several displays at once. Information ☏ 020/8365 2121.

SECOND SATURDAY IN NOVEMBER

Lord Mayor's Show
The newly appointed Lord Mayor begins his or her day of investiture at Westminster, leaving there at around 9am for Guildhall. At 11.10am, the vast ceremonial procession, headed by the 1756 State Coach, begins its journey from Guildhall to the

NOVEMBER

Law Courts in the Strand, where the oath of office is taken at 11.50am. From there the coach and its train of 140-odd floats make their way back towards Guildhall, arriving at 2.20pm. Later in the day there's a firework display from a barge tethered between Waterloo and Blackfriars bridges, and a small funfair on Paternoster Square, by St Paul's Cathedral. Information ☎020/7606 3030, ⓦwww.cityoflondon.gov.uk

NEAREST SUNDAY TO NOVEMBER 11

- - - - - - - - - - - - - - - - - - - -

Remembrance Sunday

A day of nationwide commemorative ceremonies for the dead and wounded of the two world wars and other conflicts. The principal ceremony, attended by the Queen, various other royals and the Prime Minister, takes place at the Cenotaph in Whitehall, beginning with a march-past of veterans and building to a one-minute silence at the stroke of 11am.

DECEMBER

- - - - - - - - - - - - - - - - - - - -

Christmas

Each year since the end of World War II, Norway has acknowledged its gratitude to the country that helped liberate it from the Nazis with the gift of a mighty spruce tree that appears in **Trafalgar Square** in early December. Decorated with lights, it becomes the focus for carol singing versus traffic noise each evening until Christmas Eve.

New Year's Eve

The **New Year** is welcomed en masse in Trafalgar Square as thousands of inebriated revellers stagger about and slur to *Auld Lang Syne* at midnight. London Transport runs free public transport all night, sponsored by various public-spirited breweries.

Kids' London

O n first sight London seems a hostile place for children, with its crowds, incessant noise and intimidating traffic. English attitudes can be discouraging as well, particularly if you've experienced the more indulgent approach of the French or Italians – London's restaurateurs, for example, tend to regard children and eating out as mutually exclusive concepts. Yet, if you pick your destination carefully, even central London can be a delight for the pint-sized, and it needn't overly strain the parental pocket.

Covent Garden's buskers and jugglers provide no-cost entertainment in a car-free setting, and there's always the chance of being plucked from the crowd to help out with a trick. The Thames Path along the **South Bank** is another great traffic-free environment. Start your stroll by the London Eye, take in some free foyer music at the Royal Festival Hall, watch the nearby skaters, and then head off for the Millennium Bridge and the Tate Modern.

Don't underestimate the value of London's **public transport** as a source of fun, either. The #11 double-decker from Victoria, for instance, will trundle you past the Houses of Parliament, Trafalgar Square and the Strand on its way to St Paul's Cathedral for 40p per child. The driverless Docklands Light Railway is another guaranteed source of amusement – grab a seat at the front of the train and pretend to be the driver, then take a boat back to the centre of town from Greenwich.

MUSEUMS AND SIGHTS

Lots of London's **museums and sights** will appeal to children. Below are those that are primarily geared towards entertaining and/or educating children – some are covered in the main part of our guide, and are cross-referenced accordingly. Most museums offer child-oriented programmes of workshops, educational story trails, special shows and suchlike during the school holidays. The weekly *Time Out* has listings of kids' events, and also produces *Kids Out*, a monthly listings magazine for those with children.

Bethnal Green Museum of Childhood

Map 2, J4. Cambridge Heath Rd, E2 ⓣ 020/8983 5200, ⓦ www.vam.ac.uk ⊖ Bethnal Green. Daily except Fri 10am–5.50pm; free. See p.104. The museum itself, with its collection of historic dolls' houses and toys, is not that great for kids, but they put on lots of weekend/holiday events and activities.

Horniman Museum

Map 2, J7. London Rd, SE23 ⓣ 020/8699 1872, ⓦ www .horniman.ac.uk Forest Hill train station, from Victoria or London Bridge. Daily

10.30am–5.30pm; free. See p.150.
An ethnographic and musical-instrument museum primarily, but with lots to interest kids, including an aquarium, a natural history section and lovely grounds.

Kew Bridge Steam Museum

Map 2, D5. Green Dragon Lane, Brentford, TW8. ⓣ 020/8568 4757, ⓦ www.kbsm.org.uk Kew Bridge train station from Waterloo, or bus #237 or #267 from ⊖ Gunnersbury. Daily 11am–5pm; Mon–Fri adults £3.50, children £1; Sat & Sun adults £4.50, children £2. See p.162.

Best visited at weekends, when the beam engines are in steam and the miniature steam railway is in operation. The Water for Life gallery features plenty of grimy details on the capital's water and sewerage network, which should appeal to kids.

London Aquarium

Map 6, A6. County Hall, SE1 ⊤ 020/7967 8000, ⓦ www.londonaquarium.co.uk ⊖ Westminster or Waterloo. Daily 10am–6pm or later; adults £8.75, children £5.25. See p.112.

London's largest aquarium is situated on the South Bank, and is very popular with kids, especially the bit where they get to stroke the (non-sting) rays.

London Zoo

Map 3, E1. Regent's Park, NW1 ⊤ 020/7722 3333, ⓦ www.londonzoo.co.uk Bus #274 from ⊖ Camden Town or Baker Street. Daily: March–Oct 10am–5.30pm; Nov–Feb 10am–4pm; adults £11, children

aged 3–15 £8. See p.140. Smaller kids love the children's enclosure, where they can actually handle the animals, and the regular "Animals in Action" live shows. The invertebrate house, known as the Web of Life, is also a guaranteed winner, as it has lots of creepy-crawlies, and much more hands-on stuff.

Natural History Museum

Map 8, D7. Cromwell Rd, SW7 ⊤ 020/7942 5000, ⓦ www.nhm.ac.uk ⊖ South Kensington. Mon–Sat 10am–5.50pm, Sun 11am–5.50pm; free. See p.131. Animatronic dinosaurs, stuffed animals, live ants, a "rainforest", an earthquake simulator and lots of rocks, fossils, crystals and gems. Older kids might enjoy going behind the scenes and meeting the scientists at the newly opened Darwin Centre.

Pollock's Toy Museum

Map 4, E2. 1 Scala St, W1 ⊤ 020/7636 3452, ⓦ www.tao2000.net/pollocks ⊖ Goodge Street. Mon–Sat

10am–5pm; adults £3, children £1.50.

Housed above a unique toy shop, every nook and cranny of this rambling old house is packed with toys, including a fine example of the Victorian paper theatres sold by Benjamin Pollock.

Science Museum

Map 8, D6. Exhibition Rd, SW7 ⓣ 020/7942 4455, ⓦ www.nmsi.ac.uk ⊖ South Kensington. Daily 10am–6pm; free. See p.130.

There's plenty for everyone here: hands-on fun for the little ones in the "Garden" or the "Launch Pad" in the basement, plus daily demonstrations and hi-tech gadgetry of the Wellcome Wing for older kids.

Syon

Map 2, C6. Syon Park, Brentford, Middlesex ⓣ 020/8560 0881, ⓦ www.syonpark.co.uk Bus #237 or #267 from ⊖ Gunnersbury. See p.163.

The stately home itself may not tempt the kids, but with the Butterfly House and the Aquatic Experience, plus a weekend miniature steam railway in the lovely gardens, it's a good place for a day out. Snakes and Ladders, an indoor children's play area with impressive apparatus, is also in the park (ⓣ 020/8847 0946; daily 10am–6pm; adults free, under-5s £3.15-3.90, over-5s £4.15-4.50).

PARKS AND CITY FARMS

Central London has plenty of **green spaces**, such as Hyde Park, which has playgrounds and ample room for general mayhem, as well as a diverting array of city wildlife. If you want something more unusual than ducks and squirrels, though, head for one of London's **city farms**.

Battersea Park

Map 2, G6. Albert Bridge Rd ⓣ 020/8871 7540 (zoo) or ⓣ 020/8871 7539 (playground), ⓦ www.wandsworth.gov.uk Battersea Park or Queenstown

Road train station, from Victoria. Zoo: Easter–Sept daily 10am–5pm; Oct–Easter Sat & Sun 11am–3pm; adults £2, children £1. Playground: term-time Tues–Fri 3.30–7pm; holidays and weekends 11am–6pm; free.

The park has an excellent free adventure playground and activity hut with pool table, a children's zoo with monkeys, reptiles, birds, otters and mongooses, and lots of open space. Every August the free "Teddy Bears' Picnic" draws thousands of children and their plush pals.

Coram's Fields

Map 3, I2. 93 Guilford St, WC1 ⊤ 020/7837 6138. ⊖ Russell Square. Daily 9am–dusk/8pm; free.

Very useful, centrally located playground with lots of water and sand play plus mini-farm with ducks, sheep, rabbits, goats and chickens. Adults admitted only if accompanied by a child.

Hampstead Heath

Map 2, G2. ⊤ 020/7485 4491. ⊖ Hampstead, or Gospel Oak or Hampstead Heath train stations. Open daily 24hr. See p.145.

Nine hundred acres of grassland and woodland, with superb views of the city. Excellent kite-flying, birdwatching and swimming potential, too. Music events and fun days throughout the summer.

Hyde Park/Kensington Gardens

Map 3, D5. W8 ⊤ 020/7298 2100, ⊛ www.royalparks.gov.uk ⊖ High Street Kensington or Lancaster Gate. Daily dawn–dusk. See p.125.

Hyde Park is central London's main open space; in Kensington Gardens, adjoining its western side, you can find the famous Peter Pan statue (near the Long Water), a groovy playground dedicated to Princess Diana, and a pond that's perfect for toy-boat sailing.

Kew Gardens

Map 2, C6. Richmond, Surrey ⊤ 020/8332 5000, ⊛ www.kew.org ⊖ Kew Gardens. Daily 9.30am–7.30pm

PARKS AND CITY FARMS

or dusk; adults £6.50, children free. See p.165.

Go here for the edifying open spaces, though the glasshouses usually go down well too, and there's a small aquarium in the basement of the Palm House.

Mudchute City Farm

Map 2, L5. Pier St, E14 ⓣ 020/7515 5901. Mudchute or Island Gardens DLR. Daily 9am–5pm; free.

Covering some 35 acres, this is London's largest city farm, with farmyard animals, llamas, a pets' corner and a café.

Richmond Park

Map 2, D7. Richmond, Surrey ⓣ 020/8948 3209, ⓦ www.royalparks.co.uk ⊖ Richmond, or Richmond train station from Waterloo.

Daily 8am–dusk; free. See p.167.

A fabulous stretch of countryside, with opportunities for duck-feeding, deer-spotting, mushroom hunting and cycling. There's a playground situated near Petersham Gate and a toddlers' play area near Kingston Gate.

Spitalfields Community Farm

Map 2, J4. Weaver St, E1 ⓣ 020/7247 8762, ⓦ www.spitalfieldscityfarm.org ⊖ Shoreditch. Tues–Sun 10.30am–5pm; free.

A tiny East End farm with sheep, donkeys, goats, pigs, ducks, geese, rabbits and guinea pigs. Also run a propagation scheme and organic vegetable garden.

THEATRE

Numerous London theatres put on **kids' shows** at the weekend, but there are one or two venues that are almost entirely child-centred. Ticket prices hover either side of the £5 mark for children and adults alike, unless the show is at a West End theatre, in which case you're looking at more like £15 and upwards.

THEATRE

349

Little Angel Theatre

Map 2, I3. 14 Dagmar Passage, off Cross St, N1 ⓣ 020/7226 1787, ⓦ www.littleangeltheatre.com ⊖ Angel or Highbury & Islington.

London's only permanent puppet theatre, with shows on Sat at 2pm and 5pm, and Sun at 11am and 2pm. Extra performances during holidays. No babies are admitted.

Polka Theatre

Map 2, F8. 240 The Broadway, SW19 ⓣ 020/8543 4888, ⓦ www.polkatheatre.com ⊖ Wimbledon or South Wimbledon.

Aimed at kids aged up to around 12, this is a specially designed junior arts centre, with two theatres, a playground, a café and a toy shop. Storytellers, puppeteers and mimes make regular appearances.

Puppet Theatre Barge

Map 3, B3. Little Venice, Blomfild Rd, W9 ⓣ 020/7249 6876 or 0836/202745, ⓦ www.puppetbarge.com ⊖ Warwick Avenue.

Wonderfully imaginative marionette shows on a fifty-seater barge moored in Little Venice from November to May, then at various points along the Thames (including Richmond). Shows usually start at 3pm at weekends and in the holidays.

Unicorn Theatre

ⓣ 020/7700 0702, ⓦ www.unicorntheatre.com The oldest professional children's theatre in London is currently performing in several venues across the capital while they await the building of their own theatre near Tower Bridge (due to open in 2004). Shows run the gamut from mime and puppetry to traditional plays.

SHOPS

Benjamin Pollock's Toy Shop
Map 4, H6. 44 Covent Garden Apple Market, WC2 ⓣ 020/7379 7866, ⓦ www .pollocks-coventgarden.co.uk ⊖ Covent Garden. Mon–Sat 10.30am–6pm, Sun 11am–6pm. Beautiful, old-fashioned toys, for grown-ups as well as children: toy theatres, glove puppets, jack-in-the-boxes and so on.

Children's Book Centre
Map 2, F5. 237 Kensington High St, W8 ⓣ 020/7937 7497, ⓦ www.childrensbookcentre.co .uk ⊖ Kensington High Street. Mon–Wed, Fri & Sat 9.30am–6.30pm, Thurs 9.30am–7pm, Sun noon–6pm. Huge bookstore for kids, with an excellent range of fiction and non-fiction, lots of gift ideas, a toy basement and a huge multimedia section.

Davenport's Magic Shop
Map 4, H8. Charing Cross Shopping Arcade, WC2 ⓣ 020/7836 0408, ⓦ www.davenportsmagic.co.uk ⊖ Charing Cross or Embankment. Mon–Fri 9.30am–5.30pm, Sat 10.15am–4.30pm. The oldest family magic business in the world, stocking magic tricks for amateurs and professionals alike, and offering good, practical advice.

Eric Snook's Toyshop
Map 4, H6. 32 Covent Garden Market, WC2 ⓣ 020/7379 7681, ⓦ wwwsnooksonline.co.uk ⊖ Covent Garden. Mon–Sat 10am–7pm, Sun 11am–6pm. Eschewing movie merchandise and cheap tat, this shop sells only the most tasteful, meticulously crafted playthings and a range of fancy-dress outfits.

Hamleys
Map 4, D6. 188 Regent St, W1 ⓣ 020/7494 2000, ⓦ www.hamleys.com ⊖ Oxford Circus. Mon–Fri 10am–8pm, Sat 9.30am–8pm, Sun noon–6pm.

SHOPS

The most celebrated toy shop on the planet, multistorey Hamleys is bursting with childish delights – from the humble Slinky to scaled-down petrol-driven Porsches.

The Kite Store

Map 4, H5. 69 Neal St, WC2 ⓣ 020/7836 1666. ⊖ Covent Garden. Mon–Fri 10am–6pm, Sat 10.30am–6pm.

Kites and air toys of all kinds for the beginner and stunt master alike, plus a few other fun little things.

Skate Attack

72 Chaseside, Southgate, N14 ⓣ 0800/252884, ⓦ www.skateattack.com ⊖ Southgate. Mon–Sat 9.15am–6pm.

Europe's largest retailer of roller skates, rollerblades, ice skates, skateboards and equipment. Roller-rental scheme with protective equipment: £10 a day, £15 a weekend or £20 a week, plus £100 deposit.

Directory

AIDS HELPLINE ⓣ 0800 /567123, ⓦ www.playingsafely .co.uk

AIRLINES Aer Lingus ⓣ 0845 /084 4444, ⓦ www.aerlingus .com; Aeroflot ⓣ 020/7355 2233, ⓦ www.aeroflot.co.uk; Air France ⓣ 0845/084 5111, ⓦ www.airfrance.com/uk; Alitalia ⓣ 0870/608 6001, ⓦ www.alitalia.co.uk; American Airlines ⓣ 020/7365 0777, ⓦ www.aa.com; British Airways ⓣ 0845/773 3377, ⓦ www .britishairways.com; Buzz ⓣ 0870/240 7070, ⓦ www .buzzaway.com; Canadian Airlines ⓣ 0870/524 7226, ⓦ www.aircanada.ca; Delta ⓣ 0800/414767, ⓦ www.delta .com; EasyJet ⓣ 0870/600 0000, ⓦ www.easyjet.com; KLM ⓣ 0870/575 0900, ⓦ www.klm .com; Lufthansa ⓣ 08457 /737747, ⓦ www.lufthansa.co .uk; Qantas ⓣ 08457/747767, ⓦ www.qantas.com.au; Ryanair ⓣ 0871/246 0000, ⓦ www .bookryanair.com; Virgin ⓣ 01293/450150, ⓦ www .virgin-atlantic.com

AIRPORT ENQUIRIES Gatwick ⓣ 0870/000 2468, ⓦ www.baa .co.uk; Heathrow ⓣ 0870/000 0123, ⓦ www.baa.co.uk; London City Airport ⓣ 020/7646 0000, ⓦ www.londoncityairport .com; Luton ⓣ 01582/405100, ⓦ www.london-luton.com; Stansted ⓣ 0870/000 0303, ⓦ www.baa.co.uk

AMERICAN EXPRESS 30–31 Haymarket, SW1 ⓣ 020/7484 9600, ⓦ www.americanexpress .com (Mon–Sat 9am–6pm, Sun 10am–5pm). ⊖ Piccadilly Circus.

BANKS Opening hours for most banks are Mon–Fri 9.30am –4.30pm, with some staying open half an hour later, and some high-street branches opening on Saturday mornings.

BIKE RENTAL On Your Bike, 52–54 Tooley St, SE1 ☎ 020/7378 6669, ⓦ www.onyourbike .net (Mon–Fri 8am–7pm, Sat 9.30am–5.30pm). ⊖ London Bridge.

CAR RENTAL Avis ☎ 0870/606 0100, ⓦ www.avis.com; easyCar ☎ 0906/333 3333, ⓦ www.easycar.com; Global Leisure Cars ☎ 0870/241 1986, ⓦ www.globalleisurecars.com; Hertz ☎ 0870/599 6699, ⓦ www.hertz.com; Holiday Autos ☎ 0870/530 0400, ⓦ www.holidayautos.com

CONSULATES AND EMBASSIES Australia, Australia House, Strand, WC2 ☎ 020/7379 4334, ⓦ www.australia .org.uk; Canada, MacDonald House, 1 Grosvenor Square, W1 ☎ 020/7258 6600, ⓦ www .canada.org.uk; Ireland, 17 Grosvenor Place, SW1 ☎ 020/7235 2171; New Zealand, New Zealand House, 80 Haymarket, SW1 ☎ 020/7930 8422, ⓦ www .nzembassy.com; South Africa, South Africa House, Trafalgar Square, WC2 ☎ 020/7451 7299, ⓦ www.southafricahouse.com; USA, 24 Grosvenor Square, W1 ☎ 020/7499 9000, ⓦ www .usembassy.org.uk

CULTURAL INSTITUTES French Institute, 17 Queensberry Place, SW7

☎ 020/7073 1350, ⓦ www.insti-tut-francais.org.uk; Goethe Institute, Princes Gate, Exhibition Rd, SW7 ☎ 020/7596 4000, ⓦ www.goethe.de; Italian Cultural Institute, 39 Belgrave Square, SW1 ☎ 020/7235 1461, ⓦ www.italcultur.org.uk

DENTISTS Emergency treatment: Guy's Hospital, St Thomas St, SE1 ☎ 020/7955 4317 (Mon–Fri 9am–3pm).

DOCTOR Walk-in consultation Great Chapel Street Medical Centre, Great Chapel St, W1 ☎ 020/7437 9360 (phone for surgery times).

ELECTRICITY Electricity supply in London conforms to the EU standard of approximately 230V.

EMERGENCIES For police, fire and ambulance services, call ☎ 999.

HOSPITALS For 24hr accident and emergency: Charing Cross Hospital, Fulham Palace Rd, W6 ☎ 020/8846 1234; Chelsea & Westminster Hospital, 369 Fulham Rd, SW10 ☎ 020/8746 8000; Royal Free Hospital, Pond St, NW3 ☎ 020/7794 0500; Royal London Hospital, Whitechapel Rd, E1 ☎ 020/7377 7000; St Mary's Hospital, Praed St, W2 ☎ 020/7886 6666; University College Hospital, Grafton Way, WC1 ☎ 020/7387

9300; Whittington Hospital, Highgate Hill, N19 ☎ 020/7272 3070.

INTERNET ACCESS

easyInternetcafe (ⓦ www.easy .everything.com) has 24hr branches at 456 Strand, off Trafalgar Square (⊖ Charing Cross); 9–16 Tottenham Court Rd (⊖ Tottenham Court); and 9–13 Wilton Rd, Victoria (⊖ Victoria). See ⓦ www .easyeverything.com for details of other branches.

LEFT LUGGAGE

Airports Gatwick: North Terminal ☎ 01293/502013 (daily 6am–10pm); South Terminal ☎ 01293/502014 (24hr). Heathrow: Terminal 1 ☎ 020 /8745 5301 (daily 6am–11pm); Terminal 2 ☎ 020/8745 4599 (daily 5.30am–11pm); Terminal 3 ☎ 020/8759 3344 (daily 5am –11pm); Terminal 4 ☎ 020/8897 6874 (daily 5.30am–11pm). London City Airport ☎ 020/7646 0000 (daily 5.30am–9.30pm). Stansted Airport ☎ 0870/0000 303 (24hr).

Train stations Charing Cross (daily 7am–11pm); Euston (Mon–Sat 6.45am–11.15pm, Sun 7.15am–11pm); Victoria (daily 7am–10.15pm); Waterloo International (daily 7am–10pm).

LOST PROPERTY

Airports Gatwick ☎ 01293 /503162 (Mon–Sat 8am–7pm, Sun 8am–4pm); Heathrow ☎ 020/8745 7727 (daily 8am –4pm); London City Airport ☎ 020/7646 0000 (Mon–Fri 5.30am–10pm, Sat 5.30am –1am, Sun 10am–10pm); Stansted ☎ 0870/0000 303 (daily 6am–midnight).

Buses ☎ 020/7222 1234, ⓦ www.londontransport.co.uk (24hr).

Heathrow Express ☎ 020/8745 7727, ⓦ www.heathrowexpress .co.uk (daily 8am–4pm).

Taxis (black cabs only) ☎ 07918/2000 (Mon–Fri 9am–4pm).

Train stations Euston ☎ 020 /7387 8699 (Mon–Fri 9am –5.30pm); King's Cross ☎ 020 /7278 3310 (Mon–Fri 9am –5.30pm); Liverpool Street ☎ 020/7247 4297 (Mon–Fri 9am–5.30pm); Paddington ☎ 020/7313 1514 (Mon–Fri 9am–5.30pm); Victoria ☎ 020 /7922 9887 (daily 7am–mid- night); Waterloo ☎ 020/7401 7861 (Mon–Fri 7.30am–8pm).

Tube trains London Regional Transport ☎ 020/7486 2496.

MOTORBIKE RENTAL

Raceways, 201–203 Lower Rd, SE16 ☎ 020/7237 6494, and 17 The Vale, Uxbridge Rd, W3

INTERNET ACCESS–MOTORBIKE RENTAL

ⓣ 020/8749 8181, ⓦ www
.raceways.net; Mon–Sat
9am–5pm.

POLICE Central police stations
include: Charing Cross, Agar St,
WC2 ⓣ 020/7240 1212;
Holborn, 70 Theobald's Rd,
WC1 ⓣ 020/7404 1212; King's
Cross, 76 King's Cross Rd,
WC1 ⓣ 020/7704 1212; West
End Central, 10 Vine St, W1
ⓣ 020/7437 1212; City of
London Police, Bishopsgate,
EC2 ⓣ 020/7601 2222.

POSTAL SERVICES The only
(vaguely) late-opening post
office is the Trafalgar Square
branch at 24–28 William IV St,
WC2 4DL ⓣ 020/7484 9304
(Mon–Fri 8.30am–6.30pm, Sat
9am–5.30pm); it's also the city's
poste restante collection point.
For general postal enquiries,
phone ⓣ 08457/740740
(Mon–Fri 8am–7.30pm, Sat
8am–6pm) or visit the website
ⓦ www.royalmail.co.uk

PUBLIC HOLIDAYS January 1,
Good Friday, Easter Monday,
First Monday in May, Last
Monday in May, Last Monday in
August, December 25,
December 26; if January 1,
December 25 or 26 fall on a
Saturday or Sunday, the holiday
falls on the following weekday.

TELEPHONES A variety of
companies have public pay-
phones on the street, the largest
one being British Telecom (BT).
Most phones take all coins from
10p upwards, though some only
take phonecards, available from
post offices and newsagents,
and/or credit cards.
International calls can be made
from any phonebox, by dialling
00, then the country code; to
reach the operator, phone
ⓣ 100, or for the international
operator phone ⓣ 155.

TIME Greenwich Mean Time
(GMT) is used Oct–March; for
the rest of the year the country
switches to British Summer
Time (BST), one hour ahead of
GMT.

TRAIN ENQUIRIES For national
train enquiries, call ⓣ 08457
/484950 or visit ⓦ www
.railtrack.co.uk

TRAVEL AGENTS STA Travel,
33 Bedford St, WC1, ⓣ 020
/7240 9821, ⓦ www.statravel
.co.uk; Trailfinders, Lower
Ground Floor, Waterstone's,
203–205 Piccadilly, W1 ⓣ 020
/7292 1888, ⓦ www.trailfinders
.co.uk

CONTEXTS

A brief history of London

Roman Londinium

There is evidence of scattered **Celtic settlements** along the Thames, but no firm proof that central London was permanently settled by the Celts before the arrival of the **Romans** in 43 AD. Although the Romans' principal settlement was at Camulodunum (Colchester) to the northeast, **Londinium** (London) was established as a permanent military camp, and became an important hub of the Roman road system.

In 60 AD, when the Iceni tribe rose up against the invaders under their queen **Boudicca** (or Boadicea), Londinium was burned to the ground, along with Camulodunum. According to the Roman historian Tacitus, the inhabitants were "massacred, hanged, burned and crucified", but the Iceni were eventually defeated and Boudicca committed suicide. In the aftermath, Londinium emerged as the new commercial and administrative (though not military) capital of **Britannia**, and was endowed with an imposing basilica and forum, a governor's palace, temples, bathhouses and an amphitheatre. To protect against further attacks, fortifications were built, three miles long, fifteen feet high and eight feet thick.

Saxon Lundenwic and the Danes

By the fourth century, the Roman Empire was on its last legs, and the Romans officially abandoned the city in 410 AD (when Rome was sacked by the Visigoths), leaving the country – and Londinium – at the mercy of marauding Saxon pirates. The **Saxon** invaders, who controlled most of southern England by the sixth century, appear to have settled, initially at least, to the west of the Roman city.

In 841 and 851 London suffered Danish Viking attacks, and it may have been in response to these raids that the Anglo-Saxons decided to reoccupy the walled Roman city. After numerous sporadic attacks, and the odd extended sojourn, the Danish leader Cnut (or Canute), became King of All England in 1016, and made London the national capital, a position it has held ever since.

Danish rule only lasted 26 years, and with the accession of **Edward the Confessor** (1042–66), the court and church moved upstream to Thorney Island. Here Edward built a splendid new palace so that he could oversee construction of his "West Minster" (later to become Westminster Abbey). Thus it was Edward who was responsible for the geographical separation of power, with royal government based in **Westminster** and commerce centred upstream in the **City of London**.

From 1066 to the Black Death

On his deathbed, the celibate Edward appointed Harold, Earl of Wessex, as his successor. Having crowned himself in the new Abbey – establishing a tradition that continues to this day – Harold was defeated by **William of Normandy** (William the Conqueror) and his invading army at the Battle of Hastings. On Christmas Day, 1066, William crowned himself king in Westminster Abbey. The new king granted the City numerous privileges and, as an insurance policy, also constructed three defensive towers, one of which survives as the nucleus of the Tower of London.

Over the next few centuries, the City waged a continuous struggle with the monarchy for a degree of self-government and independence. In the Magna Carta of 1215, for instance, London was granted the right to elect its own sheriff, or **Lord Mayor**. However, in 1348, the city was hit by the worst natural disaster in its entire history – the arrival of the Europe-wide bubonic plague outbreak known as the **Black Death**. This disease, carried by black rats, and transmitted to humans by flea bites, wiped out something like half the capital's population in the space of two years.

Tudor London

It was under the **Tudor royal family** that London began to prosper, and the population, which had remained constant at around 50,000 since the Black Death, increased dramatically, trebling in size during the course of the century.

The most crucial development of the sixteenth century was the English **Reformation**, the separation of the English Church from Rome. A far-reaching consequence of this split was Henry VIII's **Dissolution of the Monasteries**, begun in 1536 in order to bump up the royal coffers. The Dissolution changed the entire fabric of the city: previously dominated by its religious institutions, London's property market was suddenly flooded with confiscated estates, which were quickly snapped up and redeveloped by the Tudor nobility.

Henry VIII may have kick-started the English Reformation, but he was a religious conservative, and in the last ten years of his reign he executed as many Protestants as Catholics. Henry's sickly son, **Edward VI** (1547–53), however, pursued an even more staunchly anti-Catholic policy. By the end of his brief reign, London's churches had lost their altars, their paintings, their relics and virtually all their statuary. With the accession of "**Bloody Mary**" (1553–58) the religious pendulum swung the other way. This time, it was Protestants who were martyred with abandon at Tyburn and Smithfield.

Despite all the religious strife, the Tudor economy remained in good health, reaching its height in the reign of **Elizabeth I** (1558–1603). London's commercial success was epitomized by the millionaire merchant Thomas Gresham, who erected the **Royal Exchange** in 1572, establishing London as the premier world trade market. The 45 years of Elizabeth's reign also witnessed the efflorescence of a specifically **English Renaissance**, especially in the field of literature, which reached its apogee in the brilliant careers of **Christopher Marlowe**, **Ben Jonson** and **William Shakespeare**, whose plays were performed in the theatres of Southwark, the city's entertainment district.

Stuart London

In 1603, James VI of Scotland became **James I** of England (1603–25), thereby uniting the two crowns and marking the beginning of the **Stuart dynasty**. His intention of exercising religious tolerance was thwarted by the public outrage that followed the **Gunpowder Plot** of 1605, when Guy Fawkes, in cahoots with a group of Catholic conspirators, was discovered attempting to blow up the king at the State opening of Parliament.

Under James's successor, **Charles I** (1625–49), the ani-

STUART LONDON

mosity between Crown and Parliament culminated in full-blown **Civil War**. London was the key to victory for both sides, and as a Parliamentarian stronghold it came under attack from Royalist forces almost immediately. However, having defeated the Parliamentary forces to the west of London in 1642, Charles hesitated and withdrew to Reading, thus missing his greatest chance of victory. After a series of defeats in 1645, Charles surrendered to the Scots, who handed him over to Parliament. Eventually, in January 1649, the king was tried and executed in Whitehall, and England became a **Commonwealth** under Oliver Cromwell. London found itself in the grip of the Puritans' zealous laws, which closed down all theatres, enforced strict observance of the Sabbath, and banned the celebration of Christmas, which was considered a papist superstition.

In 1660, the city gave an ecstatic reception to **Charles II** (1660–85) when he arrived in the capital to announce the **Restoration** of the monarchy, and the "Merry Monarch" immediately caught the mood of the public by opening up the theatres and concert halls. However, the good times that rolled came to an abrupt end with the onset of the **Great Plague** of 1665, which claimed 100,000 lives. The following year, London had to contend with yet another disaster, the **Great Fire** (see p.94). Some eighty percent of the City was razed to the ground; the death toll didn't even reach double figures, but more than 100,000 were left homeless.

Within five years, 9000 houses had been rebuilt with bricks and mortar (timber was banned), and fifty years later **Christopher Wren** had almost single-handedly rebuilt all the City churches and completed the world's first Protestant cathedral, **St Paul's**. The **Great Rebuilding**, as it was known, was one of London's most remarkable achievements, and extinguished virtually all traces of the medieval city.

STUART LONDON

Georgian London

With the accession of **George I** (1714–27), the first of the Hanoverian dynasty, London's expansion continued unabated. The shops of the newly developed **West End** stocked the most fashionable goods in the country, the volume of trade more than tripled, and London's growing population – it was by now the world's largest city, with a population approaching one million – created a huge market, as well as fuelling a building boom.

Wealthy though London was, it was also experiencing the worst mortality rates since records began. Disease was rife, but the real killer was **gin**. It's difficult to exaggerate the effects of the gin-drinking orgy that took place among the poor between 1720 and 1751. At its height, gin consumption was averaging two pints a week, and the burial rate exceeded the baptism rate by more than two to one. Eventually, in the face of huge vested interests, the government passed an act that restricted gin retailing and halted the epidemic.

Policing the metropolis was also an increasing preoccupation for the government, who introduced **capital punishment** for the most minor misdemeanours. Nevertheless, crime continued unabated throughout the eighteenth century, the prison population swelled, transportations to the colonies began, and 1200 Londoners were hanged at Tyburn's gallows. Rioting became an ever-more-popular form of protest among the poorer classes in London, the most serious insurrection being the **Gordon Riots** of 1780, when up to 50,000 Londoners went on a five-day rampage through the city.

The nineteenth century

The **nineteenth century** witnessed the emergence of London as the capital of an empire that stretched across the globe. The city's population grew from just over one million in 1801 to nearly seven million by 1901. The world's largest enclosed **dock system** was built in the marshes to the east of the City, and the world's first public transport network was created, with horse-buses, trains, trams and an underground railway. **Industrialization**, however, brought pollution and overcrowding, especially in the slums of the East End; smallpox, measles, scarlet fever and cholera killed thousands of working-class families. It is this era of slum-life, and huge social divides, that Dickens evoked in his novels.

The accession of **Queen Victoria** (1837–1901) coincided with a period in which the country's international standing reached unprecedented heights, and as a result Victoria became as much a national icon as Elizabeth I had been. The spirit of the era was perhaps best embodied by the **Great Exhibition** of 1851, a display of manufacturing achievements from all over the world, which took place in the Crystal Palace erected in Hyde Park.

Local government arrived in 1855 with the establishment of the **Metropolitan Board of Works** (MBW), followed in 1888 by the directly elected **London County Council** (LCC). The achievements of the MBW and the LCC were immense, in particular those of its chief engineer, Joseph Bazalgette, who helped create an underground sewer system (much of it still in use), and greatly improved transport routes.

While half of London struggled to make ends meet, the other half enjoyed the fruits of the richest nation in the world. Luxury establishments such as the *Ritz* and Harrods belong to this period, personified by the dissolute Prince of Wales, later **Edward VII** (1901–10). For the masses, too, there were new entertainments to be enjoyed: music halls boomed and public houses prospered. The first "Test" cricket match between England and Australia took place in 1880 at the Kennington

THE NINETEENTH CENTURY

Oval and, during the following 25 years, nearly all of London's professional football clubs were founded.

From World War I to World War II

During **World War I** (1914–18), London experienced its first aerial attacks, with Zeppelin raids leaving some 650 dead, but these were minor casualties in the context of a war that destroyed millions of lives and eradicated whatever remained of the majority's respect for the ruling classes.

Between the wars, London's population increased further still, reaching close to nine million by 1939. In contrast to the nineteenth century, however, there was a marked shift in population out into the **suburbs**. After the boom of the "Swinging Twenties", the economy collapsed with the crash of the New York Stock Exchange in 1929. The arrival of the Jarrow Hunger March, the most famous protest of the Depression years, shocked London in 1936, the year in which thousands of British fascists tried to march through the predominantly Jewish East End, only to be stopped in the so-called **Battle of Cable Street**.

London was more or less unprepared for the aerial bombardments of **World War II** (1939–45). The bombing campaign, known as the **Blitz** (see p.86), began on September 7, 1940, and continued for 57 consecutive nights. Further carnage was caused towards the end of the war by the pilotless V-1 "doodlebugs" and V-2 rockets, which caused another 20,000 casualties. In total, 30,000 civilians lost their lives in the bombing of London, with 50,000 injured and some 130,000 houses destroyed.

Postwar London

To lift the country out of its postwar gloom, the **Festival of Britain** was staged in 1951 on derelict land on the south bank of the Thames, a site that was eventually transformed into the **South Bank Arts Centre**. Londoners turned up at this technological funfair in their thousands, but at the same time many were abandoning the city for good, starting a population decline that has continued ever since. The consequent labour shortage was made good by mass **immigration** from the former colonies, in particular the Indian subcontinent and the West Indies. The newcomers, a large percentage of whom settled in London, were given small welcome, and within ten years were subjected to race riots, which broke out in Notting Hill in 1958.

The riots are thought to have been carried out, for the most part, by **Teddy Boys**, working-class lads from London's slum areas and new housing estates, who formed the city's first postwar youth cult. Subsequent cults, and their accompanying music, helped turn London into the epicentre of the so-called **Swinging Sixties**, the Teddy Boys being usurped in the early 1960s by the **Mods**, whose sharp suits came from London's Carnaby Street. Fashion hit London in a big way, and – thanks to the likes of the Beatles, the Rolling Stones and Twiggy – London was proclaimed the hippest city on the planet on the front pages of *Time* magazine.

Thatcherite London

In 1979, **Margaret Thatcher** won the general election for the Conservative Party, and the country and the capital would never be quite the same again. The Conservatives were to remain in power for seventeen years, steering the country into a period of ever-greater social polarization. While taxation policies and easy credit fuelled a consumer boom for the professional classes (the "yuppies" of the 1980s), a calamitous number of people ended up trapped in long-term unemployment. The Brixton riots of 1981 and

1985, and the Tottenham riot of 1985, were reminders of the price of such divisive policies, and of the feeling of social exclusion rife among the city's black youth.

Nationally, the opposition Labour Party went into sharp decline, but in the GLC (successor to the LCC), the party won a narrow victory, led by the **radical Ken Livingstone**, or "Red Ken" as the tabloids dubbed him. Under Livingstone, the GLC poured money into projects among London's ethnic minorities, into the arts, and (most famously) into a subsidized fares policy for public transport. Such schemes endeared Livingstone to the hearts of many Londoners, but it was too much for Thatcher, who abolished the GLC in 1986, leaving London as the only European capital without a citywide elected body.

Abolition exacerbated tensions between the poorer and richer boroughs of the city. For the first time since the Victorian era, **homelessness** returned to London in a big way, with the underside of Waterloo Bridge transformed into a "Cardboard City" sheltering up to 2000 vagrants. At the same time, the so-called "**Big Bang**" took place, abolishing a whole range of restrictive practices on the Stock Exchange and fuelling the building boom in the reclaimed Docklands, the most visible legacy of Thatcherism. Stocks and shares headed into the stratosphere and, shortly after, they inevitably crashed, ushering in a recession that dragged on for the best part of the next ten years.

Millennium London

On the surface at least, twenty-first-century London has come a long way since the bleak Thatcher years. Redevelopment has begun again apace, partly fuelled by money from the National Lottery, which has funded a series of prestigious new **millennium projects** that have changed the face of the city. A new pedestrian bridge now spans the Thames, leading to the new Tate Modern gallery, spectacularly housed in a converted power station. Numerous other national institutions have transformed themselves, too – among them the British Museum, the Royal Opera House, the Science Museum, the National Portrait Gallery and the National Maritime Museum. There have been one or two millennial blunders, too, most famously the Dome, built and stuffed full of gadgetry for £750 million, but now lying empty and abandoned.

The most significant political development for London has been the creation of the **Greater London Assembly** (GLA), along with an American-style **Mayor of London**, both elected by popular mandate. The Labour government, which came to power on a wave of enthusiasm in 1997, did everything it could to prevent the election of the former GLC leader Ken Livingstone. Yet, despite being forced to leave the Labour Party and run as an independent, Livingstone won a resounding victory in the elections of May 2000. He immediately grabbed the headlines by trying to rid Trafalgar Square of its pigeons, but by far his most controversial policy is the recent introduction of a **congestion charge** of £5 for every vehicle entering central London (see p.13). It's a bold move that will undoubtedly make or break his political career.

Books

Given the enormous number of **books** on London, the list below is necessarily a very selective one. The recommendations we've made are in print and if you want to find the cheapest copy to buy online, try ⓦwww.bookbrain.co.uk.

Travel, journals and memoirs

James Boswell *London Journal*. Boswell's diary, written in 1762–3 when he was lodging in Downing Street, is remarkably candid about his frequent dealings with the city's prostitutes, and a fascinating insight into eighteenth-century life.

John Evelyn *The Diary of John Evelyn*. In contrast to his contemporary, Pepys, Evelyn gives away very little of his personal life, but his diaries cover a much greater period of English history and a much wider range of topics.

George Orwell *Down and Out in Paris and London*. Orwell's tramp's-eye view of the 1930s, written from firsthand experience. The London section is particularly harrowing.

Samuel Pepys *The Shorter Pepys*; *The Illustrated Pepys*. Pepys kept a voluminous diary while he was living in London from 1660 until 1669, recording the fall of the Commonwealth, the Restoration, the Great Plague and the Great Fire, as well as describing the daily life of the nation's capital. The unabridged version is published in eleven volumes; *The Shorter Pepys* is abridged, though still massive; *The Ilustrated Pepys* is made up of just the choicest extracts accompanied by contemporary illustrations.

Iain Sinclair *Lights Out for the Territory*. Sinclair is one of the most original London writers of his generation. A series of ramblings across London starting in Hackney, this is probably his most accessible work.

History, society and politics

Peter Ackroyd *London: The Biography*. This massive, densely written, 800-page tome is the culmination of a lifetime's love affair with a living city and its intimate history. Much praised, though it's no easy read.

Angus Calder *The Myth of the Blitz*. A useful antidote to the backs-against-the-wall, "London can take it" tone of most books on this period. Calder dwells instead on the capital's internees – Communists, conscientious objectors and "enemy aliens" – and the myth-making processes of the media of the day.

Jonathan Glancey *London Bread and Circuses*. In this small, illustrated book, the *Guardian*'s architecture critic extols the virtues of the old LCC and visionaries like Frank Pick,

who transformed London's transport in the 1930s; discusses the millennium projects (the "circuses" of the title); and bemoans the city's creaking infrastructure.

Roy Porter *London: A Social History*. This immensely readable history is one of the best books on London published since the war. It's particularly strong on the continuing saga of London's local government, and includes an impassioned critique of the damage done by Mrs Thatcher's administration.

Ben Weinreb and Christopher Hibbert *The London Encyclopaedia*. More than 1000 pages of concisely presented information on London past and present, accompanied by the odd illustration. The most fascinating book on the capital.

HISTORY, SOCIETY AND POLITICS

Art, architecture and archeology

Felix Barker and Ralph Hyde
London As It Might Have Been.
A richly illustrated book on the
weird and wonderful plans that
never quite made it from the
drawing board.

Samantha Hardingham *London:
A Guide to Recent Architecture*.
Wonderful pocket guide to the
architecture of the last ten years
or so, with a knowledgeable, critical text and plenty of black-and-
white photos.

Nikolaus Pevsner and others
The Buildings of England.
Magisterial series, started by

Pevsner and to which others
have added, inserting newer
buildings but generally respect-
ing the founder's personal tone.
The latest of the London volumes (there are now five in the
series) is a paperback edition
devoted to London Docklands.

**Richard Trench and Ellis
Hillman** *London under London*.
Fascinating book revealing the
secrets of every aspect of the
capital's subterranean history,
from the lost rivers of the underground to the gas and water
systems.

London in fiction

Peter Ackroyd *English Music*;
Hawksmoor; *The House of
Doctor Dee*; *The Great Fire of
London*; *Dan Leno and the
Limehouse Golem*. Ackroyd's
novels are all based on arcane
aspects of London, wrapped into
thriller-like narratives, and con-
juring up kaleidoscopic visions of
various ages of English culture.
Hawksmoor, about the great
church architect, is the most
popular and enjoyable.

Martin Amis *London Fields*.
"Ferociously witty, scabrously
scatological and balefully satirical", it says on the back cover,
though many regard Amis Jnr's
observation of lowlife London
as pretentious drivel, written by
a man who lives in comfortable
Notting Hill.

Anthony Burgess *A Dead Man
in Deptford*. Playwright
Christopher Marlowe's unex-
plained murder in a tavern in

Deptford provides the background for this historical novel, which brims over with Elizabethan life.

Angela Carter *The Magic Toyshop*. Carter's most celebrated novel, about a provincial woman moving to London.

G.K. Chesterton *The Napoleon of Notting Hill*. Written in 1904 but set eighty years in the future, in a London divided into squabbling independent boroughs – something prophetic there – and ruled by royalty selected on a rotational basis.

Liza Cody *Bucket Nut*; *Monkey Wrench*; *Gimme More*. Feisty, would-be female wrestler of uncertain sexuality, with a big mouth, in thrillers set in lowlife London.

Joseph Conrad *The Secret Agent*. Conrad's wonderful spy story based on the botched anarchist bombing of Greenwich Observatory in 1894, exposing the hypocrisies of both the police and the anarchists.

Charles Dickens *Bleak House*; *A Christmas Tale*; *Little Dorrit*; *Oliver Twist*. The descriptions in Dickens' London-based novels have become the clichés of the Victorian city: the fog, the slums and the stinking river. *Little Dorrit* is set mostly in Borough and contains some of his most trenchant pieces of social analysis, and much of *Bleak House* is set around the Inns of Court that Dickens knew so well.

Arthur Conan Doyle *The Complete Sherlock Holmes*. Deerstalkered sleuth Sherlock Holmes and dependable sidekick Dr Watson penetrate all levels of Victorian London, from Limehouse opium dens to millionaires' pads. *A Study in Scarlet* and *The Sign of Four* are set entirely in the capital.

Graham Greene *The Human Factor*; *It's a Battlefield*; *The Ministry of Fear*; *The End of the Affair*. Greene's London novels are all fairly bleak, ranging from *The Human Factor*, which probes the underworld of the city's spies, to *The Ministry of Fear*, which is set during the Blitz.

Nick Hornby *High Fidelity*. Hornby's extraordinarily

FICTION

successful second book focuses on the loves and life of a thirty-something bloke who lives near the Arsenal … rather like Hornby himself.

Hanif Kureishi *The Buddha of Suburbia*; *The Black Album*; *Love in a Blue Time*. The *Buddha of Suburbia* is a raunchy account of life as an Anglo-Asian in late 1960s suburbia, and the art scene of the 1970s. *The Black Album* is a thriller set in London in 1989, while *Love in a Blue Time* is a set of short stories set in 1990s London.

Jack London *The People of the Abyss*. London's classic London novel.

Timothy Mo *Sour Sweet*. Very funny and very sad story of a newly arrived Chinese family struggling to understand the English way of life in the 1960s, written with great insight by Mo, who is himself of mixed parentage.

Iris Murdoch *Under the Net*; *The Black Prince*; *An Accidental Man*; *Bruno's Dream*; *The Green Knight*. *Under the Net* was Murdoch's first, funniest and arguably her best novel, centred

on a hack writer living in London. Many of her subsequent novels are set in various parts of middle-class London and span several decades of the second half of the twentieth century. *The Green Knight*, her last novel, is a strange fable mixing medieval and modern London, with lashings of the Bible and attempted fratricide.

George Orwell *Keep the Aspidistra Flying*. Orwell's 1930s critique of Mammon is equally critical of its chief protagonist, whose attempt to rebel against the system only condemns him to poverty, working in a London bookshop and freezing his evenings away in a miserable rented room.

Edward Rutherfurd *London*. A big, big novel which stretches from Roman times to the present and deals with the most dramatic moments of London's history. Masses of historical detail woven in with the story of several families.

Iain Sinclair *White Chappell, Scarlet Tracings*; *Downriver*; *Radon Daughters*. Sinclair's idiosyncratic and richly textured novels are a strange mix of Hogarthian caricature, New Age mysticism and conspiracy-theory rant. Deeply offensive and highly recommended.

P.G. Wodehouse *Jeeves Omnibus*. Bertie Wooster and his stalwart butler, Jeeves, were based in Mayfair, and many of their exploits take place with London showgirls, and in the Drones gentlemen's club.

Virginia Woolf *Mrs Dalloway*. Woolf's novel relates the thoughts of a London society hostess and a shell-shocked war veteran, with her "stream of consciousness" style in full flow.

FICTION

INDEX

1. THE LONDON UNDERGROUND

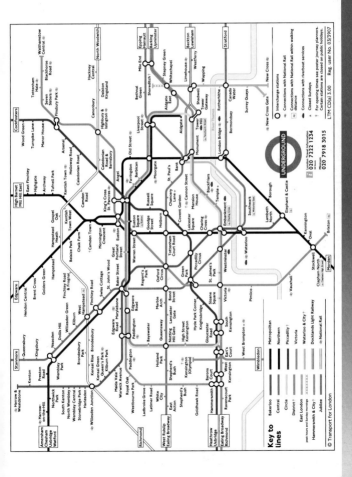

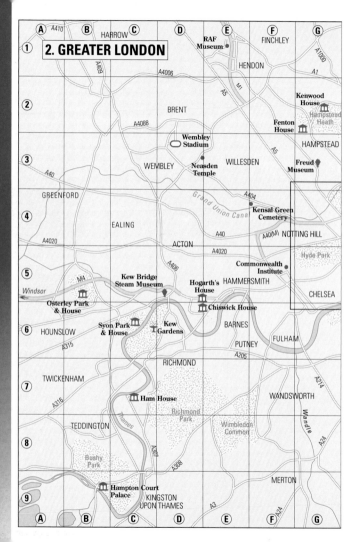

2. GREATER LONDON

HARROW
FINCHLEY
RAF Museum
HENDON
A410
A409
A4006
A5
M1
A1000
A1

Kenwood House
Hampstead Heath
Fenton House
HAMPSTEAD

BRENT
A4088
Wembley Stadium
WEMBLEY
Neasden Temple
WILLESDEN

Freud Museum

Grand Union Canal
A404
Kensal Green Cemetery
GREENFORD
A40
A40(M)
NOTTING HILL
EALING
A4020
ACTON
A4020
Commonwealth Institute
Hyde Park

M4
Kew Bridge Steam Museum
Hogarth's House
HAMMERSMITH
CHELSEA
Windsor
Osterley Park & House
Chiswick House
Syon Park & House
Kew Gardens
BARNES
HOUNSLOW
A315
PUTNEY
FULHAM
A205

TWICKENHAM
RICHMOND
A316
Ham House
Richmond Park
Wimbledon Common
WANDSWORTH
A214
Wandle
A24

TEDDINGTON
Thames
A307
A308

Bushy Park
MERTON
Hampton Court Palace
KINGSTON UPON THAMES
A3
A24

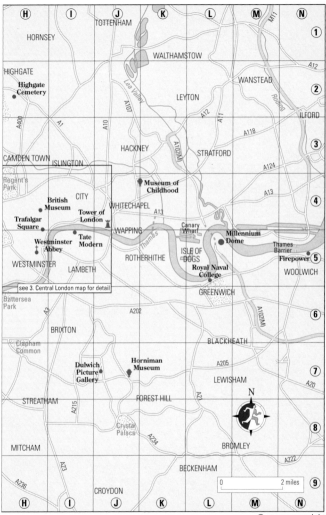

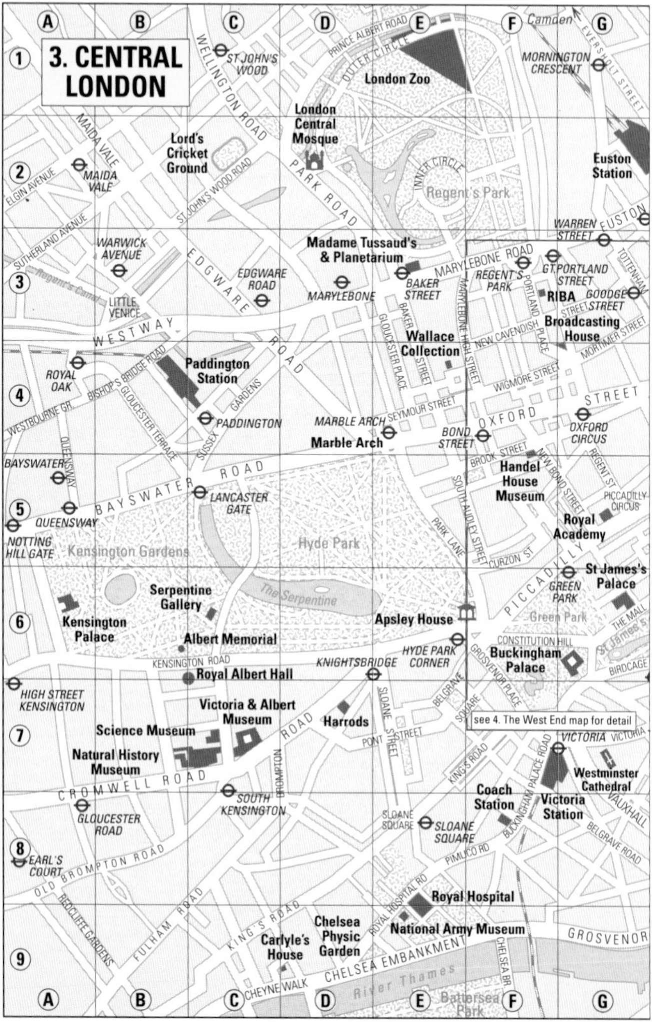
3. CENTRAL LONDON
St John's Wood
Wellington Road
Prince Albert Road
Outer Circle
London Zoo
Camden
Mornington Crescent
Eversholt Street
London Central Mosque
Lord's Cricket Ground
Maida Vale
Elgin Avenue
St John's Wood Road
Park Road
Inner Circle
Regent's Park
Euston Station
Warren Street
Euston
Sutherland Avenue
Warwick Avenue
Regent's Canal
Little Venice
Edgware Road
Madame Tussaud's & Planetarium
Marylebone
Baker Street
Marylebone Road
Regent's Park
Gt Portland Street
Tottenham
Portland Place
RIBA
Goodge Street
Broadcasting House
Mortimer Street
New Cavendish Street
Westway
Wallace Collection
Gloucester Place
Marylebone High Street
Royal Oak
Paddington Station
Bishop's Bridge Road
Gloucester Terrace
Sussex Gardens
Paddington
Wigmore Street
Westbourne Gr.
Marble Arch
Seymour Street
Bond Street
Oxford Street
Oxford Circus
Bayswater
Queensway
Bayswater Road
Lancaster Gate
Brook Street
Handel House Museum
New Bond Street
Regent St
South Audley Street
Piccadilly Circus
Royal Academy
Notting Hill Gate
Kensington Gardens
Hyde Park
Park Lane
Curzon St
Piccadilly
Green Park
St James's Palace
The Serpentine
Serpentine Gallery
Kensington Palace
Albert Memorial
Apsley House
The Mall
Constitution Hill
Buckingham Palace
St James's
Kensington Road
Royal Albert Hall
Knightsbridge
Hyde Park Corner
Grosvenor Place
Birdcage
High Street Kensington
Victoria & Albert Museum
Harrods
Sloane Street
Belgrave Square
see 4. The West End map for detail
Science Museum
Natural History Museum
Brompton Road
Pont Street
Victoria
Westminster Cathedral
Cromwell Road
South Kensington
King's Road
Coach Station
Buckingham Palace Road
Victoria Station
Vauxhall
Gloucester Road
Sloane Square
Belgrave Road
Pimlico Rd
Earl's Court
Old Brompton Road
Royal Hospital Rd
Royal Hospital
Redcliffe Gardens
Fulham Road
Chelsea Physic Garden
National Army Museum
Carlyle's House
Chelsea Embankment
Grosvenor
Chelsea Br.
River Thames
Cheyne Walk
Battersea Park

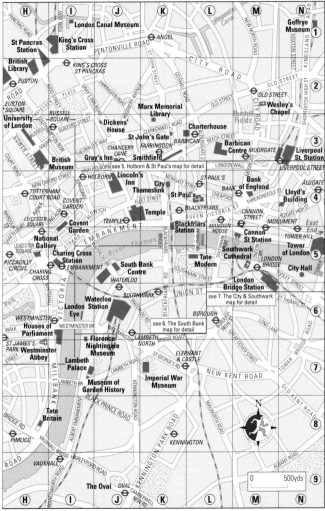

© crown copyright

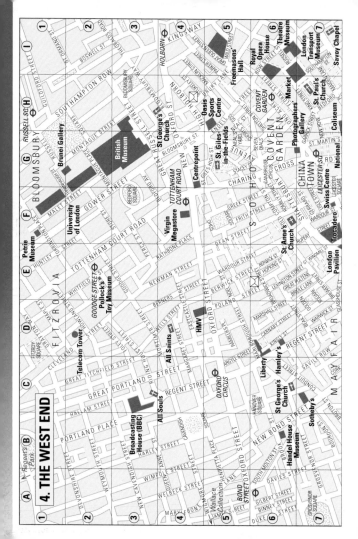

4. THE WEST END

A Regent's Park **B** **C** **D** FITZROVIA **E** **F** BLOOMSBURY **G** **H** RUSSELL SQ

1 **2** **3** **4** **5** **6** **7**

Portland Place
Broadcasting House (BBC)
All Souls
Telecom Tower
Pollock's Toy Museum
GOODGE STREET
Petrie Museum
University of London
Brunei Gallery
British Museum
St George's Church
HOLBORN
Freemasons Hall
KINGSWAY
Royal Opera House
Theatre Museum
London Transport Museum
Savoy Chapel

All Saints
HMV
Virgin Megastore
OXFORD CIRCUS
TOTTENHAM COURT ROAD
Centrepoint
St Giles-in-the-Fields
Oasis Sports Centre
COVENT GARDEN
Market
Photographers Gallery
St Paul's Church
Coliseum

Liberty
Hamley's
St George's Church
Sotheby's
SOHO
St Anne's Church
London Pavilion
Trocadero
Swiss Centre
CHINATOWN
LEICESTER SQ
National
CHARING CROSS

Wallace Collection
Handel House Museum
NEW BOND STREET
MAYFAIR
OXFORD STREET
REGENT STREET

MARYLEBONE

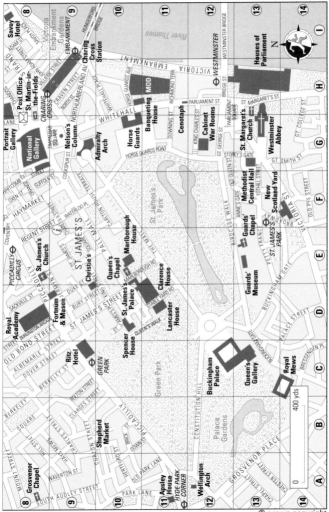

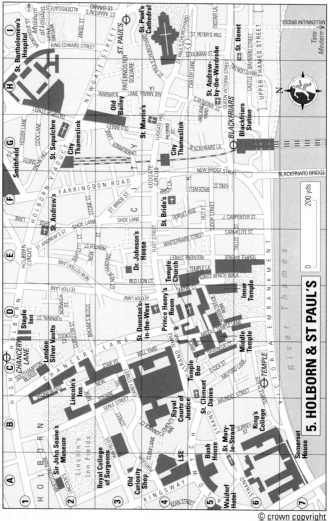

5. HOLBORN & ST PAUL'S

© crown copyright

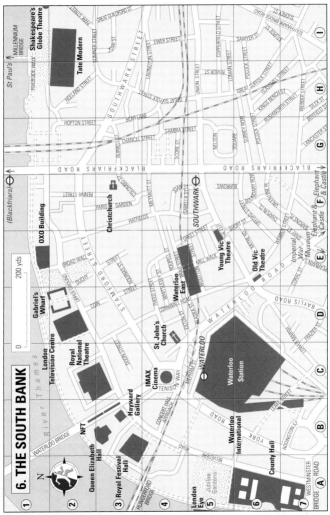

6. THE SOUTH BANK

0   200 yds

N

River Thames

Blackfriars

St Paul's

MILLENNIUM BRIDGE

Shakespeare's Globe Theatre

Tate Modern

GREAT GUILDFORD STREET
PARK STREET
ZOAR ST
SUMNER STREET
GREAT GUILDFORD STREET
EWER STREET
COPPERFIELD STREET
SAWYER ST
SUMNER STREET
HOLLAND STREET
RISBOR ST
UNION ST
LOMAN STREET
LOMAN STREET
GREAT SUFFOLK STREET
POCOCK STREET
SOUTHWARK BRIDGE ROAD
SUDREY ST
STUBBS ST
SUDREY ST

SOUTHWARK STREET

RIVERSIDE WALK
HOPTON STREET
BEAR LANE
CHANCEL STREET
GAMBIA STREET
BURRELL STREET
SCORE ST
NELSON SQUARE
SURREY ROW
KINGS BENCH ST
GLASSHILL STREET
WEBBER ROW
SILEX ST
BOYFIELD ST
LANCASTER ST

OXO Building

Gabriel's Wharf

London Television Centre

Royal National Theatre

RENNIE STREET
COLOMBO STREET
PARIS GARDEN
HATFIELDS
SELLS RD
MEYMOTT STREET
ISABELLA ST
SURREY ST
GREAT STREET

BLACKFRIARS ROAD

BLACKFRIARS ROAD

Southwark

Christchurch

BURROWS

Elephant & Castle

Hayward Gallery

NFT

Queen Elizabeth Hall

Royal Festival Hall

IMAX Cinema

St John's Church

Young Vic Theatre

Old Vic Theatre

Imperial War Museum

BROAD WALK
UPPER GROUND
STAMFORD STREET
CORNWALL ROAD
DUCHY STREET
DOON STREET
THEED STREET
WHITTLESEY ST
ROUPELL ST
EXTON ST
MILL WALK
SHORT ST
WEBBER STREET
GARDEN ROW
BROOK DRIVE
DANTE ROAD
HERCULES ROAD

Waterloo East

WATERLOO ROAD

BAYLIS ROAD

CONCERT HALL APPROACH
TENISON WAY
WATERLOO BRIDGE
HUNGERFORD BRIDGE
BELVEDERE ROAD
ADDINGTON ST
YORK ROAD
LAMBETH ROAD
FRAZIER ST

Waterloo Station

Waterloo International

County Hall

London Eye

Jubilee Gardens

WESTMINSTER BRIDGE ROAD

1   2   3   4   5   6   7

A   B   C   D   E   F   G   H   I

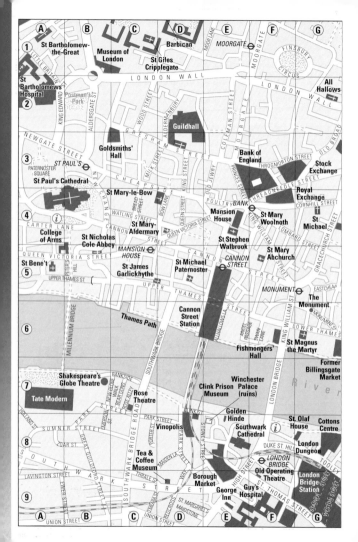

A | **B** | **C** | **D** | **E** | **F** | **G**

1
St Bartholomew-the-Great
Museum of London
St Giles Cripplegate
Barbican
MOORGATE
FINSBURY CIRCUS
LITTLE BRITAIN
MOOR LANE

2
St Bartholomew's Hospital
KING EDWARD STREET
Postman's Park
ALDERSGATE ST
WOOD STREET
LONDON WALL
COLEMAN STREET
MOORGATE
LONDON WALL
All Hallows

3
NEWGATE STREET
ST PAUL'S
PATERNOSTER SQUARE
St Paul's Cathedral
Goldsmiths' Hall
GRESHAM STREET
ALDERMANBURY
MILK STREET
KING STREET
Guildhall
PRINCES STREET
COLEMAN STREET
Bank of England
THROGMORTON STREET
OLD BROAD STREET
Stock Exchange

4
CARTER LANE
College of Arms
CHEAPSIDE
St Mary-le-Bow
St Nicholas Cole Abbey
WATLING ST
BREAD STREET
BOW LANE
QUEEN STREET
POULTRY
BANK
Mansion House
Royal Exchange
CORNHILL STREET
St Michael
GRACECHURCH STREET

5
St Bene't
QUEEN VICTORIA STREET
ST PETER'S HILL
UPPER THAMES ST
MANSION HOUSE
St Mary-Aldermary
St James Garlickhythe
CANNON STREET
St Michael Paternoster
St Stephen Walbrook
St Mary Woolnoth
LOMBARD STREET
KING WILLIAM STREET
St Mary Abchurch
MONUMENT
EASTCHEAP

6
MILLENNIUM BRIDGE
Thames Path
SOUTHWARK BRIDGE
Cannon Street Station
ALLHALLOWS LA
LAWRENCE POUNTNEY
SWAN LANE
KING WILLIAM ST
The Monument
MONUMENT
Fishmongers' Hall
St Magnus the Martyr
LOWER THAMES

7
Tate Modern
HOLLAND ST
Shakespeare's Globe Theatre
BANKSIDE
NEW GLOBE WALK
BEAR GARDENS
Rose Theatre
SOUTHWARK BRIDGE ROAD
PARK STREET
Vinopolis
Clink Prison Museum
Winchester Palace (ruins)
Golden Hinde
Southwark Cathedral
LONDON BRIDGE
Former Billingsgate Market
St Olaf House
Cottons Centre
River

8
SUMNER STREET
EMERSON ST
PORTER STREET
GREAT GUILDFORD STREET
CEDAR ST
SOUTHWARK
STREET
Tea & Coffee Museum
THRALE ST
HIGH STREET
Old Operating Theatre
DUKE ST HILL
LONDON BRIDGE
London Dungeon
TOOLEY
Guy's Hospital

9
LAVINGTON STREET
UNION STREET
SOUTHWARK BRIDGE RD
MAIDEN LANE
ST MARGARET'S
MAIDSTONE
Borough Market
George Inn
UNION STREET
REDCROSS WAY
ST THOMAS STREET
London Bridge Station
WESTON STREET
STAINER ST

A | **B** | **C** | **D** | **E** | **F** | **G**